THE EXPANDED AND ANNOTATED
MY LIFE AND WORK

Henry Ford's Universal Code for World-Class Success

THE EXPANDED AND ANNOTATED
MY LIFE AND WORK

Henry Ford's Universal Code for World-Class Success

Henry Ford • Samuel Crowther
William A. Levinson

CRC Press
Taylor & Francis Group
Boca Raton London New York

CRC Press is an imprint of the
Taylor & Francis Group, an **informa** business

CRC Press
Taylor & Francis Group
6000 Broken Sound Parkway NW, Suite 300
Boca Raton, FL 33487-2742

First issued in hardback 2019

© 2013 by Taylor & Francis Group, LLC
CRC Press is an imprint of Taylor & Francis Group, an Informa business

No claim to original U.S. Government works

ISBN-13: 978-1-4665-5771-0 (hbk)

Visit the Taylor & Francis Web site at
http://www.taylorandfrancis.com

and the CRC Press Web site at
http://www.crcpress.com

Contents

Preface

My Life and Work is easily the best and most comprehensive business leadership book ever written, and nothing has come forward in the subsequent 90 years to surpass it. What proves it best is the fact that Henry Ford wrote it only after he used its principles to achieve unprecedented world-class results in every enterprise to which he applied them. Charles Buxton Going, the managing editor of *Engineering Magazine*, described some of these results as early as 1915:

> Ford's success has startled the country, almost the world, financially, industrially, mechanically. It exhibits in higher degree than most persons would have thought possible the seemingly contradictory requirements of true efficiency, which are: constant increase of quality, great increase of pay to the workers, repeated reduction in cost to the consumer. And with these appears, as at once cause and effect, an absolutely incredible enlargement of output reaching something like one hundred fold in less than ten years, and an enormous profit to the manufacturer (Arnold and Faurote, 1915, iii).

The reconciliation of "the seemingly contradictory requirements" in question deserves particular attention. Ford overthrew the destructive paradigm that the only way to increase profits was to shortchange the worker, overcharge the customer, squeeze the supplier, or a combination of all three. Ford turned business into a win–win activity that delivered more value to everybody involved, and thereby realized the following explicit results:

- Chapter 3 will show that Ford bought out his minority stockholders for no less than $125 on the dollar. This is the language of money that gains buy-in from executives, managers, and investors.
- Ford quadrupled his workers' wages in 20 years, which corresponds to an annual growth rate of 7.2%. This is the language of money that earns buy-in from the workforce.
- The Model T, including the industries that grew to support its manufacture, contributed more than the estimated wealth of 35 of the country's 48 states to the nation's prosperity during 19 years of production (Ford and Crowther, 1930, 177). This is the language of

money that should gain buy-in from government policymakers and elected officials.

- Ford reduced the American work week from a customary 6–12 hours day, to the familiar 5-day, 40-hour work week.
- The Ford Motor Company and its Lean manufacturing methods made the United States the most productive nation on Earth, and was therefore directly responsible for the Allied victory in World War II. Ford's production chief Charles Sorensen designed the Willow Run bomber factory, which could deliver a B-24 Liberator bomber every hour.

My Life and Work is emphatically not a mechanistic or industry-specific formula that the practitioner can follow like a work instruction in a factory. It is instead an easily understandable synergy of impartial laws of economics, science, and human behavior. Ford called this synergy a *universal code*, and its mastery should be the reader's key learning objective.

This universal code delivered proven results in industries ranging from automobile manufacture to coal mines, railroads, and even healthcare as practiced in the Henry and Clara Ford Hospital. The latter has enormous implications in the context of today's out of control healthcare costs.

The Ford Motor Company prospered consistently, and even during bad economic times, while it conformed to Ford's precepts. Only when Ford's successors forgot or went against the universal code did the company decline to the extent that Ford executives who visited Japan in 1982 did not even recognize the Toyota Production System as their own company's creation.* Ford workers unionized only after the company's management violated Ford's precepts on a square deal for labor, which this book will prove almost certainly included a no-layoff policy.

Nations also prosper when they follow Ford's guidance, while economic catastrophe is the inevitable result of its contravention. The universal code, therefore, is not only impartial, scientific, and nonpartisan, it is also implacable and unforgiving like any law of nature.

My Life and Work thus offers proven solutions to the decline of the American middle class, and the offshoring of manufacturing jobs to places like China. American industrialists recognized cheap offshore labor as a

---

* One Japanese executive referred repeatedly to "the book." When Ford executives asked about the book, he responded, "It's Henry Ford's book, of course; your company's book" (Stuelpnagel, 1993).

threat more than 100 years ago, and they offered a very explicit solution of which Ford's business system was the ultimate culmination:

> We are justly proud of the high wage rates which prevail throughout our country, and jealous of any interference with them by the products of the cheaper labor of other countries. To maintain this condition, to strengthen our control of home markets, and, above all, to broaden our opportunities in foreign markets where we must compete with the products of other industrial nations, we should welcome and encourage every influence tending to increase the efficiency of our productive processes (Henry R. Towne's Preface to Taylor, 1911b, 10).

Taylor (1911a, 75) added even more explicitly:

> ... the one element more than any other which differentiates civilized from uncivilized countries—prosperous from poverty-stricken peoples—is that the average man in the one is five or six times as productive as the other.

Ford's realization of far greater per capita productivity transformed the United States from a primarily agrarian society into the wealthiest and most powerful nation on Earth during the first part of the twentieth century. *My Life and Work* shows exactly how he did it, and it contains all the basic principles necessary for the United States to regain its lead in manufacturing and service productivity

Ford wrote for ordinary workers instead of MBA and PhD candidates, although the actual content of his publications is very suitable for the latter. The original book is, therefore, an easily understandable repository of priceless concepts and principles. This edition expands on the original with modern perspectives that explain and organize Ford's thought process very explicitly. It is the specific mission of this book to lead the United States back to its rightful status as the world's most productive nation, and with corresponding prosperity, affluence, and military security for all its citizens.

William A. Levinson

Editor's Introduction

This edition of *My Life and Work* contains almost all the material of the original, plus more than 30% new content that explains and reinforces Ford's principles. The book distinguishes the two (Ford's words and those of the editor) by showing Ford's words as indented, extract text, and in the style (punctuation, spelling, and grammar) original to his book.

My Life and Work was originally an autobiography and a chronology of the Ford Motor Company, so it does not organize subjects as one would expect in a modern textbook or business book. There is usually a logical progression from one chapter to the next, but the reader will nonetheless find, for example, information on Lean manufacturing in many parts of the book as opposed to a specific chapter. The same applies to Ford's emphasis on the importance of design for reliability, selection of appropriate materials, and so on. This edition, therefore, has added second- and third-level headings to the original chapter titles to make it easier for the reader to find information. The reader may also note the authors' use of British spellings (e.g., rumour, mould, labour, and programme) for many words, which may have been common practice in the early twentieth century.

However, the first thing to do is to lay out the key principles and concepts that the reader should learn from this book. The most important is Ford's proven "universal code" for success in any enterprise.

HENRY FORD'S UNIVERSAL CODE

The Preface showed how Ford's unprecedented productivity improvements explain the enormous surge in American prosperity during the 1910s and 1920s. He achieved these world-class results not through a "one big hit" product or idea, but rather through a synergistic triad of simple, impartial, and incontrovertible laws of economics, science, and human behavior:

- **Economic Law:** No system can disburse more wealth than it produces. This is simply the economic counterpart of the physical law of conservation of matter and energy; one cannot get something from nothing. It is as inviolable as the laws of thermodynamics.
  - No ideology can create prosperity, and no government can legislate it.
  - Speculation in tulip bulbs, mortgage-backed securities, houses, dot-com stocks, and anything else that does not produce value is a zero-sum game that eventually ends in disaster for most of the speculators. A stock is worth exactly what its underlying assets can produce, and no more.
  - A supply chain also is a zero-sum game in which one stakeholder's gain is another's loss, *unless the supply chain can create more wealth for all its participants.* Application of the scientific law can change the supply chain from a zero-sum or win–lose game into a win–win activity for all its stakeholders.
- **Scientific Law:** The supply chain can create more wealth through the elimination of all wastes from its activities. The economic law says quite rightly that one cannot get something from nothing, but, as stated by Ford and Crowther (1926, p. 124), one can get something from what was considered nothing. This something is waste that often hides in plain view, and its elimination is the focus of Lean manufacturing.
  - Ford (1922, p. 329) wrote that is possible to waste exactly three things: time, material, and energy. It is useful to expand waste of time to cover the time of people (e.g., waiting and motion inefficiency) and of assets (cycle time). This allows a workforce to concentrate on four very simple key performance indicators to expose all forms of waste. Ford's workforce did, and this book will provide numerous examples.
  - Elimination of material and energy waste supports all the basic requirements of the ISO 14001 and ISO 50001 standards, respectively.
  - There is an adage to the effect that one can have high quality, low cost, or rapid delivery, but not all three. Ford proved, however, that these three goals are actually synergistic. High quality removes the cost of poor quality, while rapid delivery and, therefore, a short cycle time reduces inventory and its carrying cost.

- **Behavioral Law:** The system must provide a square deal to all its stakeholders including labor, suppliers, customers, and investors. Ford and Crowther (1926, p. 40) state explicitly that every business transaction must benefit all its participants fairly and equitably. This, in fact, defines social responsibility.

Ford proved unequivocally that this universal code works in applications ranging from manufacturing to education and healthcare. The next step is to recognize that the universal code is (1) synergistic, (2) impartial, and (3) implacable.

The Universal Code Is Synergistic

The concept of synergy is vital because none of the code's three elements can stand alone. Consider, for example, the element of a square deal for all supply chain participants. Fair compensation for labor gains employee buy-in and engagement: a "combination of an employee's loyalty, commitment and motivation" (*Industry Week*, 2011).

To this Ford adds in Chapter 8, "It ought to be the employer's ambition, as leader, to pay better wages than any similar line of business, and it ought to be the workman's ambition to make this possible." The employer's ability to pay higher wages depends significantly on labor-initiated or labor-supported productivity improvements. This was how the Ford Motor Company realized many if not most of its shop floor productivity gains. The willingness of hourly workers to improve productivity depends reciprocally on confidence that the results will show up in their paychecks. Therefore, higher wages and higher productivity are significantly if not completely interdependent.

If, on the other hand, management seeks to pay labor as little as possible and/or looks for ways to discharge workers, the workers will reciprocate with unionization, restrictive work rules, a nine-to-five mentality, productivity restrictions, and Luddism.* Then the system will produce less wealth, which may lead in turn to management efforts to wrest concessions from the union or else to ship the jobs offshore. Management and labor can lose together just as easily as they can win together. The interaction of the economic, scientific, and behavioral laws is, therefore, synergistic, whether for

---

* Luddism is the deliberate undermining of productivity improvements and mechanization.

good or bad. The same concept applies by extension to customer–supplier relationships.

The Universal Code Is Impartial

The concept of impartiality is vital because, once an organization's stakeholders understand that they are dealing with natural and scientific laws instead of ideologies, they will accept and conform to the universal code. Ford (1922, p. 56) writes explicitly:

> If a man whom we feel to be bad turns out to be a success, it is because he has fulfilled the law of success. If a man whom we feel to be a very good man is a failure, it is because he has failed to fulfill the law of success.

This "law of success" is neither Democratic nor Republican, nor is it Capitalist, Communist, or Socialist. It is an inarguable and impartial law of economic, scientific, and human nature. When people understand and accept it as such, many seemingly insurmountable problems vanish like the illusions they are. These problems include friction between Capital and Labor, which Ford proves to be a totally unnecessary dysfunction. Ford (1922, pp. 228–231) adds a chapter that contrasts "Man's Laws and Nature's Law," and shows how the latter is supreme over the former.

The concept of the law of the situation, in which everybody takes direction from the needs of the job as opposed to another person, underscores the scientific and impartial nature of Ford's business approach. This further depersonalizes the universal code and frees it of any taint of partisan or ideological origin. It is simply a proven and incontestable fact of Nature, like a mathematical equation:

Acceptance of Economic Law + Application of Scientific Law + Conformance to Behavioral Law = Success.

The reader who understands and internalizes Ford's universal code can overcome many of the self-limiting paradigms that afflict modern businesses and other organizations. These include, for example, the belief that healthcare is a zero-sum game in which escalating costs are the price of quality. The truth is that the escalating costs are the price of poor quality, inefficiency, and avoidable harm to patients. The Henry and Clara Ford

Hospital proved unequivocally that inexpensive world-class healthcare is achievable, and offshore hospitals for medical tourism are proving it yet again. If the reader must then explain the universal code to others, he or she can add that it is also implacable.

The Universal Code Is Implacable

Ford (1922, p. 290) said that copybooks, books in which children learned penmanship by copying various maxims and homilies, contained most of the world's wisdom. Rudyard Kipling's "The Gods of the Copybook Headings" is simply another expression of the impartial and inarguable laws of science, economics, and human behavior. Kipling wrote, and history has proved repeatedly, that these laws are also implacable and merciless to those who violate them. Kipling's "Gods of the Market Place" are meanwhile what Ford called Man's Laws, and they also include unrealistic expectations to the effect that a society can enjoy wealth it does not produce. The Gods of the Copybook Headings are Nature's Law, which does indeed outlast the Gods of the Market Place.

> AS I PASS through my incarnations in every age and race,
> I make my proper prostrations to the Gods of the Market Place.
> Peering through reverent fingers I watch them flourish and fall,
> And the Gods of the Copybook Headings, I notice, outlast
>   them all.
>
> … We moved as the Spirit listed. They never altered their pace,
> Being neither cloud nor wind-borne like the Gods of the
>   Market Place,
> But they always caught up with our progress, and presently
>   word would come
> That a tribe had been wiped off its icefield, or the lights had
>   gone out in Rome.
> With the Hopes that our World is built on they were utterly out
>   of touch,
> They denied that the Moon was Stilton; they denied she was
>   even Dutch;
> They denied that Wishes were Horses; they denied that a Pig
>   had Wings;

So we worshipped the Gods of the Market Who promised these
  beautiful things.
… In the Carboniferous Epoch we were promised abundance
  for all,
By robbing selected Peter to pay for collective Paul;
But, though we had plenty of money, there was nothing our
  money could buy,
And the Gods of the Copybook Headings said: *"If you don't
  work you die."*

Then the Gods of the Market tumbled, and their smooth-
  tongued wizards withdrew
And the hearts of the meanest were humbled and began to
  believe it was true
That All is not Gold that Glitters, and Two and Two make Four
And the Gods of the Copybook Headings limped up to explain
  it once more.

As it will be in the future, it was at the birth of Man
There are only four things certain since Social Progress began.
That the Dog returns to his Vomit and the Sow returns to
  her Mire,
And the burnt Fool's bandaged finger goes wabbling back to
  the Fire;

And that after this is accomplished, and the brave new world
  begins
When all men are paid for existing and no man must pay for
  his sins,
As surely as Water will wet us, as surely as Fire will burn,
The Gods of the Copybook Headings with terror and slaughter
  return!

When the Weimar Republic and Zimbabwe hyperinflated their currencies, there was indeed money, but nothing to buy with it. The fingers that
were first burned in Dutch tulip mania (if not before) wobbled back to the
Mississippi Bubble of 1720, leveraged stock speculation in 1929, and more
recently to dot-com stocks and mortgage-backed securities. Gordon Gekko's
speech in *Wall Street: Money Never Sleeps* (2010) is highly instructive: "The

mother of all evil is speculation." The Gods of the Copybook Headings are coming down very hard on Europe's Socialist systems that have promised benefits they cannot possibly pay, and Coburn (2012) warns that they are likely to slam the United States for its ballooning national debt.

Ford (1922, p. 230) added that natural or moral law, which stands even higher than the laws of economics, is godlike, impartial, and inescapable in its operation. We forget this at our collective and national peril. The Gods of the Copybook Headings make themselves known in the following situations as well:

- Price controls lead to shortages of materials and goods. If Shakespeare's Jack Cade decrees that a penny shall buy seven half-penny loaves of bread, bakers will stop selling bread. If the government cuts Medicare reimbursement rates sufficiently, doctors will stop treating senior citizens.
- Confiscatory taxes encourage a society's producers to stop producing.
- Unfairly low wages result in a nine-to-five mentality, and loss of employee loyalty and commitment.

It is not enough, however, to merely understand that no system can disburse more wealth than it creates, or that a supply chain's long-term success depends on a square deal for all its stakeholders. The reader must also learn how to remove all forms of waste from the supply chain, and then teach others how to do it. This brings us to the Henry Ford thought process.

FORD THOUGHT PROCESS

Mastery of the Ford thought process equips the practitioner to recognize all wastes of time, material, and energy on sight. This thought process is similar to that of Sir Arthur Conan Doyle's protagonist Sherlock Holmes, whose most important talent was his ability to notice seemingly trivial things that everybody else overlooked. Ford and Crowther (1930, p. 187) describe evidence of waste almost the way Holmes would describe clues at a crime scene:

It is the little things that are hard to see—the awkward little methods of doing things that have grown up and which no one notices. And since manufacturing is solely a matter of detail, these little things develop, when added together, into very big things.

Myriad forms of waste that were previously invisible become immediately obvious to anybody who has learned the Ford thought process. Recognition of waste or muda (Japanese for futility, uselessness, idleness) is a prerequisite for its removal, and the Ford culture apparently taught all its workers how to recognize waste on sight. Many if not most waste reduction projects resulted from workers' identification of waste, and this reinforces the need for worker engagement and buy-in. Norwood (1931, Chapter X) uses the phrase "it worried the men," with "it" being material waste, such as chips from machining operations, more than once to describe the process of "converting waste into millions." The millions were in the money of the early 1930s, when dollar coins were still made from silver.

Bennett (1951, pp. 32–33) meanwhile describes how Ford himself pointed to rust in a pile of slag and objected immediately to the waste of valuable iron. Ford noticed something, in this case rust, that was seemingly very trivial, but that actually indicated a significant loss of money. This story anticipates the modern concept of dumpster diving, or examination of everything that the factory throws away, to identify waste.

Ford's Holmesian powers of observation, which are easily teachable to an entire workforce, also apply to waste of time. Consider Ford's statement about railroads in Chapter 16: "A car on a siding is ... a great big question mark." A rail car that is not in motion is either adding lead time to its cargo or is else an idle capital asset, but how many people pay attention to rail cars on sidings? How many people pay attention if a factory worker walks to get parts, or bends over at the waist? Ford, or anybody who had worked for a few weeks in one of his factories, would on the other hand notice the waste motion immediately. The same applies to the accumulation of parts on a conveyor or a work slide; this indicated a stoppage at the subsequent workstation. The Ford workforce could even recognize activities that a value stream analysis would call "processes" and, therefore, value-adding, but were actually 100% rework.

This kind of thinking, in turn, resulted in enormous reductions of cycle time and inventory. Ford even went so far as to do successfully what Goldratt and Cox (1992) showed to be impossible; he operated a balanced factory at close to 100% capacity. Chapters 5 and 10 will demonstrate that he achieved this through the suppression of almost all variation in processing and material transfer times.

Meanwhile, it is useful, again because Ford and his co-author Samuel Crowther did not organize their material like that in a modern business book or textbook, to cite the most important chapters and their content. The purely autobiographical material is interesting, but the reader can probably skip it without missing anything vital. Other portions of the book, and especially those that illustrate Ford's universal code, deserve particular attention.

KEY CHAPTERS AND CHAPTER SUMMARY

The Introduction is especially important because it introduces Ford's universal code along with vital economic, Lean manufacturing, and customer service principles.

Chapter 1: "The Beginning," is primarily historical in nature, although it does provide Ford's views on so-called "nyet engineers" (people whose primary function is to say "no" rather than offer constructive advice) and also the importance of material selection.

Chapter 2: "What I Learned about Business" discusses the importance of overcoming paradigms and preconceived ideas, and it introduces continuous improvement or kaizen. It also warns against the use of the cost accounting system for managerial decisions, and this warning appears repeatedly throughout the book.

Chapter 3: "Starting the Real Business" introduces the concept of supply chain management, and it adds the need to recognize customer requirements.

Chapter 4: "The Secret of Manufacturing and Serving" revisits the importance of material selection in manufacturing, and then moves on to discuss the role of standardization in cost reduction.

Chapter 5: "Getting into Production" deserves particular attention from manufacturing professionals because it reveals Ford's job design principles. These include subdivision of labor to remove waste motion *and the variation that comes with it.* The chapter stresses the need to keep the work in continuous motion, which prevents the accumulation of inventory. It concludes with Ford's keynotes of production.

Chapter 6: "Machines and Men" introduces the concept, as discussed decades later by W. Edwards Deming and Tom Peters, of breaking down organizational barriers. It then adds the leadership principle that authority and leadership are not the same thing, and that the right to lead must be earned. The chapter then warns against letting the cost accounting system run the factory, and concludes with the need to pay attention to even seemingly insignificant forms of waste. This chapter also shows that the Ford organization was ahead of Mary Parker Follett in the identification (and implementation) of "the law of the situation," and also ahead of Burns and Stalker (1961) in the definition of mechanistic and organic management systems.

Chapter 7: "The Terror of the Machine" describes the characteristics of the ideal industrial leader.

Chapter 8: "Wages" is among the most important in the book. It teaches almost everything that anybody needs to know about industrial and labor relations: "It ought to be the employer's ambition, as leader, to pay better wages than any similar line of business, and it ought to be the workman's ambition to make this possible." Labor unions as well as employers must understand and internalize this chapter's material because no system can pay more in wages than it creates in value. The system can and must pay higher wages only when its stakeholders improve its productivity.

Chapter 9: "Why Not Always Have Good Business?" is of particular interest because Ford proved that a business can prosper even during economic downturns. There is always a market for high quality and low-cost goods, and it is the job of management to get the price down to what customers are willing to pay.

Chapter 10: "How Cheaply Can Things Be Made?" picks up where Chapter 9 leaves off by showing how to use Lean manufacturing to reduce costs and, therefore, prices. It describes just-in-time manufacturing very explicitly, as well as the need to eliminate variation from material transfer times. Achievement of the latter, along with elimination of variation in processing times, allows a factory to operate with almost no inventory whatsoever. This chapter is a particularly important element of Henry Ford's thought process.

Chapter 11: "Money and Goods" reiterates the basic fact that prosperity begins in what modern practitioners call gemba, or the value-adding workplace. An excessive focus on finance can lead to very dysfunctional results, and borrowing (and by implication government subsidies) cannot compensate for processes that simply cannot deliver value.

Chapter 12: "Money: Master or Servant?" underscores the dangers inherent in the management of any business by people whose eye is on the dollar as opposed to the job that produces the dollar. Ford contends that abuses of the financial system, including speculation in money, under-mine the creation and distribution of genuine wealth. This leads in turn to poverty. Chapter 13 then picks up where this chapter leaves off.

Chapter 13: "Why Be Poor?" exposes waste as a principal source of pov-erty, and revisits the dysfunctional effects of finance on the creation of wealth. It also raises very serious questions as to the desirability of con-tinuing to locate business in large cities. The role of the city as a center of commerce has declined enormously since the development of the Internet, so the high cost of an urban presence is almost certainly waste or muda.

Chapter 14: "The Tractor and Power Farming" is primarily of historical interest. It does, however, show the enormous influence of the application of mechanical power to farm productivity.

Chapter 15: "Why Charity?" contends very convincingly that charity should be unnecessary, and Ford's industries abolished poverty wherever they appeared. The idea is to treat the root cause of poverty rather than its symptoms, and this chapter's material applies to many of today's social welfare programs.

Chapter 16: "The Railroads" shows how elimination of bureaucracy and restrictive job classifications turned the Detroit, Toledo, and Ironton Railroad from a money loser into a profitable high-wage enterprise.

Chapter 17: "Things in General" contends very credibly that national and international prosperity can remove the economic root causes of most wars. It also describes the dangers of war propaganda, such as the kind that fomented the Spanish–American War and the United States' entry into World War I. This material is very applicable to today's events.

Chapter 18: "Democracy and Industry" has particularly important material on labor relations. It condemns impartially so-called labor leaders who foment and then exploit worker dissatisfaction, along with managers who look for ways to pay workers as little as possible. It also touches on the issue of groupthink, and reiterates the principle that the law of the situation and the requirements of the job are paramount. The rightful leader is the one who can lead the organization to the achieve-ment of its goals.

Chapter 19: "What We May Expect" reiterates Ford's basic management principles, and also introduces the concept of sustainable manufacturing. Examples include biofuels, and the need to find substitutes for nonrenew-able resources.

The Conclusion summarizes the book's key elements and learning objectives.

Henry Ford's Introduction

The first chapter of *My Life and Work* reveals its contents to be a universal code for world-class success in any enterprise, including not only manufacturing but also agriculture, mining, and service operations. Conformance to the natural laws of human and organizational behavior, which Ford calls the "Constitution of the Universe," is a prerequisite for this kind of success. This synergy of Lean manufacturing with these natural laws allows a supply chain to deliver value to all its participants including customers, suppliers, investors, and employees.

WHAT IS THE IDEA?

We have only started on our development of our country—we have not as yet, with all our talk of wonderful progress, done more than scratch the surface. The progress has been wonderful enough—but when we compare what we have done with what there is to do, then our past accomplishments are as nothing. When we consider that more power is used merely in ploughing the soil than is used in all the industrial establishments of the country put together, an inkling comes of how much opportunity there is ahead. And now, with so many countries of the world in ferment and with so much unrest everywhere, is an excellent time to suggest something of the things that may be done in the light of what has been done.

When one speaks of increasing power, machinery, and industry there comes up a picture of a cold, metallic sort of world in which great factories will drive away the trees, the flowers, the birds, and the green fields. And that then we shall have a world composed of metal machines and human machines. With all of that I do not agree. I think that unless we know more about machines and their use, unless we better understand the mechanical portion of life, we cannot have the time to enjoy the trees, and the birds, and the flowers, and the green fields.

* * *

Ford now emphasizes that he offers not a specialized business system for the manufacture of automobiles but rather "a theory that looks toward making this world a better place in which to live." The elimination of waste, which "keeps many men from getting the full return from service," removes the obstacles that stand between the simultaneous realization of high profits for the employer, high wages for the employee, fair compensation for suppliers, and low prices for the customer.

* * *

I think that we have already done too much toward banishing the pleasant things from life by thinking that there is some opposition between living and providing the means of living. We waste so much time and energy that we have little left over in which to enjoy ourselves. Power and machinery, money and goods, are useful only as they set us free to live. They are but means to an end. For instance, I do not consider the machines which bear my name simply as machines. If that was all there was to it I would do something else. I take them as concrete evidence of the working out of a theory of business, which I hope is something more than a theory of business—a theory that looks toward making this world a better place in which to live. The fact that the commercial success of the Ford Motor Company has been most unusual is important only because it serves to demonstrate, in a way which no one can fail to understand, that the theory to date is right. Considered solely in this light I can criticize the prevailing system of industry and the organization of money and society from the standpoint of one who has not been beaten by them.

As things are now organized, I could, were I thinking only selfishly, ask for no change. If I merely want money the present system is all right; it gives money in plenty to me. But I am thinking of service. The present system does not permit of the best service because it encourages every kind of waste—it keeps many men from getting the full return from service. And it is going nowhere. It is all a matter of better planning and adjustment.

I have no quarrel with the general attitude of scoffing at new ideas. It is better to be skeptical of all new ideas and to insist upon being shown rather than to rush around in a continuous brainstorm after every new idea. Skepticism, if by that we mean cautiousness, is the balance wheel of civilization. Most of the present acute troubles of the world arise out of taking on new ideas without first carefully investigating to discover if they are good ideas. An idea is not necessarily good because it is old, or necessarily bad because it is new, but if an old idea works, then the weight of the evidence is all in its favor. Ideas are of themselves extraordinarily valuable, but an idea is just an idea. Almost any one can think up an idea. The thing that counts is developing it into a practical product.

A "Universal Code" for World-Class Performance

Ford's "universal code" synergizes basic laws of economics and science with laws of human and organizational behavior. We cannot get something from nothing but we can, through the elimination of waste or muda, gain enormous wealth from what was once considered nothing. The laws of human and organizational behavior demand a square deal for all supply chain stakeholders, and the science of Lean manufacturing delivers this square deal for everybody involved.

Ford's universal code is applicable to all human endeavors, and Ford applied it successfully to mining, agriculture, transportation, and healthcare. Chapter 15 will discuss the Henry and Clara Ford Hospital, which provided outstanding and inexpensive services to its patients.

Natural Law, or the Constitution of the Universe

A thorough comprehension of the behavioral aspects of Ford's universal code relies on what Ford (1922, p. 248) called "the Constitution of the Universe."

> So, while the people are indeed supreme over the written Constitution, the spiritual constitution is supreme over them. The French Revolutionists wrote constitutions too—every drunken writer among them tossed off a constitution. Where are they? All vanished. Why? Because they were not in harmony with the constitution of the universe. The power of the Constitution is not dependent on any Government, but on its inherent rightness and practicability.

This means that it is no more possible to legislate natural laws of human and economic behavior than it is to repeal the laws of thermodynamics. These laws are natural and right, and "the way life must go if it is to go at all" (Ford and Crowther, 1926, p. 273). The foundation of Ford's business system therefore rested on impartial and inarguable laws of economic and behavioral science as well as technology.

Hindus call the Constitution of the Universe Dharma (the Right Way), while Chinese and Japanese call it Tao and Do (the Way). Hinduism warns that Dharma protects those who uphold it, and destroys those who go against it. Kipling's "The Gods of the Copybook Headings" conveys exactly the same lesson, and Ford (1922, p. 230) echoes this principle as follows:

> There is still a higher law which gets all without exception—it is the moral law. You may violate man-made law, and no one be the wiser and, apparently, no one the worse. You may violate economic law and still be carried through by the momentum of society's economic soundness. But the moral law you can never evade. You cannot even break it!
>
> ...The law stands there in its eternal integrity. You have not broken it, but you have broken something in yourself against it. In conflict with the moral law all that we can break is ourselves.[*]
>
> ...Many men have escaped man-made law, they have escaped economic law—so far, at least (nobody need be too cocksure about this, for the end of the test has not come), but no man ever lived without receiving sentence in himself upon every violation of the moral law. It gets us all, for sentence or reward. High or low, none escape. It is godlike in its impartial operation. It cannot be postponed, nor fought to a higher court, nor bribed. ...It has the final word, and its word is final.

This chapter adds explicitly, "We learn also that while men may decree social laws in conflict with natural laws, Nature vetoes those laws more ruthlessly than did the Czars." It is simply not possible to legislate prosperity, enact it through collective labor bargaining, or achieve it through any means other than creation of genuine wealth.

Ford (1922, p. 132) adds his observation of what is perhaps the biggest problem in America today: "Too many people believe that Success consists in getting your bread and butter by dickering or talking instead of producing." There was and perhaps still is a definite tendency among business school students to specialize in finance, marketing, or indeed anything but manufacturing. Hayes, Wheelwright, and Clark (1988, p. 15) cited one business manager who actually said, "Oh, business would be fine if only we didn't have to make the stuff."

Managers have avoided the need to make the stuff by outsourcing the jobs to China, but the United States is now borrowing billions of dollars

---

[*] Covey, Stephen (1991, p. 94) quotes Cecil B. DeMille to emphasize this idea. "It is impossible for us to break the law. We can only break ourselves against the law."

from that country with which to buy, whether directly or indirectly, the products in question. Coburn (2012) warns explicitly that the resulting national debt is very likely to result in economic catastrophe. The only way to avoid this catastrophe is to accept and internalize Ford's principles, which are in turn expressions of impartial and inarguable laws of economics, science, and human behavior.

The Vital Concept of Synergy

The reader who wishes to implement Ford's "universal code" must therefore apply all its aspects: economic, scientific, and behavioral. Management cannot deny workers the fruits of their labor and expect them to respond with commitment, engagement, or indeed anything more than sullen compliance with management directives. Knowledge at Wharton (2012) reports,

> ...some employees are clearly feeling disconnected from their work. Among the reasons cited for this: the recession, during which companies laid off huge swaths of their employees with little regard for loyalty or length of service; a whittling away of benefits, training and promotions for those who remain...

The reference adds that financially healthy companies have laid off employees to increase the value of their stocks, so it comes as no surprise that employees withhold anything more than perfunctory compliance. When personnel departments analyze salary and wage data to figure out how little they can pay, they should not be surprised when employees reciprocate with as little effort as they can deliver. Ford (1922, p. 250) laid it out very explicitly: "Loyalty on the part of employees must be met by loyalty on the part of the employer."

Ford's introduction to his universal code stresses the common sense principle, which is all too uncommon in a society that looks to get-rich-quick schemes like dot-com stocks and mortgage-backed securities, that honest effort is the only real source of material wealth.

* * *

I am now most interested in fully demonstrating that the ideas we have put into practice are capable of the largest application—that they have nothing peculiarly to do with motor cars or tractors but form something in the nature of a universal code. I am quite certain that it is the natural code and I want to demonstrate it so thoroughly that it will be accepted, not as a new idea, but as a natural code.

The natural thing to do is to work—to recognize that prosperity and happiness can be obtained only through honest effort. Human ills flow largely from attempting to escape from this natural course. I have no suggestion which goes beyond accepting in its fullest this principle of nature. I take it for granted that we must work. All that we have done comes as the result of a certain insistence that since we must work it is better to work intelligently and forehandedly; that the better we do our work the better off we shall be. All of which I conceive to be merely elemental common sense.

Beware of Political Progressives and Reactionaries

This chapter has already shown the natural consequences of management approaches that seek to pay workers as little as possible, or treat workers as disposable commodities. The workers reciprocate with perfunctory compliance, soldiering (marking time, limiting productivity), and unionization. "From each according to his abilities, to each according to his needs" denies the worker the rightful return for his or her work, and this makes Communism every bit as dysfunctional. Chapter 14 will show that the primary achievement of Communism was to turn a technologically advanced nation into a Third World country. This in turn reinforces the position that violation of the natural laws of human and economic behavior can render even the benefits of advanced science largely useless.

* * *

I am not a reformer. I think there is entirely too much attempt at reforming in the world and that we pay too much attention to reformers. We have two kinds of reformers. Both are nuisances. The man who calls himself a reformer wants to smash things. He is the sort of man who would tear up a whole shirt because the collar button did not fit the buttonhole. It would never occur to him to enlarge the buttonhole. This sort of reformer never under any circumstances knows what he is doing. Experience and reform do not go together. A reformer cannot keep his zeal at white heat in the presence of a fact. He must discard all facts.

Since 1914 a great many persons have received brand-new intellectual outfits. Many are beginning to think for the first time. They opened their eyes and realized that they were in the world. Then, with a thrill of independence, they realized that they could look at the world critically. They did so and found it faulty. The intoxication of assuming the masterful position of a critic of the social system—which it is every man's right to assume—is unbalancing at first. The very young critic is very much unbalanced. He is strongly in favor of wiping out the old order and starting a new one. They actually managed to start a new world in Russia. It is there that the work of the world makers can best be studied. We learn from Russia that it is the minority and not the majority who determine destructive action. We learn also that while men may decree social laws in conflict with natural laws, Nature vetoes those laws more ruthlessly than did the Czars. Nature has vetoed the whole Soviet Republic. For it sought to deny nature. It denied above all else the right to the fruits of labour. Some people say, "Russia will have to go to work," but that does not describe the case. The fact is that poor Russia is at work, but her work counts for nothing. It is not free work. In the United States a workman works eight hours a day; in Russia, he works twelve to fourteen. In the United States, if a workman wishes to lay off a day or a week, and is able to afford it, there is nothing to prevent him. In Russia, under Sovietism, the workman goes to work whether he wants to or not. The freedom of the citizen has disappeared in the discipline of a prison-like monotony in which all are treated alike. That is slavery. Freedom is the right to work a decent length of time and to get a decent living for doing so; to be able to arrange the little personal details of one's own life. It is the aggregate of these and many other items of freedom which makes up the great idealistic Freedom. The minor forms of Freedom lubricate the everyday life of all of us.

Political "Reform" Drives Out the Producers

The next paragraph applies to Zimbabwe (the former Rhodesia) every bit as much as it did to the Soviet Union. Zimbabwe's dictator Robert Mugabe forced the country's land owners off their farms in a move similar to Soviet collectivization. Mugabe soon discovered, however, that his government and the people to whom he gave the farms could not operate them. Meldrum (2005) reports that Zimbabwe then, like the former Soviet Union, attempted to get these productive elements of its society to return. The lesson is that when a society expropriates the property of its productive members, whether in terms of their wages in the Soviet Union or their land in Zimbabwe, they have no incentive to produce for the society in question.

* * *

Russia could not get along without intelligence and experience. As soon as she began to run her factories by committees, they went to rack and ruin; there was more debate than production. As soon as they threw out the skilled man, thousands of tons of precious materials were spoiled. The fanatics talked the people into starvation. The Soviets are now offering the engineers, the administrators, the foremen and superintendents, whom at first they drove out, large sums of money if only they will come back. Bolshevism is now crying for the brains and experience which it yesterday treated so ruthlessly. All that "reform" did to Russia was to block production.

There is in this country a sinister element that desires to creep in between the men who work with their hands and the men who think and plan for the men who work with their hands. The same influence that drove the brains, experience, and ability out of Russia is busily engaged in raising prejudice here. We must not suffer the stranger, the destroyer, the hater of happy humanity, to divide our people. In unity is American strength—and freedom.

* * *

The "sinister element" refers to opportunists who produce nothing while they seek to enrich themselves at the expense of those who do. These include what Ford (1922, p. 250) called the "[union] spokesperson who does not work in the shop, who does not work in any shop, whose sole ambition perhaps is to never again have to work in a shop." Ford disliked unions, but he also recognized unionization as a natural reaction to "bosses who never did a decent thing for their employees until they were compelled" (Chapter 18). This is simply the behavioral element of Ford's universal code at work.

Ford's contemporary Frederick Winslow Taylor meanwhile acknowledged soldiering (marking time, or deliberately limiting productivity) as a natural and reasonable response to cuts in piece rates when workers improved their productivity. Capitalism is therefore almost as futile as Communism and Socialism if workers do not receive the wages to which their productivity entitles them.

The "influence" to which Ford refers is Communism ("the Bolshevist"), which had by 1922 clearly become an international movement, and the next section discusses this further.

Ideology Cannot Deliver Prosperity

Ideology, whether in the form of either progressive reform or reactionary conservatism, is no substitute for conformance to the laws of physical and behavioral science. The next paragraphs have profound implications for 21st century America, where far too many people think the "correct" ideology can somehow deliver miraculous results. Shakespeare ridiculed this idea with Jack Cade's speech in Part 2 of *King Henry VI* (Act IV):

> Be brave, then, for your captain is brave and vows reformation. There shall be in England seven halfpenny loaves sold for a penny, the three-hooped pot shall have ten hoops, and I will make it felony to drink small [weak] beer. ...All shall eat and drink on my score, and I will apparel them all in one livery that they may agree like brothers, and worship me their lord.

Shakespeare included the coarse humor to appeal to the groundlings, or lower-class Britons who had to stand on the ground because they could not afford seats in the theater. Even these lower-class and quite possibly illiterate people understood that the King, whether he was Henry VI, the Duke of York, or the pretender Jack Cade, could not provide free food to everybody. They also understood that price controls that demanded the sale of seven half-penny loaves for a penny would soon make bread very scarce. People of the early 20th century apparently had less common sense than the groundlings because Ford (1922, p. 177) felt it necessary to point out the obvious:

> The demand of the disorderly element is practically that everybody be requested to raise fewer potatoes, and yet that everybody be given more potatoes. ... If everybody does less work and everybody gets more of the product of work, how long can it last?

The following material is extremely relevant today because the same delusion, namely, that any kind of ideology as opposed to production of value can deliver a free lunch, persists widely. This is simply the application of the economic part of Ford's universal code: no system can deliver more wealth than it produces.

* * *

On the other hand, we have a different kind of reformer who never calls himself one. He is singularly like the radical reformer. The radical has had no experience and does not want it. The other class of reformer has had plenty of experience but it does him no good. I refer to the reactionary—who will be surprised to find himself put in exactly the same class as the Bolshevist. He wants to go back to some previous condition, not because it was the best condition, but because he thinks he knows about that condition.

The one crowd wants to smash up the whole world in order to make a better one. The other holds the world as so good that it might well be let stand as it is—and decay. The second notion arises as does the first—out of not using the eyes to see with. It is perfectly possible to smash this world, but it is not possible to build a new one. It is possible to prevent the world from going forward, but it is not possible then to prevent it from going back—from decaying. It is foolish to expect that, if everything be overturned, everyone will thereby get three meals a day. Or, should everything be petrified, that thereby six per cent, interest may be paid. The trouble is that reformers and reactionaries alike get away from the realities—from the primary functions.

One of the counsels of caution is to be very certain that we do not mistake a reactionary turn for a return of common sense. We have passed through a period of fireworks of every description, and the making of a great many idealistic maps of progress. We did not get anywhere. It was a convention, not a march. Lovely things were said, but when we got home we found the furnace out. Reactionaries have frequently taken advantage of the recoil from such a period, and they have promised "the good old times"—which usually means the bad old abuses—and because they are perfectly void of vision they are sometimes regarded as "practical men." Their return to power is often hailed as the return of common sense.

There Are Exactly Three Sources of Material Wealth

The following discussion shows that there are only three sources of material wealth: mining, agriculture, and manufacturing, with transportation an indispensable adjunct to these activities. Ford does not mention mining specifically but it, like agriculture, is a means for the acquisition of raw materials from nature. No other activities generate material wealth, and the illusion that other activities (like dot-com stocks and mortgage-backed securities) can do so leads only to disaster.

* * *

The primary functions are agriculture, manufacture, and transporta-tion. Community life is impossible without them. They hold the world together. Raising things, making things, and earning things are as primi-tive as human need and yet as modern as anything can be. They are of the essence of physical life. When they cease, community life ceases. Things do get out of shape in this present world under the present system, but we may hope for a betterment if the foundations stand sure. The great delusion is that one may change the foundation—usurp the part of destiny in the social process. The foundations of society are the men and means to grow things, to make things, and to carry things. As long as agriculture, manu-facture, and transportation survive, the world can survive any economic or social change. As we serve our jobs we serve the world.

* * *

The following material underscores two obvious common sense principles that are unfortunately neither obvious nor common in 21st century America. "Speculation in things already produced," including Dutch tulip bulbs during the 17th century and mortgage-backed securi-ties in the 21st, does not produce wealth. The illusion that government can deliver prosperity has meanwhile led to a national debt that is rap-idly approaching the annual gross national product.

* * *

There is plenty of work to do. Business is merely work. Speculation in things already produced—that is not business. It is just more or less respectable graft. But it cannot be legislated out of existence. Laws can do very little. Law never does anything constructive. It can never be more than a policeman, and so it is a waste of time to look to our state capitals or to Washington to do that which law was not designed to do. As long as we look to legislation to cure poverty or to abolish special privilege we are going to see poverty spread and special privilege grow. We have had enough of looking to Washington and we have had enough of legislators— not so much, however, in this as in other countries—promising laws to do that which laws cannot do.

Government Cannot Deliver Prosperity

When you get a whole country—as did ours—thinking that Washington is a sort of heaven and behind its clouds dwell omniscience and omnipotence, you are educating that country into a dependent state of mind which augurs ill for the future. Our help does not come from Washington, but from ourselves; our help may, however, go to Washington as a sort of central distribution point where all our efforts are coordinated for the general good. We may help the Government; the Government cannot help us.

The slogan of "less government in business and more business in government" is a very good one, not mainly on account of business or government, but on account of the people. Business is not the reason why the United States was founded. The Declaration of Independence is not a business charter, nor is the Constitution of the United States a commercial schedule. The United States—its land, people, government, and business—are but methods by which the life of the people is made worth while. The Government is a servant and never should be anything but a servant. The moment the people become adjuncts to government, then the law of retribution begins to work, for such a relation is unnatural, immoral, and inhuman. We cannot live without business and we cannot live without government. Business and government are necessary as servants, like water and grain; as masters they overturn the natural order.

The welfare of the country is squarely up to us as individuals. That is where it should be and that is where it is safest. Governments can promise something for nothing but they cannot deliver. They can juggle the currencies as they did in Europe (and as bankers the world over do, as long as they can get the benefit of the juggling) with a patter of solemn nonsense. But it is work and work alone that can continue to deliver the goods—and that, down in his heart, is what every man knows.

There is little chance of an intelligent people, such as ours, ruining the fundamental processes of economic life. Most men know they cannot get something for nothing. Most men feel—even if they do not know—that money is not wealth. The ordinary theories which promise everything to everybody, and demand nothing from anybody, are promptly denied by the instincts of the ordinary man, even when he does not find reasons against them. He knows they are wrong. That is enough. The present order, always clumsy, often stupid, and in many ways imperfect, has this advantage over any other—it works. Doubtless our order will merge by degrees into another, and the new one will also work—but not so much by reason of what it is as by reason of what men will bring into it. The reason why Bolshevism did not work, and cannot work, is not economic. It does not matter whether industry is privately managed or socially controlled; it does not matter whether you call the workers' share "wages" or "dividends"; it does not matter whether you regimentalize the people as to food, clothing, and shelter, or whether you allow them to eat, dress, and live as they like. Those are mere matters of detail. The incapacity of the Bolshevist leaders is indicated by the fuss they made over such details. Bolshevism failed because it was both unnatural and immoral. Our system stands. Is it wrong? Of course it is wrong, at a thousand points! Is it clumsy? Of course it is clumsy. By all right and reason it ought to break down. But it does not—because it is instinct with certain economic and moral fundamentals.

Capitalism Must Conform to Economic and Moral Fundamentals

Capitalism works not necessarily because it is an inherently superior economic system but because its practice—at least in the United States during the 1920s—conformed to "certain economic and moral fundamentals." The next paragraph defines these as a worker's natural human right to the fruits of his labor. A system that denies the worker this right, whether it be Socialism, Communism, or a Capitalist system that squeezes profits from worker's wages instead of the business' ability to produce value, is inherently dysfunctional.

To this Ford adds, "Capitalists who become such because they provide better means of production are of the foundation of society," i.e., a capitalist who can develop a more efficient system as Ford did, or an entirely new economic sector as Bill Gates did, has earned his or her wealth and place in society. Capitalists whose sole function is to profit from distribution barriers (e.g., non-value-adding middlemen) instead of eliminating them are on the other hand waste or muda, and the Internet now provides the means to circumvent or eliminate many of them.

* * *

The economic fundamental is labour. Labour is the human element which makes the fruitful seasons of the earth useful to men. It is men's labour that makes the harvest what it is. That is the economic fundamental: every one of us is working with material which we did not and could not create, but which was presented to us by Nature.

The moral fundamental is man's right in his labour. This is variously stated. It is sometimes called "the right of property." It is sometimes masked in the command, "Thou shalt not steal." It is the other man's right in his property that makes stealing a crime. When a man has earned his bread, he has a right to that bread. If another steals it, he does more than steal bread; he invades a sacred human right.

If we cannot produce we cannot have—but some say if we produce it is only for the capitalists. Capitalists who become such because they provide better means of production are of the foundation of society. They have really nothing of their own. They merely manage property for the benefit of others. Capitalists who become such through trading in money are a temporarily necessary evil. They may not be evil at all if their money goes to production. If their money goes to complicating distribution—to raising barriers between the producer and the consumer—then they are evil capitalists and they will pass away when money is better adjusted to work; and money will become better adjusted to work when it is fully realized that through work and work alone may health, wealth, and happiness inevitably be secured.

The Right to Work, and to Be Paid for Work

Ford now describes the biggest problem in the United States today. Millions of people are willing to work but they cannot do so because shortsighted and incompetent—at least by Ford's standards—businesses have moved the jobs offshore for cheap labor. Lean manufacturing as practiced at the Ford Motor Company on the other hand allowed anybody with a decent basic education to earn a very high wage while producing enough value to justify that wage.

* * *

There is no reason why a man who is willing to work should not be able to work and to receive the full value of his work. There is equally no reason why a man who can but will not work should not receive the full value of his services to the community. He should most certainly be permitted to take away from the community an equivalent of what he contributes to it. If he contributes nothing he should take away nothing. He should have the freedom of starvation. We are not getting anywhere when we insist that every man ought to have more than he deserves to have—just because some do get more than they deserve to have.

There can be no greater absurdity and no greater disservice to humanity in general than to insist that all men are equal. Most certainly all men are not equal, and any democratic conception which strives to make men equal is only an effort to block progress. Men cannot be of equal service. The men of larger ability are less numerous than the men of smaller ability; it is possible for a mass of the smaller men to pull the larger ones down—but in so doing they pull themselves down. It is the larger men who give the leadership to the community and enable the smaller men to live with less effort.

The conception of democracy which names a leveling-down of ability makes for waste. No two things in nature are alike. We build our cars absolutely interchangeable. All parts are as nearly alike as chemical analysis, the finest machinery, and the finest workmanship can make them. No fitting of any kind is required, and it would certainly seem that two Fords standing side by side, looking exactly alike and made so exactly alike that any part could be taken out of one and put into the other, would be alike. But they are not. They will have different road habits. We have men who have driven hundreds, and in some cases thousands of Fords and they say that no two ever act precisely the same—that, if they should drive a new car for an hour or even less and then the car were mixed with a bunch of other new ones, also each driven for a single hour and under the same conditions, that although they could not recognize the car they had been driving merely by looking at it, they could do so by driving it.

I have been speaking in general terms. Let us be more concrete. A man ought to be able to live on a scale commensurate with the service that he renders. This is rather a good time to talk about this point, for we have recently been through a period when the rendering of service was the last thing that most people thought of. We were getting to a place where no one cared about costs or service. Orders came without effort. Whereas once it was the customer who favored the merchant by dealing with him, conditions changed until it was the merchant who favored the customer by selling to him. That is bad for business. Monopoly is bad for business. Profiteering is bad for business. The lack of necessity to hustle is bad for business. Business is never as healthy as when, like a chicken, it must do a certain amount of scratching for what it gets. Things were coming too easily. There was a let-down of the principle that an honest relation ought to obtain between values and prices. The public no longer had to be "catered to." There was even a "public be damned" attitude in many places. It was intensely bad for business. Some men called that abnormal condition

"prosperity." It was not prosperity—it was just a needless money chase.
Money chasing is not business.

Businesses Are Servants and Not Masters

When a business focuses on rendering service to its customers, the money will usually take care of itself. When the business focuses on money, however, service takes a secondary role if any at all, and then the money stops coming because the poorly served customers go elsewhere: "When the people wake up to the fact that they are not being served, the end of that producer is in sight." It is particularly telling that Ford's successors were exactly the kind of people whom Ford said should never be put in charge of anything because their eye was always on the dollar and rarely on the job that produced it:

> In the decade following World War II, Ford's Whiz Kids created a corporate culture based on a financial paradigm, in which virtually every business decision was a function only of profitability. (Hoyer, 2001)

The concept of service also ties in with China's Mandate of Heaven, the authority a leader derives through effective service to stakeholders. The Chinese would say that a leader or manager who does not serve has lost the Mandate of Heaven. Ford later applies the same concept to leadership in an organization by saying that (1) people may fear and comply with a bad leader's authority but they will never respect that leader, and (2) people recognize a genuine leader regardless of his or her official title.

* * *

It is very easy, unless one keeps a plan thoroughly in mind, to get burdened with money and then, in an effort to make more money, to forget all about selling to the people what they want. Business on a money-making basis is most insecure. It is a touch-and-go affair, moving irregularly and rarely over a term of years amounting to much. It is the function of business to produce for consumption and not for money or speculation. Producing for consumption implies that the quality of the article produced will be high and that the price will be low—that the article be one which serves the people and not merely the producer. If the money feature is twisted out of its proper perspective, then the production will be twisted to serve the producer.

The producer depends for his prosperity upon serving the people. He may get by for a while serving himself, but if he does, it will be purely accidental, and when the people wake up to the fact that they are not being served, the end of that producer is in sight. During the boom period the larger effort of production was to serve itself and hence, the moment the people woke up, many producers went to smash. They said that they had entered into a "period of depression." Really they had not. They were simply trying to pit nonsense against sense which is something that cannot successfully be done. Being greedy for money is the surest way not to get it, but when one serves for the sake of service—for the satisfaction of doing that which one believes to be right—then money abundantly takes care of itself.

Money comes naturally as the result of service. And it is absolutely necessary to have money. But we do not want to forget that the end of money is not ease but the opportunity to perform more service. In my mind nothing is more abhorrent than a life of ease. None of us has any right to ease. There is no place in civilization for the idler. Any scheme looking to abolishing money is only making affairs more complex, for we must have a measure. That our present system of money is a satisfactory basis for exchange is a matter of grave doubt. That is a question which I shall talk of in a subsequent chapter. The gist of my objection to the present monetary system is that it tends to become a thing of itself and to block instead of facilitate production.

Lean Manufacturing Turns Luxuries into Everyday Items

Ford not only believed but proved that everybody in society is entitled to luxury goods, which automobiles once were. Achievement of this goal required ongoing questions as to whether long-accepted ways of doing jobs are the best ways: "Things in past ages were made in certain ways and makers since then have just followed."

The following paragraphs also introduce very clearly the principle of design for manufacturing: "Start with an article that suits and then study to find some way of eliminating the entirely useless parts." Ford adds that this simplification should come before the item goes into production; in other words, the leanest manufacturing process on Earth can do only so much with a bad design.

* * *

My effort is in the direction of simplicity. People in general have so little and it costs so much to buy even the barest necessities (let alone that share of the luxuries to which I think everyone is entitled) because nearly every-thing that we make is much more complex than it needs to be. Our cloth-ing, our food, our household furnishings—all could be much simpler than they now are and at the same time be better looking. Things in past ages were made in certain ways and makers since then have just followed.

I do not mean that we should adopt freak styles. There is no necessity for that. Clothing need not be a bag with a hole cut in it. That might be easy to make but it would be inconvenient to wear. A blanket does not require much tailoring, but none of us could get much work done if we went around Indian-fashion in blankets. Real simplicity means that which gives the very best service and is the most convenient in use. The trouble with drastic reforms is they always insist that a man be made over in order to use certain designed articles. I think that dress reform for women— which seems to mean ugly clothes—must always originate with plain women who want to make everyone else look plain. That is not the right process. Start with an article that suits and then study to find some way of eliminating the entirely useless parts. This applies to everything—a shoe, a dress, a house, a piece of machinery, a railroad, a steamship, an airplane. As we cut out useless parts and simplify necessary ones we also cut down the cost of making. This is simple logic, but oddly enough the ordinary process starts with a cheapening of the manufacturing instead of with a simplifying of the article. The start ought to be with the article. First we ought to find whether it is as well made as it should be—does it give the best possible service? Then—are the materials the best or merely the most expensive? Then—can its complexity and weight be cut down? And so on.

Weight Is Not a Substitute for Strength

A well-designed product will not substitute weight for strength, especially in vehicles. If the vehicle's weight can be reduced with no loss in power or performance, it can carry a greater load and therefore more value. Non-value-adding weight such as water in green wood should meanwhile be eliminated from the load itself. Air has no value whatsoever (except to astronauts and divers, and it is significant that their supplies often exclude the non-value-adding nitrogen), which argues against the shipment of empty containers, popped popcorn, puffed cereals, and the like.

* * *

There is no more sense in having extra weight in an article than there is in the cockade on a coachman's hat. In fact, there is not as much. For the cockade may help the coachman to identify his hat while the extra weight means only a waste of strength. I cannot imagine where the delusion that weight means strength came from. It is all well enough in a pile-driver, but why move a heavy weight if we are not going to hit anything with it? In transportation why put extra weight in a machine? Why not add it to the load that the machine is designed to carry? Fat men cannot run as fast as thin men but we build most of our vehicles as though dead-weight fat increased speed! A deal of poverty grows out of the carriage of excess weight.

Some day we shall discover how further to eliminate weight. Take wood, for example. For certain purposes wood is now the best substance we know, but wood is extremely wasteful. The wood in a Ford car contains thirty pounds of water. There must be some way of doing better than that. There must be some method by which we can gain the same strength and elasticity without having to lug useless weight. And so through a thousand processes.

Basic Lean Manufacturing Principle: Waste Hides in Plain View

The next paragraph underscores the fact that most forms of waste hide in plain view. People become used to living with the waste, or working around it, so nobody does anything to remove it. Anybody who learns the Henry Ford thought process will on the other hand recognize such waste immediately. The following paragraph embodies the key element of the scientific aspect of Ford's universal code.

* * *

The farmer makes too complex an affair out of his daily work. I believe that the average farmer puts to a really useful purpose only about 5 per cent of the energy that he spends. If any one ever equipped a factory in the style, say, the average farm is fitted out, the place would be cluttered with men. The worst factory in Europe is hardly as bad as the average farm barn. Power is utilized to the least possible degree. Not only is everything done by hand, but seldom is a thought given to logical arrangement. A farmer doing his chores will walk up and down a rickety ladder a dozen times. He will carry water for years instead of putting in a few lengths of pipe. His whole idea, when there is extra work to do, is to hire extra men. He thinks of putting money into improvements as an expense. Farm products at their lowest prices are dearer than they ought to be. Farm profits at their highest are lower than they ought to be. It is waste motion—waste effort—that makes farm prices high and profits low.

* * *

The implications of this paragraph cannot possibly be overemphasized, and they reinforce statements by other Lean manufacturing, business, and even military practitioners:

- Dr. Shigeo Shingo (Robinson, 1990, p. 14) says of waste or muda, "Unfortunately, real waste lurks in forms that do not look like waste. Only through careful observation and goal orientation can waste be identified. We must always keep in mind that the greatest waste is the waste we don't see."
- General Carl von Clausewitz (1976, p. 119) defined friction as "...the force that makes the apparently easy so difficult. ...countless minor incidents—the kind you can never really foresee—combine to lower the general level of performance, so that one always falls short of the intended goal."
- Tom Peters (1987, p. 323) adds of bringing new products to market, "The accumulation of little items, each too trivial to trouble the boss with, is a prime cause of miss-the-market delays." The key phrase is "each too trivial to trouble the boss with" because it shows that people become used to waste and therefore live with it instead of getting rid of it.
- Taiichi Ohno (1988, p. 59) underscores the need to identify and remove all forms of waste. "In reality, however, such waste is usually hidden, making it difficult to eliminate. ...To implement the Toyota production system in your own business, there must be a total understanding of waste. Unless all sources of waste are detected and crushed, success will always be just a dream."
- Halpin (1966, pp. 60–61) adds the statement, "They turned out to be the little things that get under a worker's skin but are never quite important enough to make him come to management for a change."

The successful implementation of Henry Ford's universal code therefore requires an organization-wide culture of zero tolerance for any form of waste. Elimination of the waste requires its recognition, and mastery of this book's contents equips the reader to recognize waste that would otherwise hide in plain view.

Ford (1922, p. 329) added that there are exactly three kinds of waste: time, material, and energy. It is convenient for analytical and workforce education purposes to expand them into four key performance indicators (KPIs):

1. Waste of the time of things (parts or services, and equipment for which paying work is available; do not build unsaleable inventory to keep equipment busy). This includes cycle time; any time the product or service spends in a non-value-adding activity is waste.
   - Ford and Crowther (1926, pp. 112–121) include an entire chapter called "The Meaning of Time," which shows that inventory, which is inversely proportional to cycle time per Little's Law, is waste. The chapter also discusses the need for reliable transportation.
2. Waste of the time of people, e.g., due to motion inefficiency.
3. Waste of materials, elimination of which supports ISO 14001.
   - Ford and Crowther (1926, pp. 92–100) elaborate on this substantially in a chapter called "Learning from Waste."
   - Norwood (1931, pp. 124–136) features an entire chapter called "Converting Waste into Millions," and it addresses the same subject.
4. Waste of energy, elimination of which supports ISO 50001.

These KPIs encompass completely the Toyota Production System's Seven Wastes and also the three key performance indicators of Goldratt's Theory of Constraints. Consider, for example, money tied up in inventory, which is a TPS waste and also an undesirable Theory of Constraints performance indicator. Inventory equals throughput multiplied by cycle time, so shorter cycle times reduce inventory. Ford's workers were meanwhile so intolerant of waste of materials that even recyclable metal from punching and machining operations drew immediate attention.

Application of Ford's Principles to Agriculture

The next paragraph adds the need for a paradigm shift in agriculture, in which the farmer should regard himself as an industrialist instead of a farmer. Hydroponic farms, vertical farms, and similar plant and equipment for food production allow 21st century agricultural industrialists to eliminate much of the land required for traditional agriculture, along with risks involving frost, droughts, and other causes of crop failure.

* * *

On my own farm at Dearborn we do everything by machinery. We have eliminated a great number of wastes, but we have not as yet touched on real economy. We have not yet been able to put in five or ten years of intense night-and-day study to discover what really ought to be done. We have left more undone than we have done. Yet at no time—no matter what the value of crops—have we failed to turn a first-class profit. We are not farmers—we are industrialists on the farm. The moment the farmer considers himself as an industrialist, with a horror of waste either in material or in men, then we are going to have farm products so low-priced that all will have enough to eat, and the profits will be so satisfactory that farming will be considered as among the least hazardous and most profitable of occupations.

Lack of knowledge of what is going on and lack of knowledge of what the job really is and the best way of doing it are the reasons why farming is thought not to pay. Nothing could pay the way farming is conducted. The farmer follows luck and his forefathers. He does not know how economically to produce, and he does not know how to market. A manufacturer who knew how neither to produce nor to market would not long stay in business. That the farmer can stay on shows how wonderfully profitable farming can be.

The way to attain low-priced, high-volume production in the factory or on the farm—and low-priced, high-volume production means plenty for everyone—is quite simple. The trouble is that the general tendency is to complicate very simple affairs. Take, for an instance, an "improvement."

The Role of Design for Manufacture (DFM)

Ford next describes how the design and development of the product play a vital role in its success. Ricoh Copier (Lorenzen, 1992) learned that a design correction (or by implication improvement) delivered a 100:1 payoff, a process correction a 10:1 payoff, and a manufacturing fix only a 1:1 payoff. If quality must be built into the product as opposed to inspected into it, profitability must similarly be designed into the product. The leanest process or the best kaizen blitz cannot make a poorly designed product or service truly profitable.

* * *

When we talk about improvements usually we have in mind some change in a product. An "improved" product is one that has been changed. That is not my idea. I do not believe in starting to make until I have discovered the best possible thing. This, of course, does not mean that a product should never be changed, but I think that it will be found more economical in the end not even to try to produce an article until you have fully satisfied yourself that utility, design, and material are the best. If your researches do not give you that confidence, then keep right on searching until you find confidence. The place to start manufacturing is with the article. The factory, the organization, the selling, and the financial plans will shape themselves to the article. You will have a cutting, edge on your business chisel and in the end you will save time. Rushing into manufacturing without being certain of the product is the unrecognized cause of many business failures. People seem to think that the big thing is the factory or the store or the financial backing or the management. The big thing is the product, and any hurry in getting into fabrication before designs are completed is just so much waste time. I spent twelve years before I had a Model T—which is what is known to-day as the Ford car—that suited me. We did not attempt to go into real production until we had a real product. That product has not been essentially changed.

We are constantly experimenting with new ideas. If you travel the roads in the neighbourhood of Dearborn you can find all sorts of models of Ford cars. They are experimental cars—they are not new models. I do not believe in letting any good idea get by me, but I will not quickly decide whether an idea is good or bad. If an idea seems good or seems even to have possibilities, I believe in doing whatever is necessary to test out the idea from every angle. But testing out the idea is something very different from making a change in the car. Where most manufacturers find themselves quicker to make a change in the product than in the method of manufacturing—we follow exactly the opposite course.

The Role of Vertical Integration in Supply Chain Management

The next paragraph underscores the virtues of vertical integration, or at least the ability to manufacture independently any supplied part in case the supplier is unable to deliver. The tsunami that ravaged Japan interrupted many supply chains. *Chemical Week* (2011) reported, for example, that there is now a shortage of bis-maleimide triazine resin (BT resin), which is used in many electronic products.

* * *

Our big changes have been in methods of manufacturing. They never stand still. I believe that there is hardly a single operation in the making of our car that is the same as when we made our first car of the present model. That is why we make them so cheaply. The few changes that have been made in the car have been in the direction of convenience in use or where we found that a change in design might give added strength. The materials in the car change as we learn more and more about materials. Also we do not want to be held up in production or have the expense of production increased by any possible shortage in a particular material, so we have for most parts worked out substitute materials. Vanadium steel, for instance, is our principal steel. With it we can get the greatest strength with the least weight, but it would not be good business to let our whole future depend upon being able to get vanadium steel. We have worked out a substitute. All our steels are special, but for every one of them we have at least one, and sometimes several, fully proved and tested substitutes. And so on through all of our materials and likewise with our parts. In the beginning we made very few of our parts and none of our motors. Now we make all our motors and most of our parts because we find it cheaper to do so. But also we aim to make some of every part so that we cannot be caught in any market emergency or be crippled by some outside manufacturer being unable to fill his orders. The prices on glass were run up outrageously high during the war; we are among the largest users of glass in the country. Now we are putting up our own glass factory. If we had devoted all of this energy to making changes in the product we should be nowhere; but by not changing the product we are able to give our energy to the improvement of the making.

Eliminate Waste Effort from All Jobs

Ford now emphasizes the need to eliminate all forms of waste effort from all activities: "For any one to be required to use more force than is absolutely necessary for the job in hand is waste."

* * *

The principal part of a chisel is the cutting edge. If there is a single principle on which our business rests it is that. It makes no difference how finely made a chisel is or what splendid steel it has in it or how well it is forged—if it has no cutting edge it is not a chisel. It is just a piece of metal. All of which being translated means that it is what a thing does—not what it is supposed to do—that matters. What is the use of putting a tremendous force behind a blunt chisel if a light blow on a sharp chisel will do the work? The chisel is there to cut, not to be hammered. The hammering is only incidental to the job. So if we want to work why not concentrate on the work and do it in the quickest possible fashion? The cutting edge of merchandising is the point where the product touches the consumer. An unsatisfactory product is one that has a dull cutting edge. A lot of waste effort is needed to put it through. The cutting edge of a factory is the man and the machine on the job. If the man is not right the machine cannot be; if the machine is not right the man cannot be. For any one to be required to use more force than is absolutely necessary for the job in hand is waste.

Ford's Four Principles of Service

The last part of the following paragraph ties in again with the Mandate of Heaven: "Everyone who is connected with us—either as a manager, worker, or purchaser—is the better for our existence. The institution that we have erected is performing a service." The leader and organization justify their existence through service to all stakeholders.

* * *

The essence of my idea then is that waste and greed block the delivery of true service. Both waste and greed are unnecessary. Waste is due largely to not understanding what one does, or being careless in doing of it. Greed is merely a species of nearsightedness. I have striven toward manufacturing with a minimum of waste, both of materials and of human effort, and then toward distribution at a minimum of profit, depending for the total profit upon the volume of distribution. In the process of manufacturing I want to distribute the maximum of wage—that is, the maximum of buying power. Since also this makes for a minimum cost and we sell at a minimum profit, we can distribute a product in consonance with buying power. Thus everyone who is connected with us—either as a manager, worker, or purchaser—is the better for our existence. The institution that we have erected is performing a service. That is the only reason I have for talking about it. The principles of that service are these:

1. *An absence of fear of the future and of veneration for the past. One who fears the future, who fears failure, limits his activities. Failure is only the opportunity more intelligently to begin again. There is no disgrace in honest failure; there is disgrace in fearing to fail. What is past is useful only as it suggests ways and means for progress.*
2. *A disregard of competition. Whoever does a thing best ought to be the one to do it. It is criminal to try to get business away from another man—criminal because one is then trying to lower for personal gain the condition of one's fellow man—to rule by force instead of by intelligence.*
3. *The putting of service before profit. Without a profit, business cannot extend. There is nothing inherently wrong about making a profit. Well-conducted business enterprise cannot fail to return a profit, but profit must and inevitably will come as a reward for good service. It cannot be the basis—it must be the result of service.*
4. *Manufacturing is not buying low and selling high. It is the process of buying materials fairly and, with the smallest possible addition of cost, transforming those materials into a consumable product and giving it to the consumer. Gambling, speculating, and sharp dealing, tend only to clog this progression.*

How all of this arose, how it has worked out, and how it applies generally are the subjects of these chapters.

1

The Beginning of Business

This chapter describes how Ford got into business, and cites some of the early influences on his thought processes. The previous chapter discussed how his observation of farm work awakened him to the enormous amount of waste that can be built into a job, and this chapter discusses the agricultural influences even further. Note Ford's observation that the hand labor on farms did not deliver commensurate results.

*   *   *

On May 31, 1921, the Ford Motor Company turned out Car No. 5,000,000. It is out in my museum along with the gasoline buggy that I began work on thirty years before and which first ran satisfactorily along in the spring of 1893. I was running it when the bobolinks came to Dearborn and they always come on April 2nd. There is all the difference in the world in the appearance of the two vehicles and almost as much difference in construction and materials, but in fundamentals the two are curiously alike— except that the old buggy has on it a few wrinkles that we have not yet quite adopted in our modern car. For that first car or buggy, even though it had but two cylinders, would make twenty miles an hour and run sixty miles on the three gallons of gas the little tank held and is as good to-day as the day it was built. The development in methods of manufacture and in materials has been greater than the development in basic design. The whole design has been refined; the present Ford car, which is the "Model T," has four cylinders and a self starter—it is in every way a more convenient and an easier riding car. It is simpler than the first car. But almost every point in it may be found also in the first car. The changes have been brought about through experience in the making and not through any change in the basic principle—which I take to be an important fact demonstrating that, given a good idea to start with, it is better to concentrate on perfecting it than to hunt around for a new idea. One idea at a time is about as much as any one can handle.

It was life on the farm that drove me into devising ways and means to better transportation. I was born on July 30, 1863, on a farm at Dearborn, Michigan, and my earliest recollection is that, considering the results, there was too much work on the place. That is the way I still feel about farming. There is a legend that my parents were very poor and that the early days were hard ones. Certainly they were not rich, but neither were they poor. As Michigan farmers went, we were prosperous. The house in which I was born is still standing, and it and the farm are part of my present holding.

There was too much hard hand labour on our own and all other farms of the time. Even when very young I suspected that much might somehow be done in a better way. That is what took me into mechanics—although my mother always said that I was born a mechanic. I had a kind of workshop with odds and ends of metal for tools before I had anything else. In those days we did not have the toys of to-day; what we had were home made. My toys were all tools—they still are! And every fragment of machinery was a treasure.

FORD'S INSPIRATION: THE STEAM-POWERED ROAD ENGINE

Ford's boyhood encounter with a steam-powered road engine, which was effectively a locomotive that ran on roads instead of tracks, suggested to him the idea of passenger vehicles that could do the same. Ford's age of 12 years would have made the year about 1875. The Prussian field marshal Helmuth von Moltke was actually seven years ahead of Ford per Hughes (1993, p. 257):

> If a truck can take the place of forty horses, the advantage is evident. It can travel by itself, consumes but a fraction of its load, and covers greater distances. Military authorities will undoubtedly gain much from the use of trucks when they have been invented.

Hughes makes it clear that Moltke meant Strassenlokomotives, or "street locomotives," such as the one Ford saw later.

The purpose of the road engine that Ford saw was farm work as opposed to transportation. It could move itself to a farm, which could then connect it to farm machinery to deliver power for various tasks. Ford foresaw, however, that machines like these also could move people and goods.

* * *

The biggest event of those early years was meeting with a road engine about eight miles out of Detroit one day when we were driving to town. I was then twelve years old. The second biggest event was getting a watch—which happened in the same year. I remember that engine as though I had seen it only yesterday, for it was the first vehicle other than horse-drawn that I had ever seen. It was intended primarily for driving threshing machines and sawmills and was simply a portable engine and boiler mounted on wheels with a water tank and coal cart trailing behind. I had seen plenty of these engines hauled around by horses, but this one had a chain that made a connection between the engine and the rear wheels of the wagon-like frame on which the boiler was mounted. The engine was placed over the boiler and one man standing on the platform behind the boiler shoveled coal, managed the throttle, and did the steering. It had been made by Nichols, Shepard, & Company of Battle Creek. I found that out at once. The engine had stopped to let us pass with our horses and I was off the wagon and talking to the engineer before my father, who was driving, knew what I was up to. The engineer was very glad to explain the whole affair. He was proud of it. He showed me how the chain was disconnected from the propelling wheel and a belt put on to drive other machinery. He told me that the engine made two hundred revolutions a minute and that the chain pinion could be shifted to let the wagon stop while the engine was still running. This last is a feature which, although in different fashion, is incorporated into modern automobiles. It was not important with steam engines, which are easily stopped and started, but it became very important with the gasoline engine. It was that engine which took me into automotive transportation. I tried to make models of it, and some years later I did make one that ran very well, but from the time I saw that road engine as a boy of twelve right forward to to-day, my great interest has been in making a machine that would travel the roads. Driving to town I always had a pocket full of trinkets—nuts, washers, and odds and ends of machinery. Often I took a broken watch and tried to put it together. When I was thirteen I managed for the first time to put a watch together so that it would keep time. By the time I was fifteen I could do almost anything in watch repairing—although my tools were of the crudest. There is an immense amount to be learned simply by tinkering with things. It is not possible to learn from books how everything is made—and a real mechanic ought to know how nearly everything is made. Machines are to a mechanic what books are to a writer. He gets ideas from them, and if he has any brains he will apply those ideas.

CLOCKS: THE INSPIRATION FOR THE SYNCHRONIZED MOVING ASSEMBLY LINE

Ford's fascination with watches is significant because he later synchronized his moving assembly lines to operate like giant timepieces. Gourley (1997, 30) elaborates:

> The speed of the work was carefully timed so that the assembly line did not run too fast or too slow. Where the workers put together the chassis, the line moved six feet per minute. Where the workers bolted the front axle to the chassis, the line moved faster, 15 feet per minute.
> It was like setting the mechanism of a clock.
> Henry had created a giant moving timepiece.

This depiction suggests a production control scheme that, while not a formal pull system like kanban or drum-buffer rope, ensures that there are no shortages or surpluses of work anywhere in the system. Achievement of this goal requires extremely reliable processes because a stoppage anywhere will result very quickly in shortages down the line.

* * *

From the beginning I never could work up much interest in the labour of farming. I wanted to have something to do with machinery. My father was not entirely in sympathy with my bent toward mechanics. He thought that I ought to be a farmer. When I left school at seventeen and became an apprentice in the machine shop of the Drydock Engine Works I was all but given up for lost. I passed my apprenticeship without trouble—that is, I was qualified to be a machinist long before my three-year term had expired—and having a liking for fine work and a leaning toward watches I worked nights at repairing in a jewelry shop. At one period of those early days I think that I must have had fully three hundred watches. I thought that I could build a serviceable watch for around thirty cents and nearly started in the business. But I did not because I figured out that watches were not universal necessities, and therefore people generally would not buy them. Just how I reached that surprising conclusion I am unable to state. I did not like the ordinary jewelry and watch making work excepting where the job was hard to do. Even then I wanted to make something in quantity. It was just about the time when the standard railroad time was being arranged. We had formerly been on sun time and for quite a while, just as in our present daylight-saving days, the railroad time differed from the local time. That bothered me a good deal and so I succeeded in making a watch that kept both times. It had two dials and it was quite a curiosity in the neighbourhood.

In 1879—that is, about four years after I first saw that Nichols-Shepard machine—I managed to get a chance to run one and when my apprenticeship was over I worked with a local representative of the Westinghouse Company of Schenectady as an expert in the setting up and repair of their road engines. The engine they put out was much the same as the Nichols-Shepard engine excepting that the engine was up in front, the boiler in the rear, and the power was applied to the back wheels by a belt. They could make twelve miles an hour on the road even though the self-propelling feature was only an incident of the construction. They were sometimes used as tractors to pull heavy loads and, if the owner also happened to be in the threshing-machine business, he hitched his threshing machine and other paraphernalia to the engine in moving from farm to farm. What bothered me was the weight and the cost. They weighed a couple of tons and were far too expensive to be owned by other than a farmer with a great deal of land. They were mostly employed by people who went into threshing as a business or who had sawmills or some other line that required portable power.

Even before that time I had the idea of making some kind of a light steam car that would take the place of horses—more especially, however, as a tractor to attend to the excessively hard labour of ploughing. It occurred to me, as I remember somewhat vaguely, that precisely the same idea might be applied to a carriage or a wagon on the road. A horseless carriage was a common idea. People had been talking about carriages without horses for many years back—in fact, ever since the steam engine was invented—but the idea of the carriage at first did not seem so practical to me as the idea of an engine to do the harder farm work, and of all the work on the farm ploughing was the hardest. Our roads were poor and we had not the habit of getting around. One of the most remarkable features of the automobile on the farm is the way that it has broadened the farmer's life. We simply took for granted that unless the errand were urgent we would not go to town, and I think we rarely made more than a trip a week. In bad weather we did not go even that often.

Horses as a Wasteful Source of Transportation

Ford recognized very early that horses were an expensive form of transportation because one must feed them whether or not one uses them. A steam engine (or internal combustion engine) requires fuel only when it delivers service. Ford also predicted the utility of farm tractors, but he realized that farmers would not buy them, at least not until they saw what automobiles could do.

The original Model T could actually be modified to do farm work. There are pictures of Model Ts with studded metal back wheels for such tasks, and of Model Ts with caterpillar treads and skis in place of front wheels for use as snowmobiles.

* * *

Being a full-fledged machinist and with a very fair workshop on the farm, it was not difficult for me to build a steam wagon or tractor. In the building of it came the idea that perhaps it might be made for road use. I felt perfectly certain that horses, considering all the bother of attending them and the expense of feeding, did not earn their keep. The obvious thing to do was to design and build a steam engine that would be light enough to run an ordinary wagon or to pull a plough. I thought it more important first to develop the tractor. To lift farm drudgery off flesh and blood and lay it on steel and motors has been my most constant ambition. It was circumstances that took me first into the actual manufacture of road cars. I found eventually that people were more interested in something that would travel on the road than in something that would do the work on the farms. In fact, I doubt that the light farm tractor could have been introduced on the farm had not the farmer had his eyes opened slowly but surely by the automobile. But that is getting ahead of the story. I thought the farmer would be more interested in the tractor.

I built a steam car that ran. It had a kerosene-heated boiler and it developed plenty of power and a neat control—which is so easy with a steam throttle. But the boiler was dangerous. To get the requisite power without too big and heavy a power plant required that the engine work under high pressure; sitting on a high-pressure steam boiler is not altogether pleasant. To make it even reasonably safe required an excess of weight that nullified the economy of the high pressure. For two years I kept experimenting with various sorts of boilers— the engine and control problems were simple enough—and then I definitely abandoned the whole idea of running a road vehicle by steam. I knew that in England they had what amounted to locomotives running on the roads hauling lines of trailers and also there was no difficulty in designing a big steam tractor for use on a large farm. But ours were not then English roads; they would have stalled or racked to pieces the strongest and heaviest road tractor. And anyway the manufacturing of a big tractor which only a few wealthy farmers could buy did not seem to me worth while.

FORD ON NYET ENGINEERS AND OTHER WET BLANKETS

The lesson of the next paragraph is that experts whose experience tells them that something cannot be done are entirely right, at least as far as they are personally concerned. Shigeo Shingo called such persons "nyet engineers" ("nyet" is Russian for "no"). Chapter 5 will show that Field Marshal von Moltke referred to such individuals as "men of the negative" or people upon whom one could always rely to say why something could not be done.

* * *

But I did not give up the idea of a horseless carriage. The work with the Westinghouse representative only served to confirm the opinion I had formed that steam was not suitable for light vehicles. That is why I stayed only a year with that company. There was nothing more that the big steam tractors and engines could teach me and I did not want to waste time on something that would lead nowhere. A few years before— t'was while I was an apprentice—I read in the World of Science, an English publication, of the "silent gas engine" which was then coming out in England. I think it was the Otto engine. It ran with illuminating gas, had a single large cylinder, and the power impulses being thus intermittent required an extremely heavy fly-wheel. As far as weight was concerned, it gave nothing like the power per pound of metal that a steam engine gave, and the use of illuminating gas seemed to dismiss it as even a possibility for road use. It was interesting to me only as all machinery was interesting. I followed in the English and American magazines, which we got in the shop, the development of the engine and most particularly the hints of the possible replacement of the illuminating gas fuel by a gas formed by the vaporization of gasoline. The idea of gas engines was by no means new, but this was the first time that a really serious effort had been made to put them on the market. They were received with interest rather than enthusiasm and I do not recall any one who thought that the internal combustion engine could ever have more than a limited use. All the wise people demonstrated conclusively that the engine could not compete with steam. They never thought that it might carve out a career for itself. That is the way with wise people—they are so wise and practical that they always know to a dot just why something cannot be done; they always know the limitations. That is why I never employ an expert in full bloom. If ever I wanted to kill opposition by unfair means I would endow the opposition with experts. They would have so much good advice that I could be sure they would do little work.

The gas engine interested me and I followed its progress, but only from curiosity, until about 1885 or 1886 when, the steam engine being discarded as the motive power for the carriage that I intended some day to build, I had to look around for another sort of motive power. In 1885 I repaired an Otto engine at the Eagle Iron Works in Detroit. No one in town knew anything about them. There was a rumour that I did and, although I had never before been in contact with one, I undertook and carried through the job. That gave me a chance to study the new engine at first hand and in 1887 I built one on the Otto four-cycle model just to see if I understood the principles. "Four cycle" means that the piston traverses the cylinder four times to get one power impulse. The first stroke draws in the gas, the second compresses it, the third is the explosion or power stroke, while the fourth stroke exhausts the waste gas. The little model worked well enough; it had a one-inch bore and a three-inch stroke, operated with gasoline, and while it did not develop much power, it was slightly lighter in proportion than the engines being offered commercially. I gave it away later to a young man who wanted it for something or other and whose name I have forgotten; it was eventually destroyed. That was the beginning of the work with the internal combustion engine.

I was then on the farm to which I had returned, more because I wanted to experiment than because I wanted to farm, and, now being an all-around machinist, I had a first-class workshop to replace the toy shop of earlier days. My father offered me forty acres of timber land, provided I gave up being a machinist. I agreed in a provisional way, for cutting the timber gave me a chance to get married. I fitted out a sawmill and a portable engine and started to cut out and saw up the timber on the tract. Some of the first of that lumber went into a cottage on my new farm and in it we began our married life. It was not a big house—thirty-one feet square and only a story and a half high—but it was a comfortable place. I added to it my workshop, and when I was not cutting timber I was working on the gas engines—learning what they were and how they acted. I read everything I could find, but the greatest knowledge came from the work. A gas engine is a mysterious sort of thing—it will not always go the way it should. You can imagine how those first engines acted!

HOW RECIPROCATING MOTION ELIMINATES WASTE

Ford recognized very quickly the virtues of reciprocating motion in a two-cylinder engine, in contrast to a single cylinder engine in which the mechanical energy required for intake, compression, and exhaust had to come from a flywheel. Ford and Crowther (1926, pp. 75–76) describe application of the same principle to a lathe:

Instead of being thrown out of gear every few seconds, the direction of the feed is reversed, and rather than have the machine run idle while the finished bushing is being replaced by one in the rough, two arbors are supplied, the cutting tool operating between them like a shuttle.

This put the reverse motion of the tool to good use, just as the two-cylinder engine that Ford describes below used the power stroke of one cylinder to drive the exhaust stroke of the other. Note also the transformation of internal setup (setup that requires the tool to stop or wait for a new piece of work) into external setup. A finished bushing can be removed from one arbor and replaced with a rough one while the tool works on the other. Elimination of internal setup is now a basic principle of single-minute exchange of die (single-minute exchange of die (SMED)).

Arnold and Faurote (1915, pp. 312–313) add that Ford's Highland Park plant applied the same principle to a machine that rammed radiator tubes into a mold. "The machine works in both directions so that when the ram is being withdrawn from one set of molds, it is forcing the tubes into the corresponding one on the other side." The basic idea is to ensure, if possible, that every motion adds value. This is the Ford thought process at work.

Note also how Ford adapted existing technology (bicycle wheels, tractor transmissions, and steering mechanisms) to his new product. The elimination of unnecessary weight, whose conveyance is waste, was among Ford's critical to quality characteristics.

* * *

It was in 1890 that I began on a double-cylinder engine. It was quite impractical to consider the single cylinder for transportation purposes—the flywheel had to be entirely too heavy. Between making the first four-cycle engine of the Otto type and the start on a double cylinder I had made a great many experimental engines out of tubing. I fairly knew my way about. The double cylinder I thought could be applied to a road vehicle and my original idea was to put it on a bicycle with a direct connection to the crankshaft and allowing for the rear wheel of the bicycle to act as the balance wheel. The speed was going to be varied only by the throttle. I never carried out this plan because it soon became apparent that the engine, gasoline tank, and the various necessary controls would be entirely too heavy for a bicycle. The plan of the two opposed cylinders was that, while one would be delivering power the other would be exhausting. This naturally would not require so heavy a fly-wheel to even the application of power. The work started in my shop on the farm. Then I was offered a job with the Detroit Electric Company as an engineer and machinist at forty-five dollars a month. I took it because that was more money than the farm was bringing me and I had decided to get away from farm life anyway. The timber had all been cut. We rented a house on Bagley Avenue, Detroit. The workshop came along and I set it up in a brick shed at the back of the house. During the first several months I was in the night shift at the electric-light plant—which gave me very little time for experimenting—but after that I was in the day shift and every night and all of every Saturday night I worked on the new motor. I cannot say that it was hard work. No work with interest is ever hard. I always am certain of results. They always come if you work hard enough. But it was a very great thing to have my wife even more confident than I was. She has always been that way.

I had to work from the ground up—that is, although I knew that a number of people were working on horseless carriages, I could not know what they were doing. The hardest problems to overcome were in the making and breaking of the spark and in the avoidance of excess weight. For the transmission, the steering gear, and the general construction, I could draw on my experience with the steam tractors. In 1892 I completed my first motor car, but it was not until the spring of the following year that it ran to my satisfaction. This first car had something of the appearance of a buggy. There were two cylinders with a two-and-a-half-inch bore and a six-inch stroke set side by side and over the rear axle. I made them out of the exhaust pipe of a steam engine that I had bought. They developed about four horsepower. The power was transmitted from the motor to the countershaft by a belt and from the countershaft to the rear wheel by a chain. The car would hold two people, the seat being suspended on posts and the body on elliptical springs. There were two speeds—one of ten and the other of twenty miles per hour—obtained by shifting the belt, which was done by a clutch lever in front of the driving seat. Thrown forward, the lever put in the high speed; thrown back, the low speed; with the lever upright the engine could run free. To start the car it was necessary to turn the motor over by hand with the clutch free. To stop the car one simply released the clutch and applied the foot brake. There was no reverse, and speeds other than those of the belt were obtained by the throttle. I bought the iron work for the frame of the carriage and also the seat and the springs. The wheels were twenty-eight-inch wire bicycle wheels with rubber tires. The balance wheel I had cast from a pattern that I made and all of the more delicate mechanism I made myself. One of the features that I discovered necessary was a compensating gear that permitted the same power to be applied to each of the rear wheels when turning corners. The machine altogether weighed about five hundred pounds. A tank under the seat held three gallons of gasoline which was fed to the motor through a small pipe and a mixing valve. The ignition was by electric spark. The original machine was air-cooled— or to be more accurate, the motor simply was not cooled at all. I found that on a run of an hour or more the motor heated up, and so I very shortly put a water jacket around the cylinders and piped it to a tank in the rear of the car over the cylinders.

MATERIAL SELECTION IN DESIGN FOR MANUFACTURING

Ford emphasized the importance of selecting the right materials for a given job. He later discovered the merits of vanadium steel, such as strength and relative lightness. The next section also underscores the importance of foresight during the product design phase. It is generally not possible for the manufacturing process to make up for a bad initial design.

Nearly all of these various features had been planned in advance. That is the way I have always worked. I draw a plan and work out every detail on the plan before starting to build. For otherwise one will waste a great deal of time in makeshifts as the work goes on and the finished article will not have coherence. It will not be rightly proportioned. Many inventors fail because they do not distinguish between planning and experimenting. The largest building difficulties that I had were in obtaining the proper materials. The next were with tools. There had to be some adjustments and changes in details of the design, but what held me up most was that I had neither the time nor the money to search for the best material for each part. But in the spring of 1893, the machine was running to my partial satisfaction and giving an opportunity further to test out the design and material on the road.

2

What I Learned about Business

The first part of the chapter shows that there was discussion of electric vehicles even at the beginning of the twentieth century. The storage capacity of the battery is still a major issue, although hybrid electrics now recover much of the braking energy instead of dissipating it as heat. The rest of the chapter, which focuses on the need to overcome paradigms and practice continuous improvement (kaizen) is considerably more important.

* * *

My "gasoline buggy" was the first and for a long time the only automobile in Detroit. It was considered to be something of a nuisance, for it made a racket and it scared horses. Also it blocked traffic. For if I stopped my machine anywhere in town a crowd was around it before I could start up again. If I left it alone even for a minute some inquisitive person always tried to run it. Finally, I had to carry a chain and chain it to a lamp post whenever I left it anywhere. And then there was trouble with the police. I do not know quite why, for my impression is that there were no speed-limit laws in those days. Anyway, I had to get a special permit from the mayor and thus for a time enjoyed the distinction of being the only licensed chauffeur in America. I ran that machine about one thousand miles through 1895 and 1896 and then sold it to Charles Ainsley of Detroit for two hundred dollars. That was my first sale. I had built the car not to sell but only to experiment with. I wanted to start another car. Ainsley wanted to buy. I could use the money and we had no trouble in agreeing upon a price.

It was not at all my idea to make cars in any such petty fashion. I was looking ahead to production, but before that could come I had to have something to produce. It does not pay to hurry. I started a second car in 1896; it was much like the first but a little lighter. It also had the belt drive which I did not give up until some time later; the belts were all right excepting in hot weather. That is why I later adopted gears. I learned a great deal from that car. Others in this country and abroad were building cars by that time, and in 1895 I heard that a Benz car from Germany was on exhibition in Macy's store in New York. I traveled down to look at it but it had no features that seemed worth while. It also had the belt drive, but it was much heavier than my car. I was working for lightness; the foreign makers have never seemed to appreciate what light weight means. I built three cars in all in my home shop and all of them ran for years in Detroit. I still have the first car; I bought it back a few years later from a man to whom Mr. Ainsley had sold it. I paid one hundred dollars for it.

During all this time I kept my position with the electric company and gradually advanced to chief engineer at a salary of one hundred and twenty-five dollars a month. But my gas-engine experiments were no more popular with the president of the company than my first mechanical leanings were with my father. It was not that my employer objected to experiments—only to experiments with a gas engine. I can still hear him say:

"Electricity, yes, that's the coming thing. But gas—no."

He had ample grounds for his skepticism—to use the mildest terms. Practically no one had the remotest notion of the future of the internal combustion engine, while we were just on the edge of the great electrical development. As with every comparatively new idea, electricity was expected to do much more than we even now have any indication that it can do. I did not see the use of experimenting with electricity for my purposes. A road car could not run on a trolley even if trolley wires had been less expensive; no storage battery was in sight of a weight that was practical. An electrical car had of necessity to be limited in radius and to contain a large amount of motive machinery in proportion to the power exerted. That is not to say that I held or now hold electricity cheaply; we have not yet begun to use electricity. But it has its place, and the internal combustion engine has its place. Neither can substitute for the other—which is exceedingly fortunate.

I have the dynamo that I first had charge of at the Detroit Edison Company. When I started our Canadian plant I bought it from an office building to which it had been sold by the electric company, had it revamped a little, and for several years it gave excellent service in the Canadian plant. When we had to build a new power plant, owing to the increase in business, I had the old motor taken out to my museum—a room out at Dearborn that holds a great number of my mechanical treasures.

The Edison Company offered me the general superintendency of the company but only on condition that I would give up my gas engine and devote myself to something really useful. I had to choose between my job and my automobile. I chose the automobile, or rather I gave up the job—there was really nothing in the way of a choice. For already I knew that the car was bound to be a success. I quit my job on August 15, 1899, and went into the automobile business.

OVERCOME PARADIGMS TO ACHIEVE RESULTS

The following shows how preconceived ideas result in the loss of enormous opportunities, and Peters (1987, p. 244) provided these additional examples. Harry Warner, the founder of Warner Brothers Studio, said this about soundtracks in 1927: "Who in the hell wants to hear actors talk?" IBM's Thomas Watson, Sr. predicted in 1943, "I think there is a world market for about five computers." Digital Equipment's Ken Olsen said of home computers in 1973, "There is no reason for any individual to have a computer in their home."

One should note the requirement to foresee needs that prospective customers have yet to recognize. In this case, there was no widespread demand for automobiles; they were luxuries because of their cost. Ford created a demand for them by getting their price low enough for the middle class to afford.

* * *

It might be thought something of a step, for I had no personal funds. What money was left over from living was all used in experimenting. But my wife agreed that the automobile could not be given up—that we had to make or break. There was no "demand" for automobiles—there never is for a new article. They were accepted in much the fashion as was more recently the airplane. At first the "horseless carriage" was considered merely a freak notion and many wise people explained with particularity why it could never be more than a toy. No man of money even thought of it as a commercial possibility. I cannot imagine why each new means of transportation meets with such opposition. There are even those to-day who shake their heads and talk about the luxury of the automobile and only grudgingly admit that perhaps the motor truck is of some use. But in the beginning there was hardly any one who sensed that the automobile could be a large factor in industry. The most optimistic hoped only for a development akin to that of the bicycle. When it was found that an automobile really could go and several makers started to put out cars, the immediate query was as to which would go fastest. It was a curious but natural development—that racing idea. I never thought anything of racing, but the public refused to consider the automobile in any light other than as a fast toy. Therefore, later we had to race. The industry was held back by this initial racing slant, for the attention of the makers was diverted to making fast rather than good cars. It was a business for speculators.

A group of men of speculative turn of mind organized, as soon as I left the electric company, the Detroit Automobile Company to exploit my car. I was the chief engineer and held a small amount of the stock. For three years we continued making cars more or less on the model of my first car. We sold very few of them; I could get no support at all toward making better cars to be sold to the public at large. The whole thought was to make to order and to get the largest price possible for each car. The main idea seemed to be to get the money. And being without authority other than my engineering position gave me, I found that the new company was not a vehicle for realizing my ideas but merely a money-making concern—that did not make much money. In March, 1902, I resigned, determined never again to put myself under orders. The Detroit Automobile Company later became the Cadillac Company under the ownership of the Lelands, who came in subsequently.

I rented a shop—a one-story brick shed—at 81 Park Place to continue my experiments and to find out what business really was. I thought that it must be something different from what it had proved to be in my first adventure.

The year from 1902 until the formation of the Ford Motor Company was practically one of investigation. In my little one-room brick shop I worked on the development of a four-cylinder motor and on the outside I tried to find out what business really was and whether it needed to be quite so selfish a scramble for money as it seemed to be from my first short experience. From the period of the first car, which I have described, until the formation of my present company I built in all about twenty-five cars, of which nineteen or twenty were built with the Detroit Automobile Company. The automobile had passed from the initial stage where the fact that it could run at all was enough, to the stage where it had to show speed. Alexander Winton of Cleveland, the founder of the Winton car, was then the track champion of the country and willing to meet all comers. I designed a two-cylinder enclosed engine of a more compact type than I had before used, fitted it into a skeleton chassis, found that I could make speed, and arranged a race with Winton. We met on the Grosse Point track at Detroit. I beat him. That was my first race, and it brought advertising of the only kind that people cared to read.

The public thought nothing of a car unless it made speed—unless it beat other racing cars. My ambition to build the fastest car in the world led me to plan a four-cylinder motor. But of that more later.

CUSTOMER SATISFACTION IS A KEY SELLING POINT

Ford now stresses the need to focus on the work and not the money, along with the need for fuel efficiency and reliability. A dissatisfied customer is not an opportunity to make more money from fixing work that had not been done right the first time, but a living and angry bad advertisement.

* * *

The most surprising feature of business as it was conducted was the large attention given to finance and the small attention to service. That seemed to me to be reversing the natural process which is that the money should come as the result of work and not before the work. The second feature was the general indifference to better methods of manufacture as long as whatever was done got by and took the money. In other words, an article apparently was not built with reference to how greatly it could serve the public but with reference solely to how much money could be had for it—and that without any particular care whether the customer was satisfied. To sell him was enough. A dissatisfied customer was regarded not as a man whose trust had been violated, but either as a nuisance or as a possible source of more money in fixing up the work which ought to have been done correctly in the first place. For instance, in automobiles there was not much concern as to what happened to the car once it had been sold. How much gasoline it used per mile was of no great moment; how much service it actually gave did not matter; and if it broke down and had to have parts replaced, then that was just hard luck for the owner. It was considered good business to sell parts at the highest possible price on the theory that, since the man had already bought the car, he simply had to have the part and would be willing to pay for it.

STOCKS AND BONDS ARE DANGEROUS BUSINESS ILLUSIONS

The next section anticipates by almost 80 years the inherent problem with dot-com stocks, mortgage-backed securities, and similar so-called investments: "A good business was one that would give the opportunity for the floating of a large amount of stocks and bonds at high prices. It was the stocks and bonds, not the work, that mattered." It is one matter to invest in an actual means of production like a mine or a factory, and quite another to gamble on worthless paper (e.g., dot-com companies that had not produced earnings and were unlikely to do so), or on paper whose sole value is the assumption that house prices will rise indefinitely. Any such speculation is a zero-sum game because there is either limited or no value behind the paper in question.

The actual value of a house is, of course, the number of people it can shelter comfortably along with whatever amenities it might have, and these characteristics do not change no matter what the current price might be. This reinforces Ford's subsequent observation that the only real value of any asset consists of what the owner can do with it.

The following material also stresses the point that the sole legitimate function of invested money is to buy tools, and by implication an entire means of production, with which to produce material wealth. Material wealth consists solely of mined, grown, or manufactured goods. The means of production, of course, can deliver a useful or vital service, such as transportation or healthcare, but it needs to deliver something.

Ford also points out a possible dysfunctional effect of charges against the business, whether in interest on debt or the need to pay dividends on invested money. If the business did not pay dividends (and/or capital appreciation), it could not attract investors. Dividends, however, should come after the business has delivered profits and not before. Ford bought out his own stockholders in 1919 because they wanted higher dividends instead of reinvestment to allow the company to deliver more service.

* * *

The automobile business was not on what I would call an honest basis, to say nothing of being, from a manufacturing standpoint, on a scientific basis, but it was no worse than business in general. That was the period, it may be remembered, in which many corporations were being floated and financed. The bankers, who before then had confined themselves to the railroads, got into industry. My idea was then and still is that if a man did his work well, the price he would get for that work, the profits and all financial matters, would care for themselves and that a business ought to start small and build itself up and out of its earnings. If there are no earnings then that is a signal to the owner that he is wasting his time and does not belong in that business. I have never found it necessary to change those ideas, but I discovered that this simple formula of doing good work and getting paid for it was supposed to be slow for modern business. The plan at that time most in favor was to start off with the largest possible capitalization and then sell all the stock and all the bonds that could be sold. Whatever money happened to be left over after all the stock and bond-selling expenses and promoters, charges and all that, went grudgingly into the foundation of the business. A good business was not one that did good work and earned a fair profit. A good business was one that would give the opportunity for the floating of a large amount of stocks and bonds at high prices. It was the stocks and bonds, not the work, that mattered. I could not see how a new business or an old business could be expected to be able to charge into its product a great big bond interest and then sell the product at a fair price. I have never been able to see that.

I have never been able to understand on what theory the original investment of money can be charged against a business. Those men in business who call themselves financiers say that money is "worth" 6 per cent, or 5 per cent, or some other per cent, and that if a business has one hundred thousand dollars invested in it, the man who made the investment is entitled to charge an interest payment on the money, because, if instead of putting that money into the business he had put it into a savings bank or into certain securities, he could have a certain fixed return. Therefore they say that a proper charge against the operating expenses of a business is the interest on this money. This idea is at the root of many business failures and most service failures. Money is not worth a particular amount. As money it is not worth anything, for it will do nothing of itself. The only use of money is to buy tools to work with or the product of tools. Therefore money is worth what it will help you to produce or buy and no more. If a man thinks that his money will earn 5 per cent, or 6 per cent, he ought to place it where he can get that return, but money placed in a business is not a charge on the business—or, rather, should not be. It ceases to be money and becomes, or should become, an engine of production, and it is therefore worth what it produces—and not a fixed sum according to some scale that has no bearing upon the particular business in which the money has been placed. Any return should come after it has produced, not before.

Business men believed that you could do anything by "financing" it. If it did not go through on the first financing then the idea was to "refinance." The process of "refinancing" was simply the game of sending good money after bad. In the majority of cases the need of refinancing arises from bad management, and the effect of refinancing is simply to pay the poor managers to keep up their bad management a little longer. It is merely a postponement of the day of judgment. This makeshift of refinancing is a device of speculative financiers. Their money is no good to them unless they can connect it up with a place where real work is being done, and that they cannot do unless, somehow, that place is poorly managed. Thus, the speculative financiers delude themselves that they are putting their money out to use. They are not; they are putting it out to waste.

Pay Attention to the Work, and Money Will Take Care of Itself

Ford states explicitly that nobody should join (or by implication invest in) a company in which finance takes priority over the work. He adds that bankers and financiers are unfit to manage any business (other than banking) because their eye is always on the dollar and rarely on the work that produces it. Countless businesses have been undermined or even destroyed by finance-related metrics that have little relevance to the delivery of actual value.

Sorensen (1956, pp. 167–169) provides valuable detail on how Ford developed his dislike of bankers and financiers. A banker named Joseph Bowers visited Ford on the assumption that Ford wanted to borrow money, and "talked to him like a teacher talks to a boy kept after school." Bowers added that, as a condition of making the loan, his bank would want a director on the company's board and also control of the treasurer. Ford later blamed his treasurer, Frank Klingensmith, for bringing in Bowers in the first place. Sorensen added that, as a person whose expertise was primarily in finance, Klingensmith could not grasp the simple idea of liquidating inventory instead of taking a loan to produce capital. This required, however, a one-third reduction in cycle time. Chapter 12 elaborates on this in detail.

* * *

I determined absolutely that never would I join a company in which finance came before the work or in which bankers or financiers had a part. And further that, if there were no way to get started in the kind of business that I thought could be managed in the interest of the public, then I simply would not get started at all. For my own short experience, together with what I saw going on around me, was quite enough proof that business as a mere money-making game was not worth giving much thought to and was distinctly no place for a man who wanted to accomplish anything. Also it did not seem to me to be the way to make money. I have yet to have it demonstrated that it is the way. For the only foundation of real business is service.

THE ROLE OF RELIABILITY IN CUSTOMER SATISFACTION

Reliability and maintainability are critical selling, or at least reselling, characteristics of the product or service. The worst possible advertisement is a dissatisfied customer. The quality profession now recognizes customer dissatisfaction as a cost of external failure, but there were actually people during the early twentieth century who regarded field failures as an opportunity to make money. It could easily be argued that manufacturers of nonrepairable or nonmaintainable consumer appliances have the same attitude today, as do software manufacturers that charge users for technical support for problems with the software in question.

Ford then reiterates that control by finance, which puts the dollar ahead of the job, results in poor service that costs future sales.

*   *   *

A manufacturer is not through with his customer when a sale is completed. He has then only started with his customer. In the case of an automobile the sale of the machine is only something in the nature of an introduction. If the machine does not give service, then it is better for the manufacturer if he never had the introduction, for he will have the worst of all advertisements— a dissatisfied customer. There was something more than a tendency in the early days of the automobile to regard the selling of a machine as the real accomplishment and that thereafter it did not matter what happened to the buyer. That is the shortsighted salesman-on-commission attitude. If a salesman is paid only for what he sells, it is not to be expected that he is going to exert any great effort on a customer out of whom no more commission is to be made. And it is right on this point that we later made the largest selling argument for the Ford. The price and the quality of the car would undoubtedly have made a market, and a large market. We went beyond that. A man who bought one of our cars was in my opinion entitled to continuous use of that car, and therefore if he had a breakdown of any kind it was our duty to see that his machine was put into shape again at the earliest possible moment. In the success of the Ford car the early provision of service was an outstanding element. Most of the expensive cars of that period were ill provided with service stations. If your car broke down you had to depend on the local repair man—when you were entitled to depend upon the manufacturer. If the local repair man were a forehanded sort of a person, keeping on hand a good stock of parts (although on many of the cars the parts were not interchangeable), the owner was lucky. But if the repair man were a shiftless person, with an adequate knowledge of automobiles and an inordinate desire to make a good thing out of every car that came into his place for repairs, then even a slight breakdown meant weeks of laying up and a whopping big repair bill that had to be paid before the car could be taken away. The repair men were for a time the largest menace to the automobile industry. Even as late as 1910 and 1911 the owner of an automobile was regarded as essentially a rich man whose money ought to be taken away from him. We met that situation squarely and at the very beginning. We would not have our distribution blocked by stupid, greedy men.

That is getting some years ahead of the story, but it is control by finance that breaks up service because it looks to the immediate dollar. If the first consideration is to earn a certain amount of money, then, unless by some stroke of luck matters are going especially well and there is a surplus over for service so that the operating men may have a chance, future business has to be sacrificed for the dollar of to-day.

CONTINUOUS IMPROVEMENT (KAIZEN)

The next section cites the need for continuous improvement (kaizen), whether personal or organizational, and Ford (1922, pp. 34–25) expands on it as follows:

* * *

The man receives his last advancement—and usually it is his last—with the feeling that at length he has arrived. … Any man who thinks he is a success, has come to his terminal. He is about ready to get off.

* * *

Personal continuous improvement is a deeply ingrained ideal in Japanese society. Organizational stewardship is meanwhile a key element of Bushido, the warrior code that Japan's ruling class once followed and that guides its managers and executives today. Ford's principles, therefore, aligned very closely with Japanese culture, and this made it easy for Japan to adopt Ford's methods on an industrial scale. Peters (1987, p. 282) elaborates that the Japanese view life itself as "a battle to achieve continuous improvement."

* * *

And also I noticed a tendency among many men in business to feel that their lot was hard—they worked against a day when they might retire and live on an income—get out of the strife. Life to them was a battle to be ended as soon as possible. That was another point I could not understand, for as I reasoned, life is not a battle except with our own tendency to sag with the downpull of "getting settled." If to petrify is success, all one has to do is to humour the lazy side of the mind, but if to grow is success, then one must wake up anew every morning and keep awake all day. I saw great businesses become but the ghost of a name because someone thought they could be managed just as they were always managed, and though the management may have been most excellent in its day, its excellence consisted in its alertness to its day, and not in slavish following of its yesterdays. Life, as I see it, is not a location, but a journey. Even the man who most feels himself "settled" is not settled—he is probably sagging back. Everything is in flux, and was meant to be. Life flows. We may live at the same number of the street, but it is never the same man who lives there.

Overcome Ingrained Habits to Achieve Continuous Improvement

Paradigms and ingrained habits are a major barrier to necessary change. Ford and Crowther (1926, p. 2) elaborate, "Only the old, outworn notions stand in the way of these new ideas. The world shackles itself, blinds its eyes, and then wonders why it cannot run!"

The following material also explains how waste can easily become an accepted part of a job; people become used to living with it or working around it. "Habit conduces to a certain inertia," and the Ford thought process overcomes this inertia by encouraging every member of the workforce to identify and challenge wasteful practices on the spot.

Ford himself, however, fell victim to the complacency against which he warned others when he resisted introduction of a successor to the Model T. He wanted to continue to get the Model T's cost down and its quality up, but he failed to recognize that people now wanted vehicles with more features than the Model T could possibly deliver. This should be a lesson to any person who believes that he or she is too smart to make the same mistake, and the same applies to organizations.

* * *

And out of the delusion that life is a battle that may be lost by a false move grows, I have noticed, a great love for regularity. Men fall into the half-alive habit. Seldom does the cobbler take up with the new-fangled way of soling shoes, and seldom does the artisan willingly take up with new methods in his trade. Habit conduces to a certain inertia, and any disturbance of it affects the mind like trouble. It will be recalled that when a study was made of shop methods, so that the workmen might be taught to produce with less useless motion and fatigue, it was most opposed by the workmen themselves. Though they suspected that it was simply a game to get more out of them, what most irked them was that it interfered with the well-worn grooves in which they had become accustomed to move. Business men go down with their businesses because they like the old way so well they cannot bring themselves to change. One sees them all about—men who do not know that yesterday is past, and who woke up this morning with their last year's ideas. It could almost be written down as a formula that when a man begins to think that he has at last found his method he had better begin a most searching examination of himself to see whether some part of his brain has not gone to sleep. There is a subtle danger in a man thinking that he is "fixed" for life. It indicates that the next jolt of the wheel of progress is going to fling him off.

Preconceived Ideas and Paradigms Are Obstacles to Success

The following section illustrates the concept of the Fool of the Tarot, a card that symbolizes freedom from preconceived and, therefore, self-restricting paradigms. The Diesel clothing company's "Official Be Stupid Philosophy" illustrates the underlying concept even further: "The smart might recognize things for how they are. The stupid see things for how they could be." Ford phrases the idea almost identically: "Fools usually live long enough to prove that they were not fools."

Ford elaborates throughout this book and his others that the problem with "experts" consists not of their experience or education, but rather preconceived ideas whose primary function is usually to tell the expert why something cannot be done. Examples of such dysfunctional thinking include the belief of American military planners that the water at Pearl Harbor was too shallow for aircraft torpedoes to function properly, and the delusion of French military planners that tanks could not penetrate the Ardennes Forest. Countless business organizations have similarly concluded that something cannot be done, only to have a competitor do it to them. Sorensen (1956, pp. 172–173) adds that the Ford Motor Company knew nothing at all about glassmaking. It, therefore, did not "know" it was impossible to cast plate glass in a continuous strip and, therefore, succeeded in doing so.

Ford reiterates in the subsequent paragraph the need to put the work ahead of the money, which reflects, in turn, the economic realities of his universal code.

* * *

There is also the great fear of being thought a fool. So many men are afraid of being considered fools. I grant that public opinion is a powerful police influence for those who need it. Perhaps it is true that the majority of men need the restraint of public opinion. Public opinion may keep a man better than he would otherwise be—if not better morally, at least better as far as his social desirability is concerned. But it is not a bad thing to be a fool for righteousness' sake. The best of it is that such fools usually live long enough to prove that they were not fools—or the work they have begun lives long enough to prove they were not foolish.

The money influence—the pressing to make a profit on an "investment"— and its consequent neglect of or skimping of work and hence of service showed itself to me in many ways. It seemed to be at the bottom of most troubles. It was the cause of low wages—for without well-directed work high wages cannot be paid. And if the whole attention is not given to the work it cannot be well directed. Most men want to be free to work; under the system in use they could not be free to work. During my first experience I was not free—I could not give full play to my ideas. Everything had to be planned to make money; the last consideration was the work. And the most curious part of it all was the insistence that it was the money and not the work that counted. It did not seem to strike any one as illogical that money should be put ahead of work— even though everyone had to admit that the profit had to come from the work. The desire seemed to be to find a short cut to money and to pass over the obvious short cut—which is through the work.

Reduce Costs and Improve Quality to Expand a Market

The next segment dispels the paradigm that markets are limited in size, and that one competitor's success must come at the expense of another. A continuous reduction in cost and prices, whether for automobiles during the 1910s or computers in the late twentieth century, expands the pool of available buyers. The necessary continual improvement, however, is possible only when the organization's focus is on the job and not on the money.

* * *

Take competition; I found that competition was supposed to be a menace and that a good manager circumvented his competitors by getting a monopoly through artificial means. The idea was that there were only a certain number of people who could buy and that it was necessary to get their trade ahead of someone else. Some will remember that later many of the automobile manufacturers entered into an association under the Selden Patent just so that it might be legally possible to control the price and the output of automobiles. They had the same idea that so many trades unions have—the ridiculous notion that more profit can be had doing less work than more. The plan, I believe, is a very antiquated one. I could not see then and am still unable to see that there is not always enough for the man who does his work; time spent in fighting competition is wasted; it had better be spent in doing the work.

There are always enough people ready and anxious to buy, provided you supply what they want and at the proper price—and this applies to personal services as well as to goods.

During this time of reflection I was far from idle. We were going ahead with a four-cylinder motor and the building of a pair of big racing cars. I had plenty of time, for I never left my business. I do not believe a man can ever leave his business. He ought to think of it by day and dream of it by night. It is nice to plan to do one's work in office hours, to take up the work in the morning, to drop it in the evening—and not have a care until the next morning. It is perfectly possible to do that if one is so constituted as to be willing through all of his life to accept direction, to be an employee, possibly a responsible employee, but not a director or manager of anything. A manual labourer must have a limit on his hours, otherwise he will wear himself out. If he intends to remain always a manual labourer, then he should forget about his work when the whistle blows, but if he intends to go forward and do anything, the whistle is only a signal to start thinking over the day's work in order to discover how it might be done better.

The man who has the largest capacity for work and thought is the man who is bound to succeed. I cannot pretend to say, because I do not know, whether the man who works always, who never leaves his business, who is absolutely intent upon getting ahead, and who therefore does get ahead—is happier than the man who keeps office hours, both for his brain and his hands. It is not necessary for any one to decide the question. A ten-horsepower engine will not pull as much as a twenty. The man who keeps brain office hours limits his horsepower. If he is satisfied to pull only the load that he has, well and good, that is his affair—but he must not complain if another who has increased his horsepower pulls more than he does. Leisure and work bring different results. If a man wants leisure and gets it—then he has no cause to complain. But he cannot have both leisure and the results of work.

A COST ACCOUNTING SYSTEM IS NOT A SUICIDE PACT

Concretely, what I most realized about business in that year—and I have been learning more each year without finding it necessary to change my first conclusions—is this:

1. That finance is given a place ahead of work and, therefore, tends to kill the work and destroy the fundamental of service.
2. That thinking first of money instead of work brings on fear of failure and this fear blocks every avenue of business—it makes a man afraid

of competition, of changing his methods, or of doing anything which might change his condition.

3. That the way is clear for any one who thinks first of service—of doing the work in the best possible way.

Ford's conclusion to this chapter, which again stresses the dysfunctional effects of financial control of the work, deserves elaboration. The sole legitimate purpose of a cost accounting system is to satisfy the financial reporting requirements of the Securities and Exchange Commission and the Internal Revenue Services. GAAP (Generally Accepted Accounting Principles) standardizes financial reports for these purposes, but investors should not rely on them to compare the performances of two organizations. They are absolutely not suitable for management decision purposes; a cost accounting system is emphatically not a suicide pact.

Assets that depreciate and absorb overhead costs do so only on paper, and for very specific tax and financial reporting purposes. Ford and Crowther (1930, p. 25) said of this, "As for the buildings and machinery, they must be valued in dollars according to the meaningless methods of accounting that are required by law. Actually they are worth only what we can do with them." The same reference adds (p. 24) that book value is a generally useless and potentially misleading estimate of an asset's or a business's value.

Consider for example a million-dollar piece of equipment that depreciates over five years; 10, 20, 20, 20, 20, and 10% is a typical formula for straight-line depreciation. This means only that, for example, the company can write off $100,000 against its income for tax purposes after the first (partial) year of ownership, and $200,000 after the following year, which is the first complete year of ownership.

The machine is then worth $700,000 on paper as a capital asset, but this does not answer the question as to what it is actually worth. If it can no longer do the job for which it was purchased, or any other job, it is worth only what the company can get for it by selling it to somebody who can use it. If it can still do its job, and if its replacement would cost a million dollars, it is still worth a million dollars. It is, as Ford said, worth exactly what the company can do with it.

Overhead is another dysfunctional financial metric that has no place whatsoever outside of tax preparation and financial reports. Chapter 6 elaborates, "The foremen and superintendents would only be wasting time were they to keep a check on the costs in their departments. There are certain costs—such as the rate of wages, the overhead, the price of materials, and the like, which they could not in any way control, so they do not bother about them." The truth is that the business incurs the underlying cost no matter what, and it is merely an accounting convention that assigns it to individual units of production. It is easy to see that application of overhead to actual decision making can have disastrous effects.

Consider for example a product whose bill of materials (BOM) incorporates $10 in materials, and which requires an hour of labor at $25 an hour. The cost accounting system assigns 40% of labor plus $10 in capital equipment cost to this product, for a standard cost of $55.

Suppose the company has excess labor and equipment capacity, and it receives an offer of $20 per unit. If the business allows itself to be managed by the cost accounting system, it will reject the order with the claim that it would be selling at a loss ($35 per unit) and making it up on the volume. The truth is, however, that the $20 price offers a marginal profit of $10 per unit, and this leads to the concept of managerial economics.

Managerial or Engineering Economics

Managerial economics or *engineering economics* deals with marginal revenues, costs, and profits as shown in equation 2.1. The derivatives are for any given level of production N, e.g., 100 units per day, and dn refers to an incremental change in production.

$$Marginal\ Revenue: \left. \frac{d\ Revenue}{dn} \right]_N = sales\ price$$

$$Marginal\ Cost: \left. \frac{d\ Cost}{dn} \right]_N =$$

$$materials\ cost\ plus\ genuinely\ variable\ labor \qquad (2.1)$$

$$Marginal\ Profit: \left. \frac{d\ Profit}{dn} \right]_N =$$

$$Marginal\ Revenue\ minus\ Marginal\ Cost$$

The phrase "genuinely variable labor" is important because cost accounting systems generally treat all hourly labor as a variable cost. The truth is that this cost is a fixed cost, just like that of the plant and equipment, unless the business is paying overtime. The workers are there whether or not they have value-adding work to do. In this example, then, the only marginal cost consists of the $10 in materials. This is why every unit the company can sell for $20 brings a marginal profit of $10.

If, however, the company has no excess labor capacity and must pay overtime to fill this order, the marginal cost is now $10 for the materials plus $37.50 (at time and a half) for labor, for a marginal cost of $47.50. In this case, the order should be rejected.

Another dysfunctional effect of overhead is the desire to make as much inventory as possible to "absorb" it, i.e., distribute the overhead over as many units as possible. This might even yield a favorable overhead variance (difference between standard and actual cost) for the product. This looks good to cost accounting systems that treat inventory as a short-term and, therefore, liquid asset, but this is the only place in which inventory is an asset. Goldratt and Cox (1992) define inventory along with operating costs as undesirable performance indicators, i.e., less of both is better. Throughput, or finished goods *with customers who want them*, is the only indicator of which more is desirable.

We therefore conclude that Ford's avoidance of the use of cost accounting metrics for actual managerial decisions is worthy of particular attention and emulation.

3

Starting the Real Business

This chapter begins with the identification of what Ford calls "universal demand," whose achievement comes from a product or service that meets the needs of 95% of potential customers. These needs include high quality and low cost as well as functionality. Ford stresses that, even in his day, few people would buy without regard to quality. On the other hand, the segment that would pay for special or extraordinary product features also was very small, so it made no sense to meet that segment's needs at the expense of the 95%.

* * *

In the little brick shop at 81 Park Place I had ample opportunity to work out the design and some of the methods of manufacture of a new car. Even if it were possible to organize the exact kind of corporation that I wanted—one in which doing the work well and suiting the public would be controlling factors—it became apparent that I never could produce a thoroughly good motor car that might be sold at a low price under the existing cut-and-try manufacturing methods.

Everybody knows that it is always possible to do a thing better the second time. I do not know why manufacturing should not at that time have generally recognized this as a basic fact—unless it might be that the manufacturers were in such a hurry to obtain something to sell that they did not take time for adequate preparation. Making "to order" instead of making in volume is, I suppose, a habit, a tradition, that has descended from the old handicraft days. Ask a hundred people how they want a particular article made. About eighty will not know; they will leave it to you. Fifteen will think that they must say something, while five will really have preferences and reasons. The ninety-five, made up of those who do not know and admit it and the fifteen who do not know but do not admit it, constitute the real market for any product. The five who want something special may or may not be able to pay the price for special work. If they have the price, they can get the work, but they constitute a special and limited market. Of the ninety-five perhaps ten or fif-teen will pay a price for quality. Of those remaining, a number will buy solely on price and without regard to quality. Their numbers are thinning with each day. Buyers are learning how to buy. The majority will consider quality and buy the biggest dollar's worth of quality. If, therefore, you discover what will give this 95 per cent of people the best all-round service and then arrange to manufacture at the very highest quality and sell at the very lowest price, you will be meeting a demand which is so large that it may be called universal.

CHARGE THE LOWEST PRICE POSSIBLE, AND NOT WHAT THE MARKET WILL BEAR

The next section stresses the need to reduce prices proactively through the reduction of manufacturing costs instead of reactively in response to poor market demand. This seems to contravene the basic economic concept of price as a function of demand, but it makes considerable sense. If the producer cuts prices in response to a drop in demand, customers will believe, and often quite rightly, that the best strategy is to hold off on purchases to see if the price will fall even further. Ford and Crowther (1930, p. 9) elaborate: "If prices are used as baits for buyers, to be raised or lowered as the buyers feel about it, it is in effect a handing over of the control of the business to the buyers to do with as they like. That is a very real control and it is exercised in very drastic fashion."

If, for example, a retail store puts something on sale for 25% off, customers will realize that the store can afford to sell the product for that price all the time. Smart shoppers will, therefore, let the item sit on the shelf when the price goes back up because they know the "real" price is lower. If, on the other hand, the store sells for fair prices all of the time but never offers discounts, customers will respect the prices and not game the system by, for example, waiting until end of season sales.

The latter is the editor's recommendation for Chinese-made goods with made-in-America price tags, and the day after Christmas is a particularly good time to buy them. The lead time for delivery by container ship means that the retailer must order to forecast as opposed to actual demand. If the goods do not sell, the retailer must offer sharp discounts to clear them from the shelves to make room for the next season's items, which it must also order to forecast rather than real-time demand. Smart consumers will also wait until the end of a car's model year to buy because the auto deal-ers and manufacturers must similarly offer incentives to clear away the unsold inventory.

Ford reinforces this concept with this chapter's statement: "All the large and successful retail stores in this country are on the one-price basis." The principle, therefore, is to sell for as low a cost as possible, but never raise or lower the price in response to demand. The seller must also reduce the cost through continuous improvement, and, specifically, through removal of waste (muda) from the entire supply chain.

* * *

This is not standardizing. The use of the word "standardizing" is very apt to lead one into trouble, for it implies a certain freezing of design and method and usually works out so that the manufacturer selects whatever article he can the most easily make and sell at the highest profit. The public is not con-sidered either in the design or in the price. The thought behind most stan-dardization is to be able to make a larger profit. The result is that with the economies which are inevitable if you make only one thing, a larger and larger profit is continually being had by the manufacturer. His output also becomes larger—his facilities produce more—and before he knows it his markets are overflowing with goods which will not sell. These goods would sell if the manufacturer would take a lower price for them. There is always buying power present—but that buying power will not always respond to reductions in price. If an article has been sold at too high a price and then, because of stagnant business, the price is suddenly cut, the response is some-times most disappointing. And for a very good reason. The public is wary. It thinks that the price-cut is a fake and it sits around waiting for a real cut. We saw much of that last year. If, on the contrary, the economies of making are transferred at once to the price and if it is well known that such is the policy of the manufacturer, the public will have confidence in him and will respond. They will trust him to give honest value. So standardization may seem bad business unless it carries with it the plan of constantly reducing the price at which the article is sold. And the price has to be reduced (this is very impor-tant) because of the manufacturing economies that have come about and not because the falling demand by the public indicates that it is not satisfied with the price. The public should always be wondering how it is possible to give so much for the money.

Standardization (to use the word as I understand it) is not just taking one's best selling article and concentrating on it. It is planning day and night and probably for years, first on something which will best suit the public and then on how it should be made. The exact processes of manufacturing will develop of themselves. Then, if we shift the manufacturing from the profit to the service basis, we shall have a real business in which the profits will be all that any one could desire.

All of this seems self-evident to me. It is the logical basis of any business that wants to serve 95 per cent. of the community. It is the logical way in which the community can serve itself. I cannot comprehend why all business does not go on this basis. All that has to be done in order to adopt it is to overcome the habit of grabbing at the nearest dollar as though it were the only dollar in the world. The habit has already to an extent been overcome. All the large and successful retail stores in this country are on the one-price basis. The only further step required is to throw overboard the idea of pricing on what the traffic will bear and instead go to the common-sense basis of pricing on what it costs to manufacture and then reducing the cost of manufacture. If the design of the product has been sufficiently studied, then changes in it will come very slowly. But changes in manufacturing processes will come very rapidly and wholly naturally. That has been our experience in everything we have undertaken. How naturally it has all come about, I shall later outline. The point that I wish to impress here is that it is impossible to get a product on which one may concentrate unless an unlimited amount of study is given beforehand. It is not just an afternoon's work.

FORD AND AUTO RACING

These ideas were forming with me during this year of experimenting. Most of the experimenting went into the building of racing cars. The idea in those days was that a first-class car ought to be a racer. I never really thought much of racing, but following the bicycle idea, the manufacturers had the notion that winning a race on a track told the public something about the merits of an automobile—although I can hardly imagine any test that would tell less.

But, as the others were doing it, I, too, had to do it. In 1903, with Tom Cooper, I built two cars solely for speed. They were quite alike. One we named the "999" and the other the "Arrow." If an automobile were going to be known for speed, then I was going to make an automobile that would be known wherever speed was known. These were. I put in four great big cylinders giving 80 H.P.—which up to that time had been unheard of. The roar of those cylinders alone was enough to half kill a man. There was only one seat. One life to a car was enough. I tried out the cars. Cooper tried out the cars. We let them out at full speed. I cannot quite describe the sensation. Going over Niagara Falls would have been but a pastime after a ride in one of them. I did not want to take the responsibility of racing the "999" which we put up first, neither did Cooper. Cooper said he knew a man who lived on speed, that nothing could go too fast for him. He wired to Salt Lake City and on came a professional bicycle rider named Barney Oldfield. He had never driven a motor car, but he liked the idea of trying it. He said he would try anything once.

It took us only a week to teach him how to drive. The man did not know what fear was. All that he had to learn was how to control the monster. Controlling the fastest car of to-day was nothing as compared to controlling that car. The steering wheel had not yet been thought of. All the previous cars that I had built simply had tillers. On this one I put a two-handed tiller, for holding the car in line required all the strength of a strong man. The race for which we were working was at three miles on the Grosse Point track. We kept our cars as a dark horse. We left the predictions to the others. The tracks then were not scientifically banked. It was not known how much speed a motor car could develop. No one knew better than Oldfield what the turns meant and as he took his seat, while I was cranking the car for the start, he remarked cheerily: "Well, this chariot may kill me, but they will say afterward that I was going like hell when she took me over the bank."

And he did go. ... He never dared to look around. He did not shut off on the curves. He simply let that car go—and go it did. He was about half a mile ahead of the next man at the end of the race!

The "999" did what it was intended to do: It advertised the fact that I could build a fast motorcar. A week after the race I formed the Ford Motor Company. I was vice-president, designer, master mechanic, superintendent, and general manager. The capitalization of the company was one hundred thousand dollars, and of this I owned 25 1/2 per cent. The total amount subscribed in cash was about twenty-eight thousand dollars—which is the only money that the company has ever received for the capital fund from other than operations. In the beginning I thought that it was possible, notwithstanding my former experience, to go forward with a company in which I owned less than the controlling share. I very shortly found I had to have control and therefore in 1906, with funds that I had earned in the company, I bought enough stock to bring my holdings up to 51 per cent, and a little later bought enough more to give me 58-1/2 per cent. The new equipment and the whole progress of the company have always been financed out of earnings. In 1919 my son Edsel purchased the remaining 41-1/2 per cent of the stock because certain of the minority stockholders disagreed with my policies. For these shares he paid at the rate of $12,500 for each $100 par and in all paid about seventy-five millions [sic].

* * *

Sorensen and Williamson (1956, p. 166) report, however, that six stockholders who invested $33,100 in 1903 were bought out for $105 million, or \$3,172 on the dollar. The exact return varied by stockholder, with the Dodge brothers, John Anderson, and Horace Rackham taking \$2,500 on the dollar, while James Couzens held out for substantially more; \$2,500 would come to an annual compounded gain of 63%, but even the figure shown above, \$125 on the dollar, comes to a 35.2% annual compound gain. This does not include the dividend payouts along the way.

ROLE OF SUPPLY CHAIN MANAGEMENT

The next section introduces the concept of supply chain management, in which parts from different sources are brought together for assembly at the point of consumption. The need for all supply chain participants to adopt the same service methods is particularly important, and it means that Ford's universal code must operate across the entire supply chain. All suppliers and customers must give and receive square deals, and all must work to create more value through the elimination of waste.

* * *

The original company and its equipment, as may be gathered, were not elaborate. We rented Strelow's carpenter shop on Mack Avenue. In making my designs I had also worked out the methods of making, but, since at that time we could not afford to buy machinery, the entire car was made according to my designs, but by various manufacturers, and about all we did, even in the way of assembling, was to put on the wheels, the tires, and the body. That would really be the most economical method of manufacturing if only one could be certain that all of the various parts would be made on the manufacturing plan that I have above outlined. The most economical manufacturing of the future will be that in which the whole of an article is not made under one roof—unless, of course, it be a very simple article. The modern—or better, the future—method is to have each part made where it may best be made and then assemble the parts into a complete unit at the points of consumption. That is the method we are now following and expect to extend. It would make no difference whether one company or one individual owned all the factories fabricating the component parts of a single product, or whether such part were made in our independently owned factory, if only all adopted the same service methods. If we can buy as good a part as we can make ourselves and the supply is ample and the price right, we do not attempt to make it ourselves—or, at any rate, to make more than an emergency supply. In fact, it might be better to have the ownership widely scattered.

Transportation Is a Major Source of Waste

Ford now cites weight as a major source of waste in transportation. A passenger rail car weighs far more than the passengers and their luggage, which means only a fraction of the coal, diesel fuel, or electricity delivers value to the customers. Kilcarr (2009) reports that an 18-wheel truck that can carry 80,000 pounds under current federal regulations weighs 35,000 pounds empty. The weight of the tractor and trailer are, therefore, almost 44% nonvalue-adding. Addition of another axle with four wheels and a set of brakes would allow trucks to carry 97,000 pounds without any loss in braking ability, and without increased pressure per unit area on the road. This would reduce the vehicle's nonvalue-adding share to 36.1%.

* * *

I had been experimenting principally upon the cutting down of weight. Excess weight kills any self-propelled vehicle. There are a lot of fool ideas about weight. It is queer, when you come to think of it, how some fool terms get into current use. There is the phrase "heavyweight" as applied to a man's mental apparatus! What does it mean? No one wants to be fat and heavy of body—then why of head? For some clumsy reason we have come to confuse strength with weight. The crude methods of early building undoubtedly had much to do with this. The old ox-cart weighed a ton—and it had so much weight that it was weak! To carry a few tons of humanity from New York to Chicago, the railroad builds a train that weighs many hundred tons, and the result is an absolute loss of real strength and the extravagant waste of untold millions in the form of power. The law of diminishing returns begins to operate at the point where strength becomes weight. Weight may be desirable in a steam roller but nowhere else. Strength has nothing to do with weight. The mentality of the man who does things in the world is agile, light, and strong. The most beautiful things in the world are those from which all excess weight has been eliminated. Strength is never just weight—either in men or things. Whenever any one suggests to me that I might increase weight or add a part, I look into decreasing weight and eliminating a part! The car that I designed was lighter than any car that had yet been made. It would have been lighter if I had known how to make it so—later I got the materials to make the lighter car.

In our first year we built "Model A," selling the runabout for eight hundred and fifty dollars and the tonneau for one hundred dollars more. This model had a two-cylinder opposed motor developing eight horsepower. It had a chain drive, a seventy-two inch wheel base—which was supposed to be long—and a fuel capacity of five gallons. We made and sold 1,708 cars in the first year. That is how well the public responded.

Every one of these "Model A's" has a history. Take No. 420. Colonel D. C. Collier of California bought it in 1904. He used it for a couple of years, sold it, and bought a new Ford. No. 420 changed hands frequently until 1907 when it was bought by one Edmund Jacobs living near Ramona in the heart of the mountains. He drove it for several years in the roughest kind of work. Then he bought a new Ford and sold his old one. By 1915 No. 420 had passed into the hands of a man named Cantello who took out the motor, hitched it to a water pump, rigged up shafts on the chassis and now, while the motor chugs away at the pumping of water, the chassis drawn by a burro acts as a buggy. The moral, of course, is that you can dissect a Ford but you cannot kill it.

RECOGNITION OF CUSTOMER REQUIREMENTS

Quality function deployment (QFD) did not exist in Ford's era, but he made an obvious effort to determine what his customers wanted and needed. This included fitness for everyday use, reliability, maintainability, low price, and availability. Unlike a street car, a Model T was always available when its owner needed it for a business appointment or other time-sensitive activity.

* * *

In our first advertisement we said:

> *Our purpose is to construct and market an automobile specially designed for everyday wear and tear—business, professional, and family use; an automobile which will attain to a sufficient speed to satisfy the average person without acquiring any of those breakneck velocities which are so universally condemned; a machine which will be admired by man, woman, and child alike for its compactness, its simplicity, its safety, its all-around convenience, and—last but not least—its exceedingly reasonable price, which places it within the reach of many thousands who could not think of paying the comparatively fabulous prices asked for most machines.*

And these are the points we emphasized:

Good material.
Simplicity—most of the cars at that time required considerable skill in their management.
The engine.

The ignition—which was furnished by two sets of six dry cell batteries.
The automatic oiling.
The simplicity and the ease of control of the transmission, which was of the planetary type.
The workmanship.

We did not make the pleasure appeal. We never have. In its first advertising we showed that a motor car was a utility. We said:

> We often hear quoted the old proverb, "Time is money"—and yet how few business and professional men act as if they really believed its truth.
> Men who are constantly complaining of shortage of time and lamenting the fewness of days in the week—men to whom every five minutes wasted means a dollar thrown away—men to whom five minutes' delay sometimes means the loss of many dollars—will yet depend on the haphazard, uncomfortable, and limited means of transportation afforded by street cars, etc., when the investment of an exceedingly moderate sum in the purchase of a perfected, efficient, high-grade automobile would cut out anxiety and unpunctuality and provide a luxurious means of travel ever at your beck and call.
> Always ready, always sure.
> Built to save you time and consequent money.
> Built to take you anywhere you want to go and bring you back again on time.
> Built to add to your reputation for punctuality; to keep your customers good-humoured and in a buying mood.
> Built for business or pleasure—just as you say.
> Built also for the good of your health—to carry you "jarlessly" over any kind of half decent roads, to refresh your brain with the luxury of much "out-doorness" and your lungs with the "tonic of tonics"—the right kind of atmosphere.
> It is your say, too, when it comes to speed. You can—if you choose—loiter lingeringly through shady avenues or you can press down on the foot-lever until all the scenery looks alike to you and you have to keep your eyes skinned to count the milestones as they pass.

I am giving the gist of this advertisement to show that, from the beginning, we were looking to providing service—we never bothered with a "sporting car."

The business went along almost as by magic. The cars gained a reputation for standing up. They were tough, they were simple, and they were well made. I was working on my design for a universal single model but I had not settled the designs nor had we the money to build and equip the proper kind of plant for manufacturing. I had not the money to discover the very best and lightest *materials. We still had to accept the materials that the market offered—we got the best to be had but we had no facilities for the scientific investigation of materials or for original research.*

Quality and Reliability Are Key Selling Points

Ford now reiterates that quality and reliability, as opposed to obsolescence (and especially planned obsolescence), are key selling points. The editor recalls, for example, seeing Christmas ornaments with a particular year on them, and the seller's obvious intention was that they would be unusable in the future. It is doubtful that any but the least intelligent and least discerning customers bought even one.

Planned obsolescence brings to mind the slogan "Ending is better than mending" of Aldous Huxley's *Brave New World*, in which Henry Ford is God and *My Life and Work* is the Bible. This section of Chapter 3 shows very explicitly, however, that Ford did not think that a customer who bought a durable item from him should ever have to buy another.

* * *

My associates were not convinced that it was possible to restrict our cars to a single model. The automobile trade was following the old bicycle trade, in which every manufacturer thought it necessary to bring out a new model each year and to make it so unlike all previous models that those who had bought the former models would want to get rid of the old and buy the new. That was supposed to be good business. It is the same idea that women submit to in their clothing and hats. That is not service—it seeks only to provide something new, not something better. It is extraordinary how firmly rooted is the notion that business—continuous selling—depends not on satisfying the customer once and for all, but on first getting his money for one article and then persuading him he ought to buy a new and different one. The plan which I then had in the back of my head but to which we were not then sufficiently advanced to give expression, was that, when a model was settled upon then every improvement on that model should be interchangeable with the old model, so that a car should never get out of date. It is my ambition to have every piece of machinery, or other non-consumable product that I turn out, so strong and so well made that no one ought ever to have to buy a second one. A good machine of any kind ought to last as long as a good watch.

In the second year we scattered our energies among three models. We made a four-cylinder touring car, "Model B," which sold for two thousand dollars; "Model C," which was a slightly improved "Model A" and sold at fifty dollars more than the former price; and "Model F," a touring car which sold for a thousand dollars. That is, we scattered our energy and increased prices—and therefore we sold fewer cars than in the first year. The sales were 1,695 cars.

That "Model B"—the first four-cylinder car for general road use—had to be advertised. Winning a race or making a record was then the best kind of advertising. So I fixed up the "Arrow," the twin of the old "999"—in fact practically remade it—and a week before the New York Automobile show I drove it myself over a surveyed mile straightaway on the ice. I shall never forget that race. The ice seemed smooth enough, so smooth that if I had called off the trial we should have secured an immense amount of the wrong kind of advertising, but instead of being smooth, that ice was seamed with fissures which I knew were going to mean trouble the moment I got up speed. But there was nothing to do but go through with the trial, and I let the old "Arrow" out. At every fissure the car leaped into the air. I never knew how it was coming down. When I wasn't in the air, I was skidding, but somehow I stayed top side up and on the course, making a record that went all over the world! That put "Model B" on the map—but not enough on to overcome the price advances. No stunt and no advertising will sell an article for any length of time. Business is not a game. The moral is coming.

Our little wooden shop had, with the business we were doing, become totally inadequate, and in 1906 we took out of our working capital sufficient funds to build a three-story plant at the corner of Piquette and Beaubien streets—which for the first time gave us real manufacturing facilities. We began to make and to assemble quite a number of the parts, although still we were principally an assembling shop. In 1905–1906 we made only two models—one the four-cylinder car at $2,000 and another touring car at $1,000, both being the models of the previous year—and our sales dropped to 1,599 cars.

Some said it was because we had not brought out new models. I thought it was because our cars were too expensive—they did not appeal to the 95 per cent. I changed the policy in the next year—having first acquired stock control. For 1906–1907 we entirely left off making touring cars and made three models of runabouts and roadsters, none of which differed materially from the other in manufacturing process or in component parts, but were somewhat different in appearance. The big thing was that the cheapest car sold for $600 and the most expensive for only $750, and right there came the complete demonstration of what price meant. We sold 8,423 cars—nearly five times as many as in our biggest previous year. Our banner week was that of May 15, 1908, when we assembled 311 cars in six working days. It almost swamped our facilities. The foreman had a tallyboard on which he chalked up each car as it was finished and turned over to the testers. The tallyboard was hardly equal to the task. On one day in the following June we assembled an even one hundred cars.

In the next year we departed from the programme that had been so successful and I designed a big car—fifty horsepower, six cylinder—that would burn up the roads. We continued making our small cars, but the 1907 panic and the diversion to the more expensive model cut down the sales to 6,398 cars.

Do Not Add Unnecessary Middlemen

The next point is particularly important. Ford sold cars directly to purchasers and not through dealers who would add a markup. It was, however, apparently necessary for him to add a network of dealers later. The dealerships then added value through their ability to service the Ford vehicles.

* * *

We had been through an experimenting period of five years. The cars were beginning to be sold in Europe. The business, as an automobile business then went, was considered extraordinarily prosperous. We had plenty of money. Since the first year we have practically always had plenty of money. We sold for cash, we did not borrow money, and we sold directly to the purchaser. We had no bad debts and we kept within ourselves on every move. I have always kept well within my resources. I have never found it necessary to strain them, because, inevitably, if you give attention to work and service, the resources will increase more rapidly than you can devise ways and means of disposing of them.

We were careful in the selection of our salesmen. At first there was great difficulty in getting good salesmen because the automobile trade was not supposed to be stable. It was supposed to be dealing in a luxury—in pleasure vehicles. We eventually appointed agents, selecting the very best men we could find, and then paying to them a salary larger than they could possibly earn in business for themselves. In the beginning we had not paid much in the way of salaries. We were feeling our way, but when we knew what our way was, we adopted the policy of paying the very highest reward for service and then insisting upon getting the highest service. Among the requirements for an agent we laid down the following:

(1) A progressive, up-to-date man keenly alive to the possibilities of business.
(2) A suitable place of business clean and dignified in appearance.
(3) A stock of parts sufficient to make prompt replacements and keep in active service every Ford car in his territory.
(4) An adequately equipped repair shop which has in it the right machinery for every necessary repair and adjustment.

(5) Mechanics who are thoroughly familiar with the construction and operation of Ford cars.

(6) A comprehensive bookkeeping system and a follow-up sales system, so that it may be instantly apparent what is the financial status of the various departments of his business, the condition and size of his stock, the present owners of cars, and the future prospects.

(7) Absolute cleanliness throughout every department. There must be no unwashed windows, dusty furniture, dirty floors.

(8) A suitable display sign.

(9) The adoption of policies which will ensure absolutely square dealing and the highest character of business ethics.

And this is the general instruction that was issued:

A dealer or a salesman ought to have the name of every possible automobile buyer in his territory, including all those who have never given the matter a thought. He should then personally solicit by visitation if possible—by correspondence at the least—every man on that list and then making necessary memoranda, know the automobile situation as related to every resident so solicited. If your territory is too large to permit this, you have too much territory.

THE SELDEN PATENT SUIT

The way was not easy. We were harried by a big suit brought against the company to try to force us into line with an association of automobile manufacturers, who were operating under the false principle that there was only a limited market for automobiles and that a monopoly of that market was essential. This was the famous Selden Patent suit. At times the support of our defense severely strained our resources. Mr. Selden, who has but recently died, had little to do with the suit. It was the association which sought a monopoly under the patent. The situation was this:

George B. Selden, a patent attorney, filed an application as far back as 1879 for a patent the object of which was stated to be "The production of a safe, simple, and cheap road locomotive, light in weight, easy to control, possessed of sufficient power to overcome an ordinary inclination." This application was kept alive in the Patent Office, by methods which are perfectly legal, until 1895, when the patent was granted. In 1879, when the application was filed, the automobile was practically unknown to the general public, but by the time the patent was issued everybody was familiar with self-propelled vehicles, and most of the men, including myself, who had been for years working on motor propulsion, were surprised to learn that what we had made practicable was covered by an application of years before, although the applicant had kept his idea merely as an idea. He had done nothing to put it into practice.

The specific claims under the patent were divided into six groups and I think that not a single one of them was a really new idea even in 1879 when the application was filed. The Patent Office allowed a combination and issued a so-called "combination patent" deciding that the combination (a) of a carriage with its body machinery and steering wheel, with the (b) propelling mechanism clutch and gear, and finally (c) the engine, made a valid patent.

With all of that we were not concerned. I believed that my engine had nothing whatsoever in common with what Selden had in mind. The powerful combination of manufacturers who called themselves the "licensed manufacturers" because they operated under licenses from the patentee, brought suit against us as soon as we began to be a factor in motor production. The suit dragged on. It was intended to scare us out of business. We took volumes of testimony, and the blow came on September 15, 1909, when Judge Hough rendered an opinion in the United States District Court finding against us. Immediately that Licensed Association began to advertise, warning prospective purchasers against our cars. They had done the same thing in 1903 at the start of the suit, when it was thought that we could be put out of business. I had implicit confidence that eventually we should win our suit. I simply knew that we were right, but it was a considerable blow to get the first decision against us, for we believed that many buyers—even though no injunction was issued against us—would be frightened away from buying because of the threats of court action against individual owners. The idea was spread that if the suit finally went against me, every man who owned a Ford car would be prosecuted. Some of my more enthusiastic opponents, I understand, gave it out privately that there would be criminal as well as civil suits and that a man buying a Ford car might as well be buying a ticket to jail. We answered with an advertisement for which we took four pages in the principal newspapers all over the country. We set out our case—we set out our confidence in victory—and in conclusion said:

> In conclusion we beg to state if there are any prospective automobile buyers who are at all intimidated by the claims made by our adversaries that we will give them, in addition to the protection of the Ford Motor Company with its some $6,000,000.00 of assets, an individual bond backed by a Company of more than $6,000,000.00 more of assets, so that each and every individual owner of a Ford car will be protected until at least $12,000,000.00 of assets have been wiped out by those who desire to control and monopolize this wonderful industry.

> *The bond is yours for the asking, so do not allow yourself to be sold inferior cars at extravagant prices because of any statement made by this "Divine" body.*
>
> N. B.—*This fight is not being waged by the Ford Motor Company without the advice and counsel of the ablest patent attorneys of the East and West.*

We thought that the bond would give assurance to the buyers—that they needed confidence. They did not. We sold more than eighteen thousand cars—nearly double the output of the previous year—and I think about fifty buyers asked for bonds—perhaps it was less than that.

As a matter of fact, probably nothing so well advertised the Ford car and the Ford Motor Company as did this suit. It appeared that we were the under dog and we had the public's sympathy. The association had seventy million dollars—we at the beginning had not half that number of thousands. I never had a doubt as to the outcome, but nevertheless it was a sword hanging over our heads that we could as well do without. Prosecuting that suit was probably one of the most shortsighted acts that any group of American business men has ever combined to commit. Taken in all its sidelights, it forms the best possible example of joining unwittingly to kill a trade. I regard it as most fortunate for the automobile makers of the country that we eventually won, and the association ceased to be a serious factor in the business. By 1908, however, in spite of this suit, we had come to a point where it was possible to announce and put into fabrication the kind of car that I wanted to build.

4

The Secret of Manufacturing and Serving

This chapter contrasts a continuous search for new and better ways to do things against the inertia that might come from an initial success. This includes benchmarking, as practiced by Ford when he noticed the enormous strength of vanadium steel from a French car that was destroyed in a race. His later practice was to obtain at least one of every car ever made to identify best practices he could apply to his own products.

* * *

Now I am not outlining the career of the Ford Motor Company for any personal reason. I am not saying: "Go thou and do likewise." What I am trying to emphasize is that the ordinary way of doing business is not the best way. I am coming to the point of my entire departure from the ordinary methods. From this point dates the extraordinary success of the company.

We had been fairly following the custom of the trade. Our automobile was less complex than any other. We had no outside money in the concern. But aside from these two points we did not differ materially from the other automobile companies, excepting that we had been somewhat more successful and had rigidly pursued the policy of taking all cash discounts, putting our profits back into the business, and maintaining a large cash balance. We entered cars in all of the races. We advertised and we pushed our sales. Outside of the simplicity of the construction of the car, our main difference in design was that we made no provision for the purely "pleasure car." We were just as much a pleasure car as any other car on the market, but we gave no attention to purely luxury features. We would do special work for a buyer, and I suppose that we would have made a special car at a price. We were a prosperous company. We might easily have sat down and said: "Now we have arrived. Let us hold what we have got."

Indeed, there was some disposition to take this stand. Some of the stock-holders were seriously alarmed when our production reached one hundred cars a day. They wanted to do something to stop me from ruining the company, and when I replied to the effect that one hundred cars a day was only a trifle and that I hoped before long to make a thousand a day, they were inexpressibly shocked and I understand seriously contemplated court action. If I had followed the general opinion of my associates I should have kept the business about as it was, put our funds into a fine administration building, tried to make bargains with such competitors as seemed too active, made new designs from time to time to catch the fancy of the public, and generally have passed on into the position of a quiet, respectable citizen with a quiet, respectable business.

The temptation to stop and hang on to what one has is quite natural. I can entirely sympathize with the desire to quit a life of activity and retire to a life of ease. I have never felt the urge myself but I can comprehend what it is— although I think that a man who retires ought entirely to get out of a business. There is a disposition to retire and retain control. It was, however, no part of my plan to do anything of that sort. I regarded our progress merely as an invitation to do more—as an indication that we had reached a place where we might begin to perform a real service. I had been planning every day through these years toward a universal car. The public had given its reactions to the various models. The cars in service, the racing, and the road tests gave excellent guides as to the changes that ought to be made, and even by 1905 I had fairly in mind the specifications of the kind of car I wanted to build. But I lacked the material to give strength without weight. I came across that material almost by accident.

In 1905 I was at a motor race at Palm Beach. There was a big smash-up and a French car was wrecked. We had entered our "Model K"—the high-powered six. I thought the foreign cars had smaller and better parts than we knew anything about. After the wreck I picked up a little valve strip stem. It was very light and very strong. I asked what it was made of. Nobody knew. I gave the stem to my assistant.

"Find out all about this," I told him. "That is the kind of material we ought to have in our cars."

He found eventually that it was a French steel and that there was vanadium in it. We tried every steel maker in America—not one could make vanadium steel. I sent to England for a man who understood how to make the steel commercially. The next thing was to get a plant to turn it out. That was another problem. Vanadium requires 3,000 degrees Fahrenheit. The ordinary furnace could not go beyond 2,700 degrees. I found a small steel company in Canton, Ohio. I offered to guarantee them against loss if they would run a heat for us. They agreed. The first heat was a failure. Very little vanadium remained in the steel. I had them try again, and the second time the steel came through. Until then we had been forced to be satisfied with steel running between 60,000 and 70,000 pounds tensile strength. With vanadium, the strength went up to 170,000 pounds.

MATERIAL SELECTION AND DESIGN FOR RELIABILITY (DFR)

The book introduced these concepts earlier, and the next section expands on the need to select materials for the jobs they are to perform, e.g., tensile strength, elastic performance, and resistance to wear. The best material for one application is unlikely to be the best for another, which was a consideration that Ford's contemporaries apparently overlooked.

The following segment introduced the concept of *design for reliability* (DFR) decades before it became a recognized science. Ford recognized that a product is no more reliable than its least reliable vital component, and that any failure of said component could make the product unusable or even endanger the owner's life. This ties in with modern reliability engineering, and also failure mode effects analysis (FMEA).

* * *

Having vanadium in hand I pulled apart our models and tested in detail to determine what kind of steel was best for every part—whether we wanted a hard steel, a tough steel, or an elastic steel. We, for the first time I think, in the history of any large construction, determined scientifically the exact quality of the steel. As a result we then selected twenty different types of steel for the various steel parts. About ten of these were vanadium. Vanadium was used wherever strength and lightness were required. Of course they are not all the same kind of vanadium steel. The other elements vary according to whether the part is to stand hard wear or whether it needs spring—in short, according to what it needs. Before these experiments I believe that not more than four different grades of steel had ever been used in automobile construction. By further experimenting, especially in the direction of heat treating, we have been able still further to increase the strength of the steel and therefore to reduce the weight of the car. In 1910 the French Department of Commerce and Industry took one of our steering spindle connecting rod yokes—selecting it as a vital unit—and tried it against a similar part from what they considered the best French car, and in every test our steel proved the stronger.

The vanadium steel disposed of much of the weight. The other requisites of a universal car I had already worked out and many of them were in practice. The design had to balance. Men die because a part gives out. Machines wreck themselves because some parts are weaker than others. Therefore, a part of the problem in designing a universal car was to have as nearly as possible all parts of equal strength considering their purpose—to put a motor in a one-horse shay. Also it had to be fool proof. This was difficult because a gasoline motor is essentially a delicate instrument and there is a wonderful opportunity for any one who has a mind that way to mess it up. I adopted this slogan:

"When one of my cars breaks down I know I am to blame."

Ford next identifies vital design features as might be cited today by quality function deployment (QFD, House of Quality). These include ease of maintenance (Design for Maintenance, because most drivers are not mechanics), reliability, and lightness to reduce fuel consumption and, therefore, cost of operation. The description of the Model T underscores the importance of simplicity of design and ease of repair. The following material also reiterates the importance of simplicity in design, which makes the product not only easier to manufacture, but also simpler to maintain.

* * *

From the day the first motor car appeared on the streets it had to me appeared to be a necessity. It was this knowledge and assurance that led me to build to the one end—a car that would meet the wants of the multitudes. All my efforts were then and still are turned to the production of one car—one model. And, year following year, the pressure was, and still is, to improve and refine and make better, with an increasing reduction in price. The universal car had to have these attributes:

(1) *Quality in material to give service in use. Vanadium steel is the strongest, toughest, and most lasting of steels. It forms the foundation and super-structure of the cars. It is the highest quality steel in this respect in the world, regardless of price.*

(2) *Simplicity in operation—because the masses are not mechanics.*

(3) *Power in sufficient quantity.*

(4) *Absolute reliability—because of the varied uses to which the cars would be put and the variety of roads over which they would travel.*

(5) *Lightness. With the Ford there are only 7.95 pounds to be carried by each cubic inch of piston displacement. This is one of the reasons why Ford cars are "always going," wherever and whenever you see*

them—through sand and mud, through slush, snow, and water, up hills, across fields and roadless plains.

(6) *Control—to hold its speed always in hand, calmly and safely meeting every emergency and contingency either in the crowded streets of the city or on dangerous roads. The planetary transmission of the Ford gave this control and anybody could work it. That is the "why" of the saying: "Anybody can drive a Ford." It can turn around almost anywhere.*

(7) *The more a motor car weighs, naturally the more fuel and lubricants are used in the driving; the lighter the weight, the lighter the expense of operation. The light weight of the Ford car in its early years was used as an argument against it. Now that is all changed.*

The design which I settled upon was called "Model T." The important feature of the new model—which, if it were accepted, as I thought it would be, I intended to make the only model and then start into real production—was its simplicity. There were but four constructional units in the car—the power plant, the frame, the front axle, and the rear axle. All of these were easily accessible and they were designed so that no special skill would be required for their repair or replacement. I believed then, although I said very little about it because of the novelty of the idea, that it ought to be possible to have parts so simple and so inexpensive that the menace of expensive hand repair work would be entirely eliminated. The parts could be made so cheaply that it would be less expensive to buy new ones than to have old ones repaired. They could be carried in hardware shops just as nails or bolts are carried. I thought that it was up to me as the designer to make the car so completely simple that no one could fail to understand it.

That works both ways and applies to everything. The less complex an article, the easier it is to make, the cheaper it may be sold, and therefore the greater number may be sold.

It is not necessary to go into the technical details of the construction but perhaps this is as good a place as any to review the various models, because "Model T" was the last of the models and the policy which it brought about took this business out of the ordinary line of business. Application of the same idea would take any business out of the ordinary run.

I designed eight models in all before "Model T." They were: "Model A," "Model B," "Model C," "Model F," "Model N," "Model R," "Model S," and "Model K." Of these, Models "A," "C," and "F" had two-cylinder opposed horizontal motors. In "Model A" the motor was at the rear of the driver's seat. In all of the other models it was in a hood in front. Models "B," "N," "R," and "S" had motors of the four-cylinder vertical type. "Model K" had six cylinders. "Model A" developed eight horsepower. "Model B" developed twenty-four horsepower with a 4-1/2-inch cylinder and a 5-inch stroke. The highest horsepower was in "Model K," the six-cylinder car, which developed *forty horsepower. The largest cylinders were those of "Model B." The smallest were in Models "N," "R," and "S" which were 3-3/4 inches in diameter with a 3-3/8-inch stroke. "Model T" has a 3-3/4-inch cylinder with a 4-inch stroke. The ignition was by dry batteries in all excepting "Model B," which had storage batteries, and in "Model K" which had both battery and magneto. In the present model, the magneto is a part of the power plant and is built in. The clutch in the first four models was of the cone type; in the last four and in the present model, of the multiple disc type. The transmission in all of the cars has been planetary. "Model A" had a chain drive. "Model B" had a shaft drive. The next two models had chain drives. Since then all of the cars have had shaft drives. "Model A" had a 72-inch wheel base. Model "B," which was an extremely good car, had 92 inches. "Model K" had 120 inches. "Model C" had 78 inches. The others had 84 inches, and the present car has 100 inches. In the first five models all of the equipment was extra. The next three were sold with a partial equipment. The present car is sold with full equipment. Model "A" weighed 1,250 pounds. The lightest cars were Models "N" and "R." They weighed 1,050 pounds, but they were both runabouts. The heaviest car was the six-cylinder, which weighed 2,000 pounds. The present car weighs 1,200 lbs.*

The "Model T" had practically no features which were not contained in some one or other of the previous models. Every detail had been fully tested in practice. There was no guessing as to whether or not it would be a successful model. It had to be. There was no way it could escape being so, for it had not been made in a day. It contained all that I was then able to put into a motor car plus the material, which for the first time I was able to obtain. We put out "Model T" for the season 1908–1909.

The company was then five years old. The original factory space had been 28 acre[s]. We had employed an average of 311 people in the first year, built 1,708 cars, and had one branch house. In 1908, the factory space had increased to 2.65 acres and we owned the building. The average number of employees had increased to 1,908. We built 6,181 cars and had fourteen branch houses. It was a prosperous business.

During the season 1908-1909 we continued to make Models "R" and "S," four-cylinder runabouts and roadsters, the models that had previously been so successful, and which sold at $700 and $750. But "Model T" swept them right out. We sold 10,607 cars—a larger number than any manufacturer had ever sold. The price for the touring car was $850. On the same chassis we mounted a town car at $1,000, a roadster at $825, a coupe at $950, and a landaulet at $950.

STANDARDIZATION HOLDS DOWN COSTS

Ford's purpose in standardizing the Model T instead of offering multiple models, and dictating no choice of a color other than black, was to hold down manufacturing costs so most customers could afford the car. The Model T's successor, the Model A, did offer choices of color. The lesson is that a company that introduces a highly innovative product should first figure out how to make it cheaply, and only then move on to customization. Modern manufacturing technology, however, makes mixed-model and small-lot production relatively easy.

Ford's warning about catering to the 5% of buyers who want special options should meanwhile be a warning against stocking cars with expensive but nonfunctional features, such as moon roofs, for which many customers are simply unwilling to pay. Modern information technology should simply rule out the manufacture of any car for which there is not an actual buyer, and the minority of customers with costly desires can factory-order what they want.

* * *

This season demonstrated conclusively to me that it was time to put the new policy in force. The salesmen, before I had announced the policy, were spurred by the great sales to think that even greater sales might be had if only we had more models. It is strange how, just as soon as an article becomes successful, somebody starts to think that it would be more successful if only it were different. There is a tendency to keep monkeying with styles and to spoil a good thing by changing it. The salesmen were insistent on increasing the line. They listened to the 5 per cent, the special customers who could say what they wanted, and forgot all about the 95 per cent who just bought without making any fuss. No business can improve unless it pays the closest possible attention to complaints and suggestions. If there is any defect in service then that must be instantly and rigorously investigated, but when the suggestion is only as to style, one has to make sure whether it is not merely a personal whim that is being voiced. Salesmen always want to cater to whims instead of acquiring sufficient knowledge of their product to be able to explain to the customer with the whim that what they have will satisfy his every requirement—that is, of course, provided what they have does satisfy these requirements.

Therefore in 1909 I announced one morning, without any previous warning, that in the future we were going to build only one model, that the model was going to be "Model T," and that the chassis would be exactly the same for all cars, and I remarked:

"Any customer can have a car painted any colour that he wants so long as it is black."

I cannot say that any one agreed with me. The selling people could not of course see the advantages that a single model would bring about in production. More than that, they did not particularly care. They thought that our production was good enough as it was and there was a very decided opinion that lowering the sales price would hurt sales, that the people who wanted quality would be driven away and that there would be none to replace them. There was very little conception of the motor industry. A motor car was still regarded as something in the way of a luxury. The manufacturers did a good deal to spread this idea. Some clever persons invented the name "pleasure car" and the advertising emphasized the pleasure features. The sales people had ground for their objections and particularly when I made the following announcement:

> *"I will build a motor car for the great multitude. It will be large enough for the family but small enough for the individual to run and care for. It will be constructed of the best materials, by the best men to be hired, after the simplest designs that modern engineering can devise. But it will be so low in price that no man making a good salary will be unable to own one—and enjoy with his family the blessing of hours of pleasure in God's great open spaces."*

This announcement was received not without pleasure. The general comment was:

> *"If Ford does that he will be out of business in six months."*

The impression was that a good car could not be built at a low price, and that, anyhow, there was no use in building a low-priced car because only wealthy people were in the market for cars. The 1908-1909 sales of more than ten thousand cars had convinced me that we needed a new factory. We already had a big modern factory—the Piquette Street plant. It was as good as, perhaps a little better than, any automobile factory in the country. But I did not see how it was going to care for the sales and production that were inevitable. So I bought sixty acres at Highland Park, which was then considered away out in the country from Detroit. The amount of ground bought and the plans for a bigger factory than the world has ever seen were opposed. The question was already being asked:

> *"How soon will Ford blow up?"*

WORK FOR CONTINUOUS COST REDUCTION

The next statement, "a principle rather than an individual is at work," relates back to Ford's "universal code" and reinforces the proposition that any business can make it work equally well. The subsequent paragraph shows that Ford was able to reduce prices continuously despite higher raw material costs and higher wages. This is particularly telling because Ford's goal was to raise wages continuously, but materials are a genuine direct cost that no improvement in labor efficiency can remove from the product cost.

Ford's removal of material waste is consistent with the ISO 14001 environmental standard, and, may exceed its requirements. A manufacturer can meet ISO 14001's provisions through the identification and mitigation of environmental aspects, i.e., wastes whose discharge is subject to regulation by environmental protection laws, but plenty of material waste does not fall into this category. Ford's position was that no material waste of any kind should occur, and implementation of this policy may have offset the material costs in question.

* * *

Nobody knows how many thousand times it has been asked since. It is asked only because of the failure to grasp that a principle rather than an individual is at work, and the principle is so simple that it seems mysterious.

For 1909–1910, in order to pay for the new land and buildings, I slightly raised the prices. This is perfectly justifiable and results in a benefit, not an injury, to the purchaser. I did exactly the same thing a few years ago—or rather, in that case I did not lower the price as is my annual custom, in order to build the River Rouge plant. The extra money might in each case have been had by borrowing, but then we should have had a continuing charge upon the business and all subsequent cars would have had to bear this charge. The price of all the models was increased $100, with the exception of the roadster, which was increased only $75 and of the landaulet and town car, which were increased $150 and $200 respectively. We sold 18,664 cars, and then for 1910-1911, with the new facilities, I cut the touring car from $950 to $780 and we sold 34,528 cars. That is the beginning of the steady reduction in the price of the cars in the face of ever-increasing cost of materials and ever-higher wages.

Improve the Productivity of the Individual Worker

The next section shows that one does not have to double the workforce to double production: "You will note that men were not employed in proportion to the output." Elimination of all forms of waste, including waste motion in the case of people, makes this achievable. The subsequent story shows that handmade axe handles, which were, despite the care taken by a skilled and experienced laborer, inferior to those produced by machines.

* * *

Contrast the year 1908 with the year 1911. The factory space increased from 2.65 to 32 acres. The average number of employees from 1,908 to 4,110, and the cars built from a little over six thousand to nearly thirty-five thousand. You will note that men were not employed in proportion to the output.

We were, almost overnight it seems, in great production. How did all this come about?

Simply through the application of an inevitable principle. By the application of intelligently directed power and machinery. In a little dark shop on a side street an old man had laboured for years making axe handles. Out of seasoned hickory he fashioned them, with the help of a draw shave, a chisel, and a supply of sandpaper. Carefully was each handle weighed and balanced. No two of them were alike. The curve must exactly fit the hand and must conform to the grain of the wood. From dawn until dark the old man laboured. His average product was eight handles a week, for which he received a dollar and a half each. And often some of these were unsaleable—because the balance was not true.

To-day you can buy a better axe handle, made by machinery, for a few cents. And you need not worry about the balance. They are all alike—and every one is perfect. Modern methods applied in a big way have not only brought the cost of axe handles down to a fraction of their former cost—but they have immensely improved the product.

The machine in question was almost certainly a Blanchard lathe, or a similar tool for the mass production of irregularly shaped wooden products. Thomas Blanchard's original objective was to shape musket stocks from wooden blanks, per the National Park Service:

The so-called Blanchard lathe [actually, it's a shaper since the cutter is a rotating wheel] works much [like] a modern key-cutting machine with a stock blank [a rough gunstock form] in place of the key blank. An iron master form, in the shape of the musket stock, slowly rotates allowing a guide wheel to roll over it and to direct, in turn, the cutting wheel as it makes identical movements on the rotating wooden stock blank.

* * *

It is conceivable that the axe handle maker in Ford's story could have had an iron master made from his best piece, his master piece, and then enjoyed a very comfortable retirement while a Blanchard lathe made endless copies of his best work. The same principle could apply today to the hand-crafted wooden products that are often displayed at art fairs. The key lesson of the story, however, is that automation can deliver virtually identical copies of the best known form of the product, and in far greater quantities and lower cost than is possible through hand production.

The following from Ford introduces the concept of a supply chain and its stakeholders, and the interdependency of the supplier, its employees, and its customers.

* * *

It was the application of these same methods to the making of the Ford car that at the very start lowered the price and heightened the quality. We just developed an idea. The nucleus of a business may be an idea. That is, an inventor or a thoughtful workman works out a new and better way to serve some established human need; the idea commends itself, and people want to avail themselves of it. In this way a single individual may prove, through his idea or discovery, the nucleus of a business. But the creation of the body and bulk of that business is shared by everyone who has anything to do with it. No manufacturer can say: "I built this business"—if he has required the help of thousands of men in building it. It is a joint production. Everyone employed in it has contributed something to it. By working and producing they make it possible for the purchasing world to keep coming to that business for the type of service it provides, and thus they help establish a custom, a trade, a habit which supplies them with a livelihood. That is the way our company grew and just how I shall start explaining in the next chapter.

The Importance of Reliability

The chapter's last segment reinforces Ford's statement that reliability is a major selling point. This idea is commonplace today, when buyers of automobiles and major appliances check the reliability ratings in *Consumer Reports* and similar publications.

* * *

In the meantime, the company had become world-wide. We had branches in London and in Australia. We were shipping to every part of the world, and in England particularly we were beginning to be as well known as in America.

The introduction of the car in England was somewhat difficult on account of the failure of the American bicycle. Because the American bicycle had not been suited to English uses it was taken for granted and made a point of by the distributors that no American vehicle could appeal to the British market. Two "Model As" found their way to England in 1903. The newspapers refused to notice them. The automobile agents refused to take the slightest interest. It was rumoured that the principal components of its manufacture were string and hoop wire and that a buyer would be lucky if it held together for a fortnight! In the first year about a dozen cars in all were used; the second was only a little better. And I may say as to the reliability of that "Model A" that most of them after nearly twenty years are still in some kind of service in England.

In 1905 our agent entered a "Model C" in the Scottish Reliability Trials. In those days reliability runs were more popular in England than motor races. Perhaps there was no inkling that after all an automobile was not merely a toy. The Scottish Trials was over eight hundred miles of hilly, heavy roads. The Ford came through with only one involuntary stop against it. That started the Ford sales in England. In that same year Ford taxicabs were placed in London for the first time. In the next several years the sales began to pick up. The cars went into every endurance and reliability test and won every one of them. The Brighton dealer had ten Fords driven over the South Downs for two days in a kind of steeplechase and every one of them came through. As a result six hundred cars were sold that year. In 1911 Henry Alexander drove a "Model T" to the top of Ben Nevis, 4,600 feet. That year 14,060 cars were sold in England, and it has never since been necessary to stage any kind of a stunt. We eventually opened our own factory at Manchester; at first it was purely an assembling plant. But as the years have gone by we have progressively made more and more of the car.

5

Getting into Production

This chapter begins with the very valuable observation that organizations must look at the cost of things that are absent along with that of things that are present. The ISO 9001 (International Organization of Standardization) standard for quality management systems is an example. A quality management system is far more conspicuous by its absence, in the form of defects, poor service, and even medical malpractice, than by its presence. A good decision process, therefore, will ask: "What is the cost of not doing or having this?" as well as: "What will it cost to buy or implement this?"

This chapter repeats the common sense fact that the product (or service) and not the employer pays wages, which means that the workforce must help make the process more efficient if it wants higher pay. It adds that customers pay more than they should, and workers earn less than they should because of the huge inefficiencies that exist in most production and service operations. Lean manufacturing, the scientific element of his universal code, removes these inefficiencies.

* * *

If a device would save in time just 10 per cent. or increase results 10 per cent., then its absence is always a 10 per cent. tax. If the time of a person is worth fifty cents an hour, a 10 per cent. saving is worth five cents an hour. If the owner of a skyscraper could increase his income 10 per cent., he would willingly pay half the increase just to know how. The reason why he owns a skyscraper is that science has proved that certain materials, used in a given way, can save space and increase rental incomes. A building thirty stories high needs no more ground space than one five stories high. Getting along with the old-style architecture costs the five-story man the income of twenty-five floors. Save ten steps a day for each of twelve thousand employees and you will have saved fifty miles of wasted motion and misspent energy.

Those are the principles on which the production of my plant was built up. They all come practically as of course. In the beginning we tried to get machinists. As the necessity for production increased it became apparent not only that enough machinists were not to be had, but also that skilled men were not necessary in production, and out of this grew a principle that I later want to present in full.

It is self-evident that a majority of the people in the world are not mentally—even if they are physically—capable of making a good living. That is, they are not capable of furnishing with their own hands a sufficient quantity of the goods which this world needs to be able to exchange their unaided product for the goods which they need. I have heard it said, in fact I believe it is quite a current thought, that we have taken skill out of work. We have not. We have put in skill. We have put a higher skill into planning, management, and tool building, and the results of that skill are enjoyed by the man who is not skilled. This I shall later enlarge on.

We have to recognize the unevenness in human mental equipments. If every job in our place required skill the place would never have existed. Sufficiently skilled men to the number needed could not have been trained in a hundred years. A million men working by hand could not even approximate our present daily output. No one could manage a million men. But more important than that, the product of the unaided hands of those million men could not be sold at a price in consonance with buying power. And even if it were possible to imagine such an aggregation and imagine its management and correlation, just think of the area that it would have to occupy! How many of the men would be engaged, not in producing, but in merely carrying from place to place what the other men had produced? I cannot see how under such conditions the men could possibly be paid more than ten or twenty cents a day—for of course it is not the employer who pays wages. He only handles the money. It is the product that pays the wages and it is the management that arranges the production so that the product may pay the wages.

The more economical methods of production did not begin all at once. They began gradually—just as we began gradually to make our own parts. "Model T" was the first motor that we made ourselves. The great economies began in assembling and then extended to other sections so that, while to-day we have skilled mechanics in plenty, they do not produce automobiles—they make it easy for others to produce them. Our skilled men are the tool makers, the experimental workmen, the machinists, and the pattern makers. They are as good as any men in the world—so good, indeed, that they should not be wasted in doing that which the machines they contrive can do better. The rank and file of men come to us unskilled; they learn their jobs within a few hours or a few days. If they do not learn within that time they will never be of any use to us. These men are, many of them, foreigners, and all that is required before they are taken on is that they should be potentially able to do enough work to pay the overhead charges on the floor space they occupy. They do not have to be able-bodied men. We have jobs that require great physical strength—although they are rapidly lessening; we have other jobs that require no strength whatsoever—jobs which, as far as strength is concerned, might be attended to by a child of three.

It is not possible, without going deeply into technical processes, to present the whole development of manufacturing, step by step, in the order in which each thing came about. I do not know that this could be done, because something has been happening nearly every day and nobody can keep track. Take at random a number of the changes. From them it is possible not only to gain some idea of what will happen when this world is put on a production basis, but also to see how much more we pay for things than we ought to, and how much lower wages are than they ought to be, and what a vast field remains to be explored. The Ford Company is only a little way along on the journey.

THE BIRTH OF THE ASSEMBLY LINE

Ford now describes how division of labor made economic mass production possible. His factory began with the traditional departmental or "farm" layout, in which individual departments made specific parts that a single worker or department would later assemble. The workers' need to get and move the parts, however, created an enormous amount of waste motion that added no value to the product, and for which the worker could not be paid. This led to the assembly line that moved the work to the people, and task subdivision that eliminated the waste motion of exchanging one tool for another.

Note especially the statement that pedestrianism is not a highly paying line of work, and also Ford's two basic motion efficiency principles. No job should require a worker to take more than one step in any direction to get or move work, and no job should require anybody to bend over. The latter doubtlessly prevented back-related repetitive motion injuries in a highly repetitive working environment.

* * *

A Ford car contains about five thousand parts—that is counting screws, nuts, and all. Some of the parts are fairly bulky and others are almost the size of watch parts. In our first assembling we simply started to put a car together at a spot on the floor and workmen brought to it the parts as they were needed in exactly the same way that one builds a house. When we started to make parts it was natural to create a single department of the factory to make that part, but usually one workman performed all of the operations necessary on a small part. The rapid press of production made it necessary to devise plans of production that would avoid having the workers falling over one another. The undirected worker spends more of his time walking about for materials and tools than he does in working; he gets small pay because pedestrianism is not a highly paid line.

The first step forward in assembly came when we began taking the work to the men instead of the men to the work. We now have two general principles in all operations—that a man shall never have to take more than one step, if possibly it can be avoided, and that no man need ever stoop over.

Basic Job Design Principles

The phrase "reduction of the necessity for thought on the part of the worker" is particularly important, and it is also subject to misinterpretation. An unenlightened reader might construe this as a desire on Ford's part for mindless automata, the human equivalent of robots, or the almost mindless Deltas and Epsilons of Aldous Huxley's *Brave New World*. We have already seen that Ford encouraged his workers to identify waste and look for ways to improve their jobs, which is hardly consistent with mindless automata.

The foundation of Dr. Shigeo Shingo's poka-yoke (error proofing) is, however, the common sense premise that any job that requires worker vigilance to prevent defects will eventually produce defects. Doctors are the real world counterparts of the intellectually gifted Alphas of *Brave New World*, but 80 to 85% of all medical mistakes result from the doctor's need to think about anything other than the practice of his or her specialized skills and experience. If, for example, the doctor has to worry about misinterpretation of a prescription, or about a mix-up in patient test results, there will be serious and possibly life-threatening trouble sooner or later. This is what Ford means by "reduction of the necessity for thought on the part of the worker."

It also should, of course, be impossible to assemble parts backward or leave out a component. Ford and Crowther (1930, 198) describe a welding operation in which automatically operated plates cover all but the next button that the operator is supposed to press. "It is impossible for the operator to go wrong." This is an example of removing the need for thought, or rather close attention to a mindlessly repetitive job, from the activity.

Norwood (1931, Chap. VI) uses the phrase "Can't rather than don't" to describe Ford's application of the same principle to workplace safety. The worker does not have to devote constant thought or attention to safety because the job design makes accidents impossible.

* * *

The principles of assembly are these:

1. *Place the tools and the men in the sequence of the operation so that each component part shall travel the least possible distance while in the process of finishing.*
2. *Use work slides or some other form of carrier so that when a work-man completes his operation, he drops the part always in the same place—which place must always be the most convenient place to his hand—and if possible have gravity carry the part to the next workman for his operation.*
3. *Use sliding assembling lines by which the parts to be assembled are delivered at convenient distances.*

The net result of the application of these principles is the reduction of the necessity for thought on the part of the worker and the reduction of his move-ments to a minimum. He does as nearly as possible only one thing with only one movement.

The assembling of the chassis is, from the point of view of the non-mechanical mind, our most interesting and perhaps best known operation, and at one time it was an exceedingly important operation. We now ship out the parts for assembly at the point of distribution.

Along about April 1, 1913, we first tried the experiment of an assembly line. We tried it on assembling the flywheel magneto. We try everything in a little way first—we will rip out anything once we discover a better way, but we have to know absolutely that the new way is going to be better than the old before we do anything drastic.

Subdivision of Labor

The following discussion makes it emphatically clear how subdivision of labor can increase efficiency and, therefore, wages and profitability, enor-mously. Subdivision of the job eliminates the need to change tools, walk, or even reach very far for parts. Excellent examples include improvised fire brigades or groups of flood control volunteers that pass buckets of water, or sandbags, so nobody has to walk.

The flywheel magneto example shows how subdivision of labor allowed one worker to do the work of four, and probably with less physical effort. Application of the same principle to the motor yielded a threefold productivity improvement.

* * *

I believe that this was the first moving line ever installed. The idea came in a general way from the overhead trolley that the Chicago packers use in dressing beef. We had previously assembled the fly-wheel magneto in the usual method. With one workman doing a complete job he could turn out from thirty-five to forty pieces in a nine-hour day, or about twenty minutes to an assembly. What he did alone was then spread into twenty-nine operations; that cut down the assembly time to thirteen minutes, ten seconds. Then we raised the height of the line eight inches—this was in 1914—and cut the time to seven minutes. Further experimenting with the speed that the work should move at cut the time down to five minutes. In short, the result is this: by the aid of scientific study one man is now able to do somewhat more than four did only a comparatively few years ago. That line established the efficiency of the method and we now use it everywhere. The assembling of the motor, formerly done by one man, is now divided into eighty-four operations—those men do the work that three times their number formerly did. In a short time we tried out the plan on the chassis.

Ergonomics and the Adjustable Height Skillet

Anderson (2007) discusses the adjustable height skillet, which holds an entire automobile at a comfortable height for the worker. Its ancestor as introduced by Ford, while not adjustable, did account for workers of different heights to make the task as easy as possible. Note how the workers travel with the work, but by riding the skillet instead of walking, and with the parts ready at hand as they are needed.

* * *

About the best we had done in stationary chassis assembling was an average of twelve hours and twenty-eight minutes per chassis. We tried the experiment of drawing the chassis with a rope and windlass down a line two hundred fifty feet long. Six assemblers traveled with the chassis and picked up the parts from piles placed along the line. This rough experiment reduced the time to five hours fifty minutes per chassis. In the early part of 1914 we

elevated the assembly line. We had adopted the policy of "man-high" work;
we had one line twenty-six and three quarter inches and another twenty-
four and one half inches from the floor—to suit squads of different heights.
The waist-high arrangement and a further subdivision of work so that each
man had fewer movements cut down the labour time per chassis to one hour
thirty-three minutes. Only the chassis was then assembled in the line. The
body was placed on in "John R. Street"—the famous street that runs through
our Highland Park factories. Now the line assembles the whole car.

How to Run a Balanced Factory at (Almost) 100% Capacity

The next section will astonish readers of Goldratt and Cox's (1992) *The Goal*, whose matchsticks-and-dice production control exercise shows why it is impossible to run a balanced factory at 100% capacity. Ford's statement "… he must have every second necessary but not a single unnecessary second" contradicts Goldratt by suggesting a lack of significant excess capacity in any operation, which makes every operation a constraint.

Subdivision of tasks, which eliminates not only the nonvalue-adding time of exchanging tools or searching for parts, but also the associated variation, was the apparent key to Ford's success as shown by equation 5.1. T is the total time for a series of n process steps, while σ^2 is their variance.

$$T = \sum_{k=1}^{n} t_k \quad and \quad \sigma^2 = \sum_{k=1}^{n} \sigma_k^2 \tag{5.1}$$

The n steps include not only the value-adding actions, but also those that do not add value. These include setup, exchange of tools, transportation, waiting for transportation, and waiting to form transfer batches. Single-unit processing eliminates the latter, while conveyors and work slides remove most of the variation associated with transportation. Task subdivision eliminates considerations, such as exchange of tools.

This is why: "The man who puts in a bolt does not put on the nut; the man who puts on the nut does not tighten it." If the same person did both tasks, he or she would have to pick up and put down a wrench each time. Ford later elaborates on this (Chapter 10) by pointing out that elimination of variation in processing and material transfer times can remove almost all inventory from the system.

The Kingman Equation (Hopp and Spearman, 2000, p. 270) supports Ford's assertion. Cycle time in queue (CTQ) is proportional to $u/(1-u)$ where u is the tool utilization, and this factor does indeed approach infinity as u approaches 100%. CTQ is also, however, proportional to the sum of the squares of the coefficients of variation for (1) arrivals at the workstation and (2) effective processing time. If single-unit flow and division of labor can reduce both variation terms to effectively zero, CTQ will be zero for any utilization of less than 100%.

The subsequent paragraph adds that the work is in continuous motion, and there are no batch and queue activities. Batch and queue can do nothing but add cycle time and variation in material transfer time to the process.

* * *

It must not be imagined, however, that all this worked out as quickly as it sounds. The speed of the moving work had to be carefully tried out; in the fly-wheel magneto we first had a speed of sixty inches per minute. That was too fast. Then we tried eighteen inches per minute. That was too slow. Finally we settled on forty-four inches per minute. The idea is that a man must not be hurried in his work—he must have every second necessary but not a single unnecessary second. We have worked out speeds for each assembly, for the success of the chassis assembly caused us gradually to overhaul our entire method of manufacturing and to put all assembling in mechanically driven lines. The chassis assembling line, for instance, goes at a pace of six feet per minute; the front axle assembly line goes at one hundred eighty-nine inches per minute. In the chassis assembling are forty-five separate operations or stations. The first men fasten four mud-guard brackets to the chassis frame; the motor arrives on the tenth operation and so on in detail. Some men do only one or two small operations, others do more. The man who places a part does not fasten it—the part may not be fully in place until after several operations later. The man who puts in a bolt does not put on the nut; the man who puts on the nut does not tighten it. On operation number thirty-four the budding motor gets its gasoline; it has previously received lubrication; on operation number forty-four the radiator is filled with water, and on operation number forty-five the car drives out onto John R. Street.

Essentially the same ideas have been applied to the assembling of the motor. In October, 1913, it required nine hours and fifty-four minutes of labour time to assemble one motor; six months later, by the moving assembly method, this time had been reduced to five hours and fifty-six minutes. Every piece of work in the shops moves; it may move on hooks on overhead chains going to assembly in the exact order in which the parts are required; it may travel on a moving platform, or it may go by gravity, but the point is that there is no lifting or trucking of anything other than materials. Materials are brought in on small trucks or trailers operated by cut-down Ford chassis, which are sufficiently mobile and quick to get in and out of any aisle where they may be required to go. No workman has anything to do with moving or lifting anything. That is all in a separate department—the department of transportation.

The Introduction of Cellular Manufacturing

The next part of this chapter shows unequivocally that Ford introduced what are now known as work cells: "A department is a little factory by itself." This eliminated interdepartmental transportation, as might be identified from a modern spaghetti diagram.

* * *

We started assembling a motor car in a single factory. Then as we began to make parts, we began to departmentalize so that each department would do only one thing. As the factory is now organized each department makes only a single part or assembles a part. A department is a little factory in itself. The part comes into it as raw material or as a casting, goes through the sequence of machines and heat treatments, or whatever may be required, and leaves that department finished. It was only because of transport ease that the departments were grouped together when we started to manufacture. I did not know that such minute divisions would be possible; but as our production grew and departments multiplied, we actually changed from making automobiles to making parts. Then we found that we had made another new discovery, which was that by no means all of the parts had to be made in one factory. It was not really a discovery—it was something in the nature of going around in a circle to my first manufacturing when I bought the motors and probably ninety per cent of the parts. When we began to make our own parts we practically took for granted that they all had to be made in the one factory—that there was some special virtue in having a single roof over the manufacture of the entire car. We have now developed away from this. If we build any more large factories, it will be only because the making of a single part must be in such tremendous volume as to require a large unit. I hope that in the course of time the big Highland Park plant will be doing only one or two things. The casting has already been taken away from it and has gone to the River Rouge plant. So now we are on our way back to where we started from—excepting that, instead of buying our parts on the outside, we are beginning to make them in our own factories on the outside.

This is a development which holds exceptional consequences, for it means, as I shall enlarge in a later chapter, that highly standardized, highly subdivided industry need no longer become concentrated in large plants with all the inconveniences of transportation and housing that hamper large plants. A thousand or five hundred men ought to be enough in a single factory; then there would be no problem of transporting them to work or away from work and there would be no slums or any of the other unnatural ways of living incident to the overcrowding that must take place if the workmen are to live within reasonable distances of a very large plant.

Highland Park now has five hundred departments. Down at our Piquette plant we had only eighteen departments, and formerly at Highland Park we had only one hundred and fifty departments. This illustrates how far we are going in the manufacture of parts.

IGNORE THE NYET ENGINEERS

Chapter 1 already showed that Ford encountered (and ignored) his share of nyet or "no" engineers: people who were all too ready to tell him why something could not be done. The person who "knows" that something cannot be done is right, at least as far as he or her is concerned personally.

Ford's view of these so-called experts is consistent with the Diesel Clothing Company's advertising slogan, "Stupid might fail; smart doesn't even try." Field Marshal Helmuth von Moltke phrased the matter somewhat more scientifically (Hughes, 1993, p. 77):

> The positive recommendation has against it the most undoubted drawbacks. The negation remains in the right, and everyone agrees to do nothing. In every headquarters there are men who know how to demonstrate with great perception all the difficulties attending every proposed enterprise. The very first time something goes wrong they prove conclusively that they had "said so." They are always right. Because they never counsel anything positive, much less carry it out; success cannot refute them. These men of the negative are the ruination of senior commanders.

Moltke's "men of the negative" are equivalent to Shingo's "nyet engineers" and Yoshiki Iwata's "concrete heads," the latter from Womack and Jones (1996, pp. 128–129). These are the "experts" against whose advice Ford warns.

We do not, however, agree with Ford's practice of keeping no records of experiments. It is important to know what has not worked in the past to avoid repetition of the unsuccessful approach. Ford emphatically did keep track of successful experiments, though, and he engaged in best practice deployment to make sure all his factories exploited the knowledge.

* * *

Hardly a week passes without some improvement being made somewhere in machine or process, and sometimes this is made in defiance of what is called "the best shop practice." I recall that a machine manufacturer was once called into conference on the building of a special machine. The specifications called for an output of two hundred per hour.

"This is a mistake," said the manufacturer, "you mean two hundred a day—no machine can be forced to two hundred an hour."

The company officer sent for the man who had designed the machine and they called his attention to the specification. He said:

"Yes, what about it?"

"It can't be done," said the manufacturer positively, "no machine built will do that—it is out of the question."

"Out of the question!" exclaimed the engineer, "if you will come down to the main floor you will see one doing it; we built one to see if it could be done and now we want more like it."

The factory keeps no record of experiments. The foremen and superintendents remember what has been done. If a certain method has formerly been tried and failed, somebody will remember it—but I am not particularly anxious for the men to remember what someone else has tried to do in the past, for then we might quickly accumulate far too many things that could not be done. That is one of the troubles with extensive records. If you keep on recording all of your failures you will shortly have a list showing that there is nothing left for you to try—whereas it by no means follows because one man has failed in a certain method that another man will not succeed.

They told us we could not cast gray iron by our endless chain method and I believe there is a record of failures. But we are doing it. The man who carried through our work either did not know or paid no attention to the previous figures. Likewise we were told that it was out of the question to pour the hot iron directly from the blast furnace into mould. The usual method is to run the iron into pigs, let them season for a time, and then remelt them for casting. But at the River Rouge plant we are casting directly from cupolas that are filled from the blast furnaces. Then, too, a record of failures—particularly if it is a dignified and well-authenticated record—deters a young man from trying. We get some of our best results from letting fools rush in where angels fear to tread.

None of our men are "experts." We have most unfortunately found it necessary to get rid of a man as soon as he thinks himself an expert—because no one ever considers himself expert if he really knows his job. A man who knows a job sees so much more to be done than he has done, that he is always pressing forward and never gives up an instant of thought to how good and how efficient he is. Thinking always ahead, thinking always of trying to do more, brings a state of mind in which nothing is impossible. The moment one gets into the "expert" state of mind a great number of things become impossible.

I refuse to recognize that there are impossibilities. I cannot discover that any one knows enough about anything on this earth definitely to say what is and what is not possible. The right kind of experience, the right kind of technical training, ought to enlarge the mind and reduce the number of impossibilities. It unfortunately does nothing of the kind. Most technical training and the average of that which we call experience, provide a record of previous failures and, instead of these failures being taken for what they are worth, they are taken as absolute bars to progress. If some man, calling himself an authority, says that this or that cannot be done, then a horde of unthinking followers start the chorus: "It can't be done."

Take castings. Castings has always been a wasteful process and is so old that it has accumulated many traditions which make improvements extraordinarily difficult to bring about. I believe one authority on moulding declared—before we started our experiments—that any man who said he could reduce costs within half a year wrote himself down as a fraud.

KEEP THE WORK IN CONTINUOUS MOTION, AVOID BATCH OPERATIONS

Ford achieved the seemingly impossible (as described by the so-called "expert" above) in metal casting through the replacement of batch operations with single-unit flow. Arnold and Faurote (1915, pp. 85–86) meanwhile describe the conversion of a batch annealing process to a continuous flow operation that carried the parts through a furnace on a continuous chain. The idea of keeping the work in continuous motion while avoiding any kind of batching and queuing underscores Ford's approach to process design, and it is equally applicable today.

* * *

Our foundry used to be much like other foundries. When we cast the first "Model T" cylinders in 1910, everything in the place was done by hand; shovels and wheelbarrows abounded. The work was then either skilled or unskilled; we had moulders and we had labourers. Now we have about five per cent of thoroughly skilled moulders and core setters, but the remaining 95 per cent are unskilled, or to put it more accurately, must be skilled in exactly one operation which the most stupid man can learn within two days. The moulding is all done by machinery. Each part which we have to cast has a unit or units of its own—according to the number required in the plan of production. The machinery of the unit is adapted to the single casting; thus the men in the unit each perform a single operation that is always the same. A unit consists of an overhead railway to which at intervals are hung little platforms for the moulds. Without going into technical details, let me say the making of the moulds and the cores, and the packing of the cores, are done with the work in motion on the platforms. The metal is poured at another point as the work moves, and by the time the mould in which the metal has been poured reaches the terminal, it is cool enough to start on its automatic way to cleaning, machining, and assembling. And the platform is moving around for a new load.

SUBDIVIDE THE JOB TO ELIMINATE WASTE MOTION

This book has already shown how subdivision of labor can eliminate an enormous amount of waste motion and the associated variation in processing and material transfer times. This piston rod assembly operation provides yet another example. The result was a 67-fold productivity improvement: 325 pieces per hour by 7 workers versus 19.44 per hour by 28 workers.

* * *

Take the development of the piston-rod assembly. Even under the old plan, this operation took only three minutes and did not seem to be one to bother about. There were two benches and twenty-eight men in all; they assembled one hundred seventy-five pistons and rods in a nine-hour day—which means just five seconds over three minutes each. There was no inspection, and many of the piston and rod assemblies came back from the motor assembling line as defective. It is a very simple operation. The workman pushed the pin out of the piston, oiled the pin, slipped the rod in place, put the pin through the rod and piston, tightened one screw, and opened another screw. That was the whole operation. The foreman, examining the operation, could not discover why it should take as much as three minutes. He analyzed the motions with a stop-watch. He found that four hours out of a nine-hour day were spent in walking. The assembler did not go off anywhere, but he had to shift his feet to gather in his materials and to push away his finished piece. In the whole task, each man performed six operations. The foreman devised a new plan; he split the operation into three divisions, put a slide on the bench and three men on each side of it, and an inspector at the end.

Instead of one man performing the whole operation, one man then performed only one third of the operation—he performed only as much as he could do without shifting his feet. They cut down the squad from twenty-eight to fourteen men. The former record for twenty-eight men was one hundred seventy-five assemblies a day. Now seven men turn out twenty-six hundred assemblies in eight hours. It is not necessary to calculate the savings there!

AUTOMATE JOBS AND REDUCE MATERIAL TRANSFER DISTANCES

Automation of a job, such as riveting crankcase arms to the crankcase, can improve productivity 60-fold, which supports the premise that Lean manufacturing can make high-wage American workers more than competitive with cheap offshore labor. Ford also cited a more than 10-fold reduction in the distance that a cylinder casting had to travel in the factory. This underscores the principle that transportation of materials and parts, even inside the factory, is nonvalue-adding.

* * *

Painting the rear axle assembly once gave some trouble. It used to be dipped by hand into a tank of enamel. This required several handlings and the services of two men. Now one man takes care of it all on a special machine, designed and built in the factory. The man now merely hangs the assembly on a moving chain which carries it up over the enamel tank, two levers then thrust thimbles over the ends of the ladle shaft, the paint tank rises six feet, immerses the axle, returns to position, and the axle goes on to the drying oven. The whole cycle of operations now takes just thirteen seconds.

The radiator is a complex affair and soldering it used to be a matter of skill. There are ninety-five tubes in a radiator. Fitting and soldering these tubes in place is by hand a long operation, requiring both skill and patience. Now it is all done by a machine which will make twelve hundred radiator cores in eight hours; then they are soldered in place by being carried through a furnace by a conveyor. No tinsmith work and so no skill are required.

We used to rivet the crank-case arms to the crank-case, using pneumatic hammers which were supposed to be the latest development. It took six men to hold the hammers and six men to hold the casings, and the din was terrific. Now an automatic press operated by one man, who does nothing else, gets through five times as much work in a day as those twelve men did.

In the Piquette plant the cylinder casting traveled four thousand feet in the course of finishing; now it travels only slightly over three hundred feet.

FORD'S KEYNOTES OF PRODUCTION

This chapter's concluding section is particularly important because it states very explicitly Ford's principles for job design:

1. Too much room for workers is as bad as too little room. It wastes floor space and, more importantly, it introduces nonvalue-adding distance over which the work must move.
2. Subdivide operations to eliminate nonvalue-adding motions, along with accompanying variation in processing and material transfer times.
3. Design for manufacture or assembly.

* * *

There is no manual handling of material. There is not a single hand operation. If a machine can be made automatic, it is made automatic. Not a single operation is ever considered as being done in the best or cheapest way. At that, only about ten per cent of our tools are special; the others are regular machines adjusted to the particular job. And they are placed almost side by side. We put more machinery per square foot of floor space than any other factory in the world—every foot of space not used carries an overhead expense. We want none of that waste. Yet there is all the room needed—no man has too much room and no man has too little room. Dividing and subdividing operations, keeping the work in motion—those are the keynotes of production. But also it is to be remembered that all the parts are designed so that they can be most easily made. And the saving? Although the comparison is not quite fair, it is startling. If at our present rate of production we employed the same number of men per car that we did when we began in 1903—and those men were only for assembly—we should to-day require a force of more than two hundred thousand. We have less than fifty thousand men on automobile production at our highest point of around four thousand cars a day!

6

Machines and Men

This chapter begins with a warning against bureaucracy and a "silo mentality" in which job descriptions limit creativity and willingness to take responsibility. The first paragraphs anticipate W. Edwards Deming's and Tom Peters' advice to break down organizational barriers (Deming) and make the organization porous (Peters). The chapter later reinforces this material with the statement: "The health of every organization depends on every member—whatever his place—feeling that everything that happens to come to his notice relating to the welfare of the business is his own job."

Another key takeaway from this chapter is the principle that no official title can convey the right to lead others. This right, which China calls the Mandate of Heaven, comes instead from the prospective leader's service to his or her followers and organization. This concept ties in closely with "the law of the situation," in which the de facto leader is the person who is most qualified to guide, facilitate, and, otherwise, lead others to achieve a specific goal.

The absence of official job titles is also consistent with current practice at Honda's Marysville, Ohio plant. Participants in Y-gaya (informal and open discussion) meetings "are instructed to leave their titles at the door" (Cable, 2012, p. 28).

BREAK DOWN ORGANIZATIONAL BARRIERS

Jack Vance's "Dodkin's Job" (1959) is a humorous dystopian science fiction story that illustrates Ford's statement about bureaucracy: "... his message has to go through the subforeman, the foreman, the department head, and all the assistant superintendents, before, in the course of time, it reaches the general superintendent." This is the experience of Vance's protagonist, a low-level employee of a gigantic corporation. He wants to point out the enormous inefficiency of carrying tools to and from a storeroom, and he uses various subterfuges to take his suggestion to higher level supervisors including, finally, the CEO.

The CEO then directs him downward through another channel of the bureaucracy until he finally finds Dodkin. Dodkin is a bottom-level employee who has been feeding "interpolations" to a computer, whose output, in turn, guides the entire organization's activities. The protagonist then convinces Dodkin to retire, arranges for himself to be demoted so he can take over Dodkin's job, and then feeds the computer his own interpolations. The story becomes far less funny when one realizes that there are organizations with the kind of silo mentality and departmental barriers that make this kind of situation possible in the real world.

* * *

That which one has to fight hardest against in bringing together a large number of people to do work is excess organization and consequent red tape. To my mind there is no bent of mind more dangerous than that which is sometimes described as the "genius for organization." This usually results in the birth of a great big chart showing, after the fashion of a family tree, how authority ramifies. The tree is heavy with nice round berries, each of which bears the name of a man or of an office. Every man has a title and certain duties which are strictly limited by the circumference of his berry.

If a straw boss wants to say something to the general superintendent, his message has to go through the sub-foreman, the foreman, the department head, and all the assistant superintendents, before, in the course of time, it reaches the general superintendent. Probably by that time what he wanted to talk about is already history. It takes about six weeks for the message of a man living in a berry on the lower left-hand corner of the chart to reach the president or chairman of the board, and, if it ever does reach one of these august officials, it has by that time gathered to itself about a pound of criticisms, suggestions, and comments. Very few things are ever taken under "official consideration" until long after the time when they actually ought to have been done. The buck is passed to and fro and all responsibility is dodged by individuals—following the lazy notion that two heads are better than one.

* * *

The following segment could be construed as support for a silo mentality because it seems to discourage communication between departments. Cross-functional meetings are currently the generally accepted practice in world-class organizations. Ford apparently meant that people were not to go looking into other people's jobs, and assembly line work left little time for such extracurricular activities. If, however, the workers saw something, like a sheet of metal with holes in it, they were encouraged to ask what became of the metal that was in those holes. They also asked and discovered what might be done to reduce or eliminate the material waste in question.

The subsequent discussion meanwhile suggests the modern concept of self-directed work teams: "A group of men, wholly intent upon getting work done, have no difficulty in seeing that the work is done. They do not get into trouble about the limits of authority, because they are not thinking of titles." The person who is best able to do a necessary task simply does it.

* * *

Now a business, in my way of thinking, is not a machine. It is a collection of people who are brought together to do work and not to write letters to one another. It is not necessary for any one department to know what any other department is doing. If a man is doing his work he will not have time to take up any other work. It is the business of those who plan the entire work to see that all of the departments are working properly toward the same end. It is not necessary to have meetings to establish good feeling between individuals or departments. It is not necessary for people to love each other in order to work together. Too much good fellowship may indeed be a very bad thing, for it may lead to one man trying to cover up the faults of another. That is bad for both men.

When we are at work we ought to be at work. When we are at play we ought to be at play. There is no use trying to mix the two. The sole object ought to be to get the work done and to get paid for it. When the work is done, then the play can come, but not before. And so the Ford factories and enterprises have no organization, no specific duties attaching to any position, no line of succession or of authority, very few titles, and no conferences. We have only the clerical help that is absolutely required; we have no elaborate records of any kind, and consequently no red tape.

We make the individual responsibility complete. The workman is absolutely responsible for his work. The straw boss is responsible for the workmen under him. The foreman is responsible for his group. The department head is responsible for the department. The general superintendent is responsible for the whole factory. Every man has to know what is going on in his sphere. I say "general superintendent." There is no such formal title. One man is in charge of the factory and has been for years. He has two men with him, who, without in any way having their duties defined, have taken particular sections of the work to themselves. With them are about half a dozen other men in the nature of assistants, but without specific duties. They have all made jobs for themselves—but there are no limits to their jobs. They just work in where they best fit. One man chases stock and shortages. Another has grabbed inspection, and so on.

This may seem haphazard, but it is not. A group of men, wholly intent upon getting work done, have no difficulty in seeing that the work is done. They do not get into trouble about the limits of authority, because they are not thinking of titles. If they had offices and all that, they would shortly be giving up their time to office work and to wondering why did they not have a better office than some other fellow.

Authority Is Not Leadership

Ford now makes it clear that authority is not leadership, and abuse of authority is detrimental to the morale of any organization. This is consistent with the principle that no title can convey the genuine right to lead and direct others; this right (Mandate of Heaven) must be earned.

* * *

Because there are no titles and no limits of authority, there is no question of red tape or going over a man's head. Any workman can go to anybody, and so established has become this custom, that a foreman does not get sore if a workman goes over him and directly to the head of the factory. The workman rarely ever does so, because a foreman knows as well as he knows his own name that if he has been unjust it will be very quickly found out, and he shall no longer be a foreman. One of the things that we will not tolerate is injustice of any kind. The moment a man starts to swell with authority he is discovered, and he goes out, or goes back to a machine. A large amount of labour unrest comes from the unjust exercise of authority by those in subordinate positions, and I am afraid that in far too many manufacturing institutions it is really not possible for a workman to get a square deal.

The Law of the Situation

The concept that the needs of the job are all-important cannot be overemphasized. Juran and Gryna (1988, p. 22.60) state, "One *person* should not give orders to another *person*. Both should take their orders from the 'law of the situation,' a phrase coined by [Mary] Parker Follett. ..." This is the foundation of self-directed work teams. The Ford organization may well have been more than a decade ahead of Follet, who published "The Giving of Orders" in 1926, in the actual implementation of this principle.

> The situation controls, and the true leader is the one who responds immediately and effectively to the situation. And since a situation is always primary, authority derives from function rather than position. The responsibility is *for* and not *to*. Of course, I understand all this better today than I did in 1909 (Sorensen, 1956, p. 43).

There is meanwhile no doubt that Sorensen was at least five years ahead of Burns and Stalker (1961) in defining mechanistic and organic management systems as follows:

> … two diametrically opposed shop management practices. One is a rigid *system*, in which rules tend to be paramount; the other is a flexible *method*, in which the objective comes first (Sorensen, 1956, p. 41).

The Ford organization, of course, had put the organic model to work more than 40 years earlier, and placement of the objective first is consistent with the law of the situation.

The subsequent paragraphs underscore the Chinese concept of the Mandate of Heaven, under which a leader earns and maintains the right to lead through service to his or her stakeholders. "Everybody acknowledges a real leader—a man who is fit to plan and command." (Ford used the gender-specific language in an era in which workforces were almost entirely male.)

The person who is most qualified to plan and command *with regard to the situation at hand* is, therefore, the de facto leader regardless of official titles. This is the practice of the U.S. Special Forces (MacPherson, 2012): "When the time comes, the subject matter expert takes the lead and all other members of the team, including the officers and senior NCOs (noncommissioned officers), become highly cross-trained and supportive team members."

Note also Ford's warning that division of responsibility can often result in elimination of responsibility. It is too easy for somebody to say of a particular matter: "This does not fall into my job description." Therefore, there must be some specific responsibilities because a job that belongs to everybody soon belongs to nobody. Ford's statement: "The health of every organization depends on every member—whatever his place—feeling that everything that happens to come to his notice relating to the welfare of the business is his own job." This strikes a good balance between these extremes.

* * *

The work and the work alone controls us. That is one of the reasons why we have no titles. Most men can swing a job, but they are floored by a title. The effect of a title is very peculiar. It has been used too much as a sign of emancipation from work. It is almost equivalent to a badge bearing the legend: "This man has nothing to do but regard himself as important and all others as inferior."

Not only is a title often injurious to the wearer, but it has its effect on others as well. There is perhaps no greater single source of personal dissatisfaction among men than the fact that the title-bearers are not always the real leaders. Everybody acknowledges a real leader—a man who is fit to plan and command. And when you find a real leader who bears a title, you will have to inquire of someone else what his title is. He doesn't boast about it.

Titles in business have been greatly overdone and business has suffered. One of the bad features is the division of responsibility according to titles, which goes so far as to amount to a removal altogether of responsibility. Where responsibility is broken up into many small bits and divided among many departments, each department under its own titular head, who in turn is surrounded by a group bearing their nice sub-titles, it is difficult to find any one who really feels responsible. Everyone knows what "passing the buck" means. The game must have originated in industrial organizations where the departments simply shove responsibility along. The health of every organization depends on every member—whatever his place—feeling that everything that happens to come to his notice relating to the welfare of the business is his own job. Railroads have gone to the devil under the eyes of departments that say: "Oh, that doesn't come under our department. Department X, 100 miles away, has that in charge."

There used to be a lot of advice given to officials not to hide behind their titles. The very necessity for the advice showed a condition that needed more than advice to correct it. And the correction is just this—abolish the titles. A few may be legally necessary; a few may be useful in directing the public how to do business with the concern, but for the rest the best rule is simple: "Get rid of them."

As a matter of fact, the record of business in general just now is such as to detract very much from the value of titles. No one would boast of being president of a bankrupt bank. Business on the whole has not been so skillfully steered as to leave much margin for pride in the steersmen. The men who bear titles now and are worth anything are forgetting their titles and are down in the foundation of business looking for the weak spots. They are back again in the places from which they rose—trying to reconstruct from the bottom up. And when a man is really at work, he needs no title. His work honours him.

FORD'S HIRING PRACTICES

The following material seems to defy common sense because past performance is generally a good indicator of future performance. Ford's practice of bringing everybody in on the bottom (regardless of past experience) and then promoting from the ranks apparently worked nonetheless. "The man in charge of the big River Rouge plant [who] began as a patternmaker" was, in fact, Charles Sorensen, the same person who designed the Willow Run bomber plant in a single night.

The subsequent material elaborates that advancement should be a function entirely of a person's work as opposed to favoritism, or participation in meetings whose primary function is for people to show fancy PowerPoint® slides to one another. MacPherson (2012) warns emphatically against "death by PowerPoint," and adds that Lean leadership presentations should use flip charts or handwritten A3 reports. A3 refers to the 11 × 17-inch sheet of paper on which the entire presentation can be written.

* * *

All of our people come into the factory or the offices through the employment departments. As I have said, we do not hire experts—neither do we hire men on past experiences or for any position other than the lowest. Since we do not take a man on his past history, we do not refuse him because of his past history. I never met a man who was thoroughly bad. There is always some good in him—if he gets a chance. That is the reason we do not care in the least about a man's antecedents—we do not hire a man's history, we hire the man. If he has been in jail, that is no reason to say that he will be in jail again. I think, on the contrary, he is, if given a chance, very likely to make a special effort to keep out of jail. Our employment office does not bar a man for anything he has previously done—he is equally acceptable whether he has been in Sing Sing or at Harvard and we do not even inquire from which place he has graduated. All that he needs is the desire to work. If he does not desire to work, it is very unlikely that he will apply for a position, for it is pretty well understood that a man in the Ford plant works.

We do not, to repeat, care what a man has been. If he has gone to college he ought to be able to go ahead faster, but he has to start at the bottom and prove his ability. Every man's future rests solely with himself. There is far too much loose talk about men being unable to obtain recognition. With us every man is fairly certain to get the exact recognition he deserves.

Of course, there are certain factors in the desire for recognition which must be reckoned with. The whole modern industrial system has warped the desire so out of shape that it is now almost an obsession. There was a time when a man's personal advancement depended entirely and immediately upon his work, and not upon any one's favor; but nowadays it often depends far too much upon the individual's good fortune in catching some influential eye. That is what we have successfully fought against. Men will work with the idea of catching somebody's eye; they will work with the idea that if they fail to get credit for what they have done, they might as well have done it badly or not have done it at all. Thus the work sometimes becomes a secondary consideration. The job in hand—the article in hand, the special kind of service in hand—turns out to be not the principal job. The main work becomes personal advancement—a platform from which to catch somebody's eye. This habit of making the work secondary and the recognition primary is unfair to the work. It makes recognition and credit the real job. And this also has an unfortunate effect on the worker. It encourages a peculiar kind of ambition which is neither lovely nor productive. It produces the kind of man who imagines that by "standing in with the boss" he will get ahead. Every shop knows this kind of man. And the worst of it is there are some things in the present industrial system which make it appear that the game really pays. Foremen are only human. It is natural that they should be flattered by being made to believe that they hold the weal or woe of workmen in their hands. It is natural, also, that being open to flattery, their self-seeking subordinates should flatter them still more to obtain and profit by their favor. That is why I want as little as possible of the personal element.

It is particularly easy for any man who never knows it all to go forward to a higher position with us. Some men will work hard but they do not possess the capacity to think and especially to think quickly. Such men get as far as their ability deserves. A man may, by his industry, deserve advancement, but it cannot be possibly given him unless he also has a certain element of leadership. This is not a dream world we are living in. I think that every man in the shaking-down process of our factory eventually lands about where he belongs.

THE NEED FOR CONTINUAL IMPROVEMENT

We are never satisfied with the way that everything is done in any part of the organization; we always think it ought to be done better and that eventually it will be done better. The spirit of crowding forces the man who has the qualities for a higher place eventually to get it. He perhaps would not get the place if at any time the organization—which is a word I do not like to use— became fixed, so that there would be routine steps and dead men's shoes. But we have so few titles that a man who ought to be doing something better than he is doing, very soon gets to doing it—he is not restrained by the fact that there is no position ahead of him "open"—for there are no "positions." We have no cut-and-dried places—our best men make their places. This is easy enough to do, for there is always work, and when you think of getting the work done instead of finding a title to fit a man who wants to be promoted, then there is no difficulty about promotion. The promotion itself is not formal; the man simply finds himself doing something other than what he was doing and getting more money.

All of our people have thus come up from the bottom. The head of the factory started as a machinist. The man in charge of the big River Rouge plant began as a patternmaker. Another man overseeing one of the principal departments started as a sweeper. There is not a single man anywhere in the factory who did not simply come in off the street. Everything that we have developed has been done by men who have qualified themselves with us. We fortunately did not inherit any traditions and we are not founding any. If we have a tradition it is this: Everything can always be done better than it is being done.

DO NOT ALLOW THE COST ACCOUNTING SYSTEM TO RUN THE FACTORY

The absorption of overhead by the product is an artifact of the cost accounting system, and its use in actual decisions (such as making inventory to divide the overhead among more units) can result in very dysfunctional outcomes. Production supervisors at Ford were on the other hand responsive to a single measurement: rate of production. This did not result in unsaleable inventory because there were buyers for all the output.

The following material also shows that Ford had an informal suggestion system, and that he encouraged worker initiative. *Ford News* (1923, No. 15, 6) shows meanwhile that the company had a contest in which employees recommended uses for the waste ends of wooden wheel spokes. Distillation of the waste wood into Kingsford charcoal and wood chemicals was the winning entry, but other suggested uses included wooden mats and also the use of shorter pieces of wood to prevent the waste up front.

* * *

That pressing always to do work better and faster solves nearly every factory problem. A department gets its standing on its rate of production. The rate of production and the cost of production are distinct elements. The foremen and superintendents would only be wasting time were they to keep a check on the costs in their departments. There are certain costs—such as the rate of wages, the overhead, the price of materials, and the like, which they could not in any way control, so they do not bother about them. What they can control is the rate of production in their own departments. The rating of a department is gained by dividing the number of parts produced by the number of hands working. Every foreman checks his own department daily—he carries the figures always with him. The superintendent has a tabulation of all the scores; if there is something wrong in a department the output score shows it at once, the superintendent makes inquiries and the foreman looks alive. A considerable part of the incentive to better methods is directly traceable to this simple rule-of-thumb method of rating production. The foreman need not be a cost accountant—he is no better a foreman for being one. His charges are the machines and the human beings in his department. When they are working at their best he has performed his service. The rate of his production is his guide. There is no reason for him to scatter his energies over collateral subjects.

This rating system simply forces a foreman to forget personalities—to forget everything other than the work in hand. If he should select the people he likes instead of the people who can best do the work, his department record will quickly show up that fact.

There is no difficulty in picking out men. They pick themselves out because—although one hears a great deal about the lack of opportunity for advancement—the average workman is more interested in a steady job than he is in advancement. Scarcely more than five per cent, of those who work for wages, while they have the desire to receive more money, have also the willingness to accept the additional responsibility and the additional work which goes with the higher places. Only about twenty-five per cent are even willing to be straw bosses, and most of them take that position because it carries with it more pay than working on a machine. Men of a more mechanical turn of mind, but with no desire for responsibility, go into the tool-making departments where they receive considerably more pay than in production proper. But the vast majority of men want to stay put. They want to be led. They want to have everything done for them and to have no responsibility. Therefore, in spite of the great mass of men, the difficulty is not to discover men to advance, but men who are willing to be advanced.

The accepted theory is that all people are anxious for advancement, and a great many pretty plans have been built up from that. I can only say that we do not find that to be the case. The Americans in our employ do want to go ahead, but they by no means do always want to go clear through to the top. The foreigners, generally speaking, are content to stay as straw bosses. Why all of this is, I do not know. I am giving the facts.

As I have said, everyone in the place reserves an open mind as to the way in which every job is being done. If there is any fixed theory—any fixed rule—it is that no job is being done well enough. The whole factory management is always open to suggestion, and we have an informal suggestion system by which any workman can communicate any idea that comes to him and get action on it.

PAY ATTENTION TO EVEN SMALL SAVINGS

The saving of a cent per piece may be distinctly worth while. A saving of one cent on a part at our present rate of production represents twelve thousand dollars a year. One cent saved on each part would amount to millions a year. Therefore, in comparing savings, the calculations are carried out to the thousandth part of a cent. If the new way suggested shows a saving and the cost of making the change will pay for itself within a reasonable time—say within three months—the change is made practically as of course. These changes are by no means limited to improvements which will increase production or decrease cost. A great many—perhaps most of them—are in the line of making the work easier. We do not want any hard, man-killing work about the place, and there is now very little of it. And usually it so works out that adopting the way which is easier on the men also decreases the cost. There is most intimate connection between decency and good business. We also investigate down to the last decimal whether it is cheaper to make or to buy a part.

Frontline Workers Are the Best Guardians against Waste (Muda)

The following material is consistent with Tom Peters' (1987) observation that the person who actually does a job knows more about it than anybody else. It also makes it clear that Ford created a culture in which every employee learned to recognize waste that might otherwise hide in plain view; a skill that was among Ford's primary success secrets. Note, for example, that the workers recognized deburring of gears as 100% rework, as opposed to a value-adding activity. The same applies to the operation that was necessary to straighten camshafts that warped during heat treatment. The straightening "process" (and "process" implies a value-adding activity in value stream analysis) was actually 100% rework.

It is also particularly telling that the workforce was intolerant of a machining operation that ground 12% of the metal into easily recyclable scrap; "… the mere fact that all waste is not a dead loss is no excuse for permitting waste." Ford and Crowther (1926, p. 113) add: "Picking up and reclaiming the scrap left over after production is a public service, but planning so that there will be no scrap is a higher public service."

This attitude can be compared to the acceptance of 80% or more machining waste in modern workplaces. Mege (2000) reports that many aerospace machining processes cut billets of aluminum into 15 to 20% parts by weight, and, therefore, 80 to 85% (recyclable) scrap by weight. This reference adds that one manufacturer even bragged that his high-agility machine ground 400 tons of aluminum into chips every month, and that he had to install an extra swarf compacter to handle this waste.

Arnold and Faurote (1915, p. 212), on the other hand, objected to similarly wasteful machining operations at Ford's Highland Park plant: "… that is to say, 5/6 of the pot stock is wasted." The difference is, of course, that Ford's workers did not brag about the waste, but instead tried to do something about it.

* * *

The suggestions come from everywhere. The Polish workmen seem to be the cleverest of all of the foreigners in making them. One, who could not speak English, indicated that if the tool in his machine were set at a different angle it might wear longer. As it was it lasted only four or five cuts. He was right, and a lot of money was saved in grinding. Another Pole, running a drill press, rigged up a little fixture to save handling the part after drilling. That was adopted generally and a considerable saving resulted. The men often try out little attachments of their own because, concentrating on one thing, they can, if they have a mind that way, usually devise some improvement. The cleanliness of a man's machine also—although cleaning a machine is no part of his duty—is usually an indication of his intelligence.

Here are some of the suggestions: A proposal that castings be taken from the foundry to the machine shop on an overhead conveyor saved seventy men in the transport division. There used to be seventeen men—and this was when production was smaller—taking the burrs off gears, and it was a hard, nasty job. A man roughly sketched a special machine. His idea was worked out and the machine built. Now four men have several times the output of the seventeen men—and have no hard work at all to do. Changing from a solid to a welded rod in one part of the chassis effected an immediate saving of about one half million a year on a smaller than the present-day production. Making certain tubes out of flat sheets instead of drawing them in the usual way effected another enormous saving.

The old method of making a certain gear comprised four operations and 12 per cent of the steel went into scrap. We use most of our scrap and eventually we will use it all, but that is no reason for not cutting down on scrap—the mere fact that all waste is not a dead loss is no excuse for permitting waste. One of the workmen devised a very simple new method for making this gear in which the scrap was only one per cent. Again, the camshaft has to have heat treatment in order to make the surface hard; the cam shafts always came out of the heat-treat oven somewhat warped, and even back in 1918, we employed 37 men just to straighten the shafts. Several of our men experimented for about a year and finally worked out a new form of oven in which the shafts could not warp. In 1921, with the production much larger than in 1918, we employed only eight men in the whole operation.

Visual Controls and Error-Proofing

The following material underscores Shigeo Shingo's observation that a job that relies on worker vigilance to prevent defects will eventually produce defects. The manufacturer should instead error-proof the job, or apply Ford's "can't rather than don't" job safety principle to quality as well as safety. It also shows that Ford used what are now known as visual controls: colored lights told the heat treatment operator what to do.

* * *

And then there is the pressing to take away the necessity for skill in any job done by any one. The old-time tool hardener was an expert. He had to judge the heating temperatures. It was a hit-or-miss operation. The wonder is that he hit so often. The heat treatment in the hardening of steel is highly important—providing one knows exactly the right heat to apply. That cannot be known by rule-of-thumb. It has to be measured. We introduced a system by which the man at the furnace has nothing at all to do with the heat. He does not see the pyrometer—the instrument which registers the temperature. Coloured electric lights give him his signals.

None of our machines is ever built haphazardly. The idea is investigated in detail before a move is made. Sometimes wooden models are constructed or again the parts are drawn to full size on a blackboard. We are not bound by precedent but we leave nothing to luck, and we have yet to build a machine that will not do the work for which it was designed. About ninety per cent of all experiments have been successful.

Whatever expertness in fabrication that has developed has been due to men. I think that if men are unhampered and they know that they are serving, they will always put all of mind and will into even the most trivial of tasks.

7

The Terror of the Machine

This chapter addresses concerns about repetitive labor, and it also shows that the Ford Motor Company was a pioneer in hiring handicapped workers for meaningful jobs. The chapter later introduces modern concepts, such as job rotation, skill inventories, and workplace safety.

* * *

Repetitive labour—the doing of one thing over and over again and always in the same way—is a terrifying prospect to a certain kind of mind. It is terrifying to me. I could not possibly do the same thing day in and day out, but to other minds, perhaps I might say to the majority of minds, repetitive operations hold no terrors. In fact, to some types of mind thought is absolutely appalling. To them the ideal job is one where the creative instinct need not be expressed. The jobs where it is necessary to put in mind as well as muscle have very few takers—we always need men who like a job because it is difficult. The average worker, I am sorry to say, wants a job in which he does not have to put forth much physical exertion—above all, he wants a job in which he does not have to think. Those who have what might be called the creative type of mind and who thoroughly abhor monotony are apt to imagine that all other minds are similarly restless and therefore to extend quite unwanted sympathy to the labouring man who day in and day out performs almost exactly the same operation.

When you come right down to it, most jobs are repetitive. A business man has a routine that he follows with great exactness; the work of a bank president is nearly all routine; the work of under officers and clerks in a bank is purely routine. Indeed, for most purposes and most people, it is necessary to establish something in the way of a routine and to make most motions purely repetitive—otherwise the individual will not get enough done to be able to live off his own exertions. There is no reason why any one with a creative mind should be at a monotonous job, for everywhere the need for creative men is pressing. There will never be a dearth of places for skilled people, but we have to recognize that the will to be skilled is not general. And even if the will be present, then the courage to go through with the training is absent. One cannot become skilled by mere wishing.

CHARACTERISTICS OF THE IDEAL INDUSTRIAL LEADER

Ford's pessimistic view of the hourly worker as somebody who wants to be led, and who does not want to exercise creativity or leadership, is realistic. "Many workers prefer the mechanistic system; the worker has less initiative, but also less responsibility" (Miller, 1985). Another example consists of enlisted soldiers who, even if they have the ability to learn the job, do not want promotion to officer or even noncommissioned officer rank despite the higher pay.

Ford recognizes this issue, and he then defines the characteristics of the ideal leader who can deliver high wages to even those workers who wish only to do what they are told. This requires "plans that will profit the other fellow as he is," as opposed to the other fellow as one might like him to be. This book has already shown, though, that the Ford organization encouraged rather than stifled worker initiative and creativity. The following paragraph also reaffirms the behavioral leg of Ford's universal code. Ford ranks the ability to "deal with the laws of personality" higher than artistic laws of color or music.

The Russian field marshal Alexander V. Suvorov was even more progressive than Ford, and modern practitioners should look to his approach to worker empowerment. The Russian private, who was often a conscripted serf, was also a lower organizational participant who expected to be told what to do. Suvorov believed that even a private should understand his job instead of simply doing only what his superiors told him to do. The result was that, even if the officer became a casualty or was not present at a crisis point, the men would form self-directed teams and accomplish the desired mission.

* * *

There are far too many assumptions about what human nature ought to be and not enough research into what it is. Take the assumption that creative work can be undertaken only in the realm of vision. We speak of creative "artists" in music, painting, and the other arts. We seemingly limit the creative functions to productions that may be hung on gallery walls, or played in concert halls, or otherwise displayed where idle and fastidious people gather to admire each other's culture. But if a man wants a field for vital creative work, let him come where he is dealing with higher laws than those of sound, or line, or colour; let him come where he may deal with the laws of personality. We want artists in industrial relationship. We want masters in industrial method—both from the standpoint of the producer and the product. We want those who can mould the political, social, industrial, and moral mass into a sound and shapely whole. We have limited the creative faculty too much and have used it for too trivial ends. We want men who can create the working design for all that is right and good and desirable in our life. Good intentions plus well-thought-out working designs can be put into practice and can be made to succeed. It is possible to increase the well-being of the workingman—not by having him do less work, but by aiding him to do more. If the world will give its attention and interest and energy to the making of plans that will profit the other fellow as he is, then such plans can be established on a practical working basis. Such plans will endure—and they will be far the most profitable both in human and financial values. What this generation needs is a deep faith, a profound conviction in the practicability of righteousness, justice, and humanity in industry. If we cannot have these qualities, then we were better off without industry. Indeed, if we cannot get those qualities, the days of industry are numbered. But we can get them. We are getting them.

If a man cannot earn his keep without the aid of machinery, is it benefiting him to withhold that machinery because attendance upon it may be monotonous? And let him starve? Or is it better to put him in the way of a good living? Is a man the happier for starving? If he is the happier for using a machine to less than its capacity, is he happier for producing less than he might and consequently getting less than his share of the world's goods in exchange?

REPETITIVE MOTION INJURY AND JOB ROTATION

Repetitive motion injury is among the first problems that come to mind when one thinks of repetitive assembly line work, and Ford himself considered it as shown in the following discussion. There were, however, few if any such injuries because the repetitive motions did not require much physical effort by the worker as opposed to, for example, twisting a screwdriver for eight hours a day. Ford wrote explicitly in the Introduction: "For any one to be required to use more force than is absolutely necessary for the job in hand is waste." As shown below, Ford says explicitly of a particularly monotonous job that "no muscular energy is required."

The following discussion also shows that Ford offered job rotation, although not many workers took advantage of it.

* * *

I have not been able to discover that repetitive labour injures a man in any way. I have been told by parlour experts that repetitive labour is soul—as well as body—destroying, but that has not been the result of our investigations. There was one case of a man who all day long did little but step on a treadle release. He thought that the motion was making him one-sided; the medical examination did not show that he had been affected but, of course, he was changed to another job that used a different set of muscles. In a few weeks he asked for his old job again. It would seem reasonable to imagine that going through the same set of motions daily for eight hours would produce an abnormal body, but we have never had a case of it. We shift men whenever they ask to be shifted and we should like regularly to change them—that would be entirely feasible if only the men would have it that way. They do not like changes which they do not themselves suggest. Some of the operations are undoubtedly monotonous—so monotonous that it seems scarcely possible that any man would care to continue long at the same job. Probably the most monotonous task in the whole factory is one in which a man picks up a gear with a steel hook, shakes it in a vat of oil, then turns it into a basket. The motion never varies. The gears come to him always in exactly the same place, he gives each one the same number of shakes, and he drops it into a basket which is always in the same place. No muscular energy is required, no intelligence is required. He does little more than wave his hands gently to and fro—the steel rod is so light. Yet the man on that job has been doing it for eight solid years. He has saved and invested his money until now he has about forty thousand dollars—and he stubbornly resists every attempt to force him into a better job!

The most thorough research has not brought out a single case of a man's mind being twisted or deadened by the work. The kind of mind that does not like repetitive work does not have to stay in it. The work in each department is classified according to its desirability and skill into Classes "A," "B," and "C," each class having anywhere from ten to thirty different operations. A man comes directly from the employment office to "Class C." As he gets better he goes into "Class B," and so on into "Class A," and out of "Class A" into tool making or some supervisory capacity. It is up to him to place himself. If he stays in production it is because he likes it.

EMPLOYMENT OF DISABLED WORKERS

Ford uses the now-archaic term "cripple" for a person with disabilities, and also the gender-specific "men." Recall, however, that the workforce was then almost entirely male, and that Rosie the Riveter would not enter the workplace for another 20 years. The key point of the following discussion is that Ford looked for, and usually found, ways to employ disabled workers every bit as productively as able-bodied ones.

* * *

In a previous chapter I noted that no one applying for work is refused on account of physical condition. This policy went into effect on January 12, 1914, at the time of setting the minimum wage at five dollars a day and the working day at eight hours. It carried with it the further condition that no one should be discharged on account of physical condition, except, of course, in the case of contagious disease. I think that if an industrial institution is to fill its whole role, it ought to be possible for a cross-section of its employees to show about the same proportions as a cross-section of a society in general. We have always with us the maimed and the halt. There is a most generous disposition to regard all of these people who are physically incapacitated for labour as a charge on society and to support them by charity. There are cases where I imagine that the support must be by charity—as, for instance, an idiot. But those cases are extraordinarily rare, and we have found it possible, among the great number of different tasks that must be performed somewhere in the company, to find an opening for almost any one and on the basis of production. The blind man or cripple can, in the particular place to which he is assigned, perform just as much work and receive exactly the same pay as a wholly able-bodied man would. We do not prefer cripples—but we have demonstrated that they can earn full wages.

It would be quite outside the spirit of what we are trying to do, to take on men because they were crippled, pay them a lower wage, and be content with a lower output. That might be directly helping the men but it would not be helping them in the best way. The best way is always the way by which they can be put on a productive par with able-bodied men. I believe that there is very little occasion for charity in this world—that is, charity in the sense of making gifts. Most certainly business and charity cannot be combined; the purpose of a factory is to produce, and it ill serves the community in general unless it does produce to the utmost of its capacity. We are too ready to assume without investigation that the full possession of faculties is a condition requisite to the best performance of all jobs. To discover just what was the real situation, I had all of the different jobs in the factory classified to the kind of machine and work—whether the physical labour involved was light, medium, or heavy; whether it were a wet or a dry job, and if not, with what kind of fluid; whether it were clean or dirty; near an oven or a furnace; the condition of the air; whether one or both hands had to be used; whether the employee stood or sat down at his work; whether it was noisy or quiet; whether it required accuracy; whether the light was natural or artificial; the number of pieces that had to be handled per hour; the weight of the material handled; and the description of the strain upon the worker. It turned out at the time of the inquiry that there were then 7,882 different jobs in the factory. Of these, 949 were classified as heavy work requiring strong, able-bodied, and practically physically perfect men; 3,338 required men of ordinary physical development and strength. The remaining 3,595 jobs were disclosed as requiring no physical exertion and could be performed by the slightest, weakest sort of men. In fact, most of them could be satisfactorily filled by women or older children. The lightest jobs were again classified to discover how many of them required the use of full faculties, and we found that 670 could be filled by legless men, 2,637 by one-legged men, 2 by armless men, 715 by one-armed men, and 10 by blind men. Therefore, out of 7,882 kinds of jobs, 4,034—although some of them required strength—did not require full physical capacity. That is, developed industry can provide wage work for a higher average of standard men than are ordinarily included in any normal community. If the jobs in any one industry or, say, any one factory, were analyzed as ours have been analyzed, the proportion might be very different, yet I am quite sure that if work is sufficiently subdivided—subdivided to the point of highest economy—there will be no dearth of places in which the physically incapacitated can do a man's job and get a man's wage. It is economically most wasteful to accept crippled men as charges and then to teach them trivial tasks like the weaving of baskets or some other form of unremunerative hand labour, in the hope, not of aiding them to make a living, but of preventing despondency.

When a man is taken on by the Employment Department, the theory is to put him into a job suited to his condition. If he is already at work and he does not seem able to perform the work, or if he does not like his work, he is given a transfer card, which he takes up to the transfer department, and after an examination he is tried out in some other work more suited to his condition or disposition. Those who are below the ordinary physical standards are just as good workers, rightly placed, as those who are above. For instance, a blind man was assigned to the stock department to count bolts and nuts for shipment to branch establishments. Two other able-bodied men were already employed on this work. In two days the foreman sent a note to the transfer department releasing the able-bodied men because the blind man was able to do not only his own work but also the work that had formerly been done by the sound men.

Meaningful Tasks for Injured Workers

This salvage can be carried further. It is usually taken for granted that when a man is injured he is simply out of the running and should be paid an allowance. But there is always a period of convalescence, especially in fracture cases, where the man is strong enough to work, and, indeed, by that time usually anxious to work, for the largest possible accident allowance can never be as great as a man's wage. If it were, then a business would simply have an additional tax put upon it, and that tax would show up in the cost of the product. There would be less buying of the product and therefore less work for somebody. That is an inevitable sequence that must always be borne in mind.

We have experimented with bedridden men—men who were able to sit up. We put black oilcloth covers or aprons over the beds and set the men to work screwing nuts on small bolts. This is a job that has to be done by hand and on which fifteen or twenty men are kept busy in the Magneto Department. The men in the hospital could do it just as well as the men in the shop and they were able to receive their regular wages. In fact, their production was about 20 per cent, I believe, above the usual shop production. No man had to do the work unless he wanted to. But they all wanted to. It kept time from hanging on their hands. They slept and ate better and recovered more rapidly.

No particular consideration has to be given to deaf-and-dumb employees. They do their work one hundred per cent. The tubercular employees—and there are usually about a thousand of them—mostly work in the material salvage department. Those cases which are considered contagious work together in an especially constructed shed. The work of all of them is largely out of doors.

At the time of the last analysis of employed, there were 9,563 sub-standard men. Of these, 123 had crippled or amputated arms, forearms, or hands. One had both hands off. There were 4 totally blind men, 207 blind in one eye, 253 with one eye nearly blind, 37 deaf and dumb, 60 epileptics, 4 with both legs or feet missing, 234 with one foot or leg missing. The others had minor impediments.

The length of time required to become proficient in the various occupations is about as follows: 43 per cent of all the jobs require not over one day of training; 36 per cent require from one day to one week; 6 per cent require from one to two weeks; 14 per cent require from one month to one year; one per cent require from one to six years. The last jobs require great skill—as in tool making and die sinking.

RULES AND REGULATIONS

It is particularly noteworthy that Ford did not run a bilingual or, given the diverse origins of his workers, a multilingual workplace. The provision of work instructions and other documents in more than one language is indeed an opportunity for inconsistency and, therefore, a quality system nonconformance. The legendary Tower of Babel was, of course, the first complex engineering project that went uncompleted because the workers did not speak the same language. Ford instead provided instruction in English as a second language, which opened his factory's doors to immigrants who were willing to learn while maintaining the standardization on which successful manufacturing depends.

Ford's position that married women whose husbands worked should not work themselves, of course, is not acceptable today. It is, however, to Ford's credit that he paid the women he hired the same wage as men in the same job even though no legislation required him to do so.

* * *

The discipline throughout the plant is rigid. There are no petty rules, and no rules the justice of which can reasonably be disputed. The injustice of arbitrary discharge is avoided by confining the right of discharge to the employment manager, and he rarely exercises it. The year 1919 is the last on which statistics were kept. In that year 30,155 changes occurred. Of those 10,334 were absent more than ten days without notice and therefore dropped. Because they refused the job assigned or, without giving cause, demanded a transfer, 3,702 were let go. A refusal to learn English in the school provided accounted for 38 more; 108 enlisted; about 3,000 were transferred to other plants. Going home, going into farming or business accounted for about the same number. Eighty-two women were discharged because their husbands were working—we do not employ married women whose husbands have jobs. Out of the whole lot only 80 were flatly discharged and the causes were: Misrepresentation, 56; by order of Educational Department, 20; and undesirable, 4.

We expect the men to do what they are told. The organization is so highly specialized and one part is so dependent upon another that we could not for a moment consider allowing men to have their own way. Without the most rigid discipline we would have the utmost confusion. I think it should not be otherwise in industry. The men are there to get the greatest possible amount of work done and to receive the highest possible pay. If each man were permitted to act in his own way, production would suffer and therefore pay would suffer. Any one who does not like to work in our way may always leave. The company's conduct toward the men is meant to be exact and impartial. It is naturally to the interest both of the foremen and of the department heads that the releases from their departments should be few. The workman has a full chance to tell his story if he has been unjustly treated—he has full recourse. Of course, it is inevitable that injustices occur. Men are not always fair with their fellow workmen. Defective human nature obstructs our good intentions now and then. The foreman does not always get the idea, or mis-applies it—but the company's intentions are as I have stated, and we use every means to have them understood.

Skills Inventory

This section shows that Ford kept an inventory of available skills among his workers, which he called a "Better Advantage Notice." This made it possible to quickly find a worker with any necessary skill.

* * *

It is necessary to be most insistent in the matter of absences. A man may not come or go as he pleases; he may always apply for leave to the fore-man, but if he leaves without notice, then, on his return, the reasons for his absence are carefully investigated and are sometimes referred to the Medical Department. If his reasons are good, he is permitted to resume work. If they are not good he may be discharged. In hiring a man the only data taken concerns his name, his address, his age, whether he is married or single, the number of his dependents, whether he has ever worked for the Ford Motor Company, and the condition of his sight and his hearing. No questions are asked concerning what the man has previously done, but we have what we call the "Better Advantage Notice," by which a man who has had a trade before he came to us files a notice with the employment department stat-ing what the trade was. In this way, when we need specialists of any kind, we can get them right out of production. This is also one of the avenues by which tool makers and moulders quickly reach the higher positions. I once wanted a Swiss watch maker. The cards turned one up—he was running a drill press. The Heat Treat department wanted a skilled firebrick layer. He also was found on a drill press—he is now a general inspector.

There is not much personal contact—the men do their work and go home—a factory is not a drawing room. But we try to have justice and, while there may be little in the way of hand shaking—we have no professional hand shakers—also we try to prevent opportunity for petty personalities. We have so many departments that the place is almost a world in itself—every kind of man can find a place somewhere in it. Take fighting between men. Men will fight, and usually fighting is a cause for discharge on the spot. We find that does not help the fighters—it merely gets them out of our sight. So the foremen have become rather ingenious in devising punishments that will not take anything away from the man's family and which require no time at all to administer.

REDUCE MATERIAL TRANSPORTATION DISTANCES

The following material underscores the fact that transportation, even inside the factory, adds nothing but cost and cycle time. The arrangement of machines in the sequence of operations anticipates the modern work cell.

* * *

One point that is absolutely essential to high capacity, as well as to humane production, is a clean, well-lighted and well-ventilated factory. Our machines are placed very close together—every foot of floor space in the factory carries, of course, the same overhead charge. The consumer must pay the extra overhead and the extra transportation involved in having machines even six inches farther apart than they have to be. We measure on each job the exact amount of room that a man needs; he must not be cramped—that would be waste. But if he and his machine occupy more space than is required, that also is waste. This brings our machines closer together than in probably any other factory in the world. To a stranger they may seem piled right on top of one another, but they are scientifically arranged, not only in the sequence of operations, but to give every man and every machine every square inch that he requires and, if possible, not a square inch, and certainly not a square foot, more than he requires. Our factory buildings are not intended to be used as parks. The close placing requires a maximum of safeguards and ventilation.

KEY SAFETY PRINCIPLES

The next section underscores Ford's "can't rather than don't" safety principle, which applies error proofing (poka yoke) to workplace safety. The achievement of safety comes not from warning signs that tell workers to be careful, but rather from job and equipment designs that make accidents impossible. Note especially the investigation of every accident, and follow-up with closed-loop corrective action to preclude similar accidents.

Ford cites the danger of wearing loose clothing or ties that may be caught in machinery, and this may be the origin of the practice of putting one's tie inside one's shirt when in a factory.

* * *

Machine safeguarding is a subject all of itself. We do not consider any machine—no matter how efficiently it may turn out its work—as a proper machine unless it is absolutely safe. We have no machines that we consider unsafe, but even at that a few accidents will happen. Every accident, no matter how trivial, is traced back by a skilled man employed solely for that purpose, and a study is made of the machine to make that same accident in the future impossible.

When we put up the older buildings, we did not understand so much about ventilation as we do to-day. In all the later buildings, the supporting columns are made hollow and through them the bad air is pumped out and the good air introduced. A nearly even temperature is kept everywhere the year round and, during daylight, there is nowhere the necessity for artificial light. Something like seven hundred men are detailed exclusively to keeping the shops clean, the windows washed, and all of the paint fresh. The dark corners which invite expectoration are painted white. One cannot have morale without cleanliness. We tolerate makeshift cleanliness no more than makeshift methods.

No reason exists why factory work should be dangerous. If a man has worked too hard or through too long hours he gets into a mental state that invites accidents. Part of the work of preventing accidents is to avoid this mental state; part is to prevent carelessness, and part is to make machinery absolutely fool-proof. The principal causes of accidents as they are grouped by the experts are:

(1) Defective structures;
(2) defective machines;
(3) insufficient room;
(4) absence of safeguards;
(5) unclean conditions;
(6) bad lights;
(7) bad air;
(8) unsuitable clothing;
(9) carelessness;
(10) ignorance;
(11) mental condition;

(12) lack of cooperation.

The questions of defective structures, defective machinery, insufficient room, unclean conditions, bad light, bad air, the wrong mental condition, and the lack of cooperation are easily disposed of. None of the men work too hard. The wages settle nine tenths of the mental problems and construction gets rid of the others. We have then to guard against unsuitable clothing, carelessness, and ignorance, and to make everything we have fool-proof. This is more difficult where we have belts. In all of our new construction, each machine has its individual electric motor, but in the older construction we had to use belts. Every belt is guarded. Over the automatic conveyors are placed bridges so that no man has to cross at a dangerous point. Wherever there is a possibility of flying metal, the workman is required to wear goggles and the chances are further reduced by surrounding the machine with netting. Around hot furnaces we have railings. There is nowhere an open part of a machine in which clothing can be caught. All the aisles are kept clear. The starting switches of draw presses are protected by big red tags which have to be removed before the switch can be turned—this prevents the machine being started thoughtlessly. Workmen will wear unsuitable clothing—ties that may be caught in a pulley, flowing sleeves, and all manner of unsuitable articles. The bosses have to watch for that, and they catch most of the offenders. New machines are tested in every way before they are permitted to be installed. As a result we have practically no serious accidents.

Industry needs not exact a human toll.

8

Wages

This chapter deserves particular attention because it lays out everything that anybody other than an attorney needs to know about industrial and labor relations. Ford's principles are emphatically common sense, but costly and destructive labor disputes show that common sense is far too uncommon. The failure of Ford's successors to conform to these principles led directly to the company's decline, and also to serious and even violent conflicts with labor during the late 1930s.

Chapter 8 begins by discrediting thoroughly employers who seek to pay their workers as little as possible, and it also underscores the relationship between high wages and national prosperity. Ford and Crowther (1930, 53) state explicitly that it is a false economy to hire cheap, low-skill workers to run expensive manufacturing equipment. Ford and Crowther (1926, 119–121) add that cheap sailors will allow a ship to remain in port for one or two weeks, thus wasting the time of a very expensive asset. A well-paid, first-class crew, on the other hand, will keep the ship moving, so payment of higher wages actually saves money. This was the thought process behind the Ford Motor Company's compensation policies.

* * *

There is nothing to running a business by custom—to saying: "I pay the going rate of wages." The same man would not so easily say: "I have nothing better or cheaper to sell than any one has." No manufacturer in his right mind would contend that buying only the cheapest materials is the way to make certain of manufacturing the best article. Then why do we hear so much talk about the "liquidation of labour" and the benefits that will flow to the country from cutting wages—which means only the cutting of buying power and the curtailing of the home market? What good is industry if it be so unskillfully managed as not to return a living to everyone concerned? No question is more important than that of wages—most of the people of the country live on wages. The scale of their living—the rate of their wages—determines the prosperity of the country.

Throughout all the Ford industries we now have a minimum wage of six dollars a day; we used to have a minimum of five dollars; before that we paid whatever it was necessary to pay. It would be bad morals to go back to the old market rate of paying—but also it would be the worst sort of bad business.

CAPITAL AND LABOR ARE PARTNERS, NOT ADVERSARIES

This section summarizes the entire science of industrial and labor relations in a single sentence: "It ought to be the employer's ambition, as leader, to pay better wages than any similar line of business, and it ought to be the workman's ambition to make this possible." The interdependence of the employer and employee is common sense, but far too many businesses treat the workforce as a necessary evil and unfortunate expense.

Ford (1922, p. 42) adds explicitly that, while Labor can do very little without Capital, Capital is equally helpless without Labor. If the worker cannot produce much more than a subsistence level of existence outside an organized factory and its supply chain, the factory cannot operate without workers. It is, therefore, counterproductive and dysfunctional for either to try to exploit the other.

Ford's statement: "If an employer urges men to do their best, and the men learn after a while that their best does not bring any reward, then they naturally drop back into 'getting by'" is entirely consistent with Frederick Winslow Taylor's (1911a, p. 8) explanation of the causes of soldiering, or marking time:

> ... after a workman has had the price per piece of the work he is doing lowered two or three times as a result of his having worked harder and increased his output, he is likely entirely to lose sight of his employer's side of the case and become imbued with a grim determination to have no more cuts if soldiering can prevent it.

Note also the reiteration of the economic, scientific, and behavioral legs of Ford's universal code. Neither employee nor employer can receive more wealth than they produce, but the science of Lean manufacturing allows the production of more value. The behavioral element warns meanwhile that the frontline worker is, to use Taylor's words, "entirely likely to lose sight of his employer's side of the case" if the employer follows up on productivity improvements by cutting the workforce. Sinclair (1937, p. 81) added explicitly of the Ford Company's practices after Ford delegated control to others:

> Twenty men who had been making a certain part would see a new machine brought in and set up, and one of them would be taught to operate it and do the work of the twenty. The other nineteen wouldn't be fired right away—there appeared to be a rule against that. The foreman would put them at other work, and presently he would start to "ride" them, and the men would know exactly what that meant.

Ford (1922, p. 46) condemns explicitly the practice of laying off workers during slack times, which, in combination with Sinclair's statement, suggests almost unequivocally that there was a no-layoff rule at the company. The foremen had by 1937 found ways to work around this rule, or violate its spirit without going against its letter. Sinclair (1937, p. 76) also made it emphatically clear that Ford, regardless of his title, was no longer in charge: "Henry's plant was ten times as big, and Henry himself was old; he left his troubles to others, and avoided knowing what they were doing."

What they were doing led directly to the unionization that Ford probably regarded as an insult because he regarded unionization as a natural and even justified reaction to "bosses who never did a decent thing for their employees until they were compelled" (see Chapter 18). He simply did not realize that the people to whom he had left the management of his business had gone against his core principles.

* * *

First get at the relationships. It is not usual to speak of an employee as a partner, and yet what else is he? Whenever a man finds the management of a business too much for his own time or strength, he calls in assistants to share the management with him. Why, then, if a man finds the production part of a business too much for his own two hands should he deny the title of "partner" to those who come in and help him produce? Every business that employs more than one man is a kind of partnership. The moment a man calls for assistance in his business—even though the assistant be but a boy—that moment he has taken a partner. He may himself be sole owner of the resources of the business and sole director of its operations, but only while he remains sole manager and sole producer can he claim complete independence. No man is independent as long as he has to depend on another man to help him. It is a reciprocal relation—the boss is the partner of his worker, the worker is partner of his boss. And such being the case, it is useless for one group or the other to assume that it is the one indispensable unit. Both are indispensable. The one can become unduly assertive only at the expense of the other—and eventually at its own expense as well. It is utterly foolish for Capital or for Labour to think of themselves as groups. They are partners. When they pull and haul against each other—they simply injure the organization in which they are partners and from which both draw support.

It ought to be the employer's ambition, as leader, to pay better wages than any similar line of business, and it ought to be the workman's ambition to make this possible. Of course there are men in all shops who seem to believe that if they do their best, it will be only for the employer's benefit— and not at all for their own. It is a pity that such a feeling should exist. But it does exist and perhaps it has some justification. If an employer urges men to do their best, and the men learn after a while that their best does not bring any reward, then they naturally drop back into "getting by." But if they see the fruits of hard work in their pay envelope—proof that harder work means higher pay—then also they begin to learn that they are a part of the business, and that its success depends on them and their success depends on it.

The Business Must Create the Wages

The previous material shows what happens to employers, including the Ford Motor Company under Ford's successors, who look for ways to pay their workers as little as possible. Labor, and especially unions, must recognize in turn that no system can pay more in wages than it creates in value. Labor must help create the value through the removal of waste from the system, which is the focus of Lean manufacturing.

* * *

"What ought the employer to pay?"—"What ought the employee to receive?" These are but minor questions. The basic question is "What can the business stand?" Certainly no business can stand outgo that exceeds its income. When you pump water out of a well at a faster rate than the water flows in, the well goes dry. And when the well runs dry, those who depend on it go thirsty. And if, perchance, they imagine they can pump one well dry and then jump to some other well, it is only a matter of time when all the wells will be dry. There is now a widespread demand for more justly divided rewards, but it must be recognized that there are limits to rewards.

The business itself sets the limits. You cannot distribute $150,000 out of a business that brings in only $100,000. The business limits the wages, but does anything limit the business? The business limits itself by following bad precedents.

If men, instead of saying "the employer ought to do thus-and-so," would say, "the business ought to be so stimulated and managed that it can do thus-and-so," they would get somewhere. Because only the business can pay wages. Certainly the employer cannot, unless the business warrants. But if that business does warrant higher wages and the employer refuses, what is to be done? As a rule a business means the livelihood of too many men, to be tampered with. It is criminal to assassinate a business to which large numbers of men have given their labours and to which they have learned to look as their field of usefulness and their source of livelihood. Killing the business by a strike or a lockout does not help. The employer can gain nothing by looking over the employees and asking himself, "How little can I get them to take?" Nor the employee by glaring back and asking, "How much can I force him to give?" Eventually both will have to turn to the business and ask, "How can this industry be made safe and profitable, so that it will be able to provide a sure and comfortable living for all of us?"

But by no means all employers or all employees will think straight. The habit of acting shortsightedly is a hard one to break. What can be done? Nothing. No rules or laws will effect the changes. But enlightened self-interest will. It takes a little while for enlightenment to spread. But spread it must, for the concern in which both employer and employees work to the same end of service is bound to forge ahead in business.

What do we mean by high wages, anyway?

We mean a higher wage than was paid ten months or ten years ago. We do not mean a higher wage than ought to be paid. Our high wages of to-day may be low wages ten years from now.

If it is right for the manager of a business to try to make it pay larger dividends, it is quite as right that he should try to make it pay higher wages. But it is not the manager of the business who pays the high wages. Of course, if he can and will not, then the blame is on him. But he alone can never make high wages possible. High wages cannot be paid unless the workmen earn them. Their labour is the productive factor. It is not the only productive factor—poor management can waste labour and material and nullify the efforts of labour. Labour can nullify the results of good management. But in a partnership of skilled management and honest labour, it is the workman who makes high wages possible. He invests his energy and skill, and if he makes an honest, wholehearted investment, high wages ought to be his reward. Not only has he earned them, but he has had a big part in creating them.

It ought to be clear, however, that the high wage begins down in the shop. If it is not created there it cannot get into pay envelopes. There will never be a system invented which will do away with the necessity of work. Nature has seen to that. Idle hands and minds were never intended for any one of us. Work is our sanity, our self-respect, our salvation. So far from being a curse, work is the greatest blessing. Exact social justice flows only out of honest work. The man who contributes much should take away much. Therefore no element of charity is present in the paying of wages. The kind of workman who gives the business the best that is in him is the best kind of workman a business can have. And he cannot be expected to do this indefinitely without proper recognition of his contribution. The man who comes to the day's job feeling that no matter how much he may give, it will not yield him enough of a return to keep him beyond want, is not in shape to do his day's work. He is anxious and worried, and it all reacts to the detriment of his work.

Intrinsic Motivation: The Task Is its Own Reward

But if a man feels that his day's work is not only supplying his basic need, but is also giving him a margin of comfort and enabling him to give his boys and girls their opportunity and his wife some pleasure in life, then his job looks good to him and he is free to give it of his best. This is a good thing for him and a good thing for the business. The man who does not get a certain satisfaction out of his day's work is losing the best part of his pay.

The Role of Profit Sharing

For the day's work is a great thing—a very great thing! It is at the very foundation of the world; it is the basis of our self-respect. And the employer ought constantly to put in a harder day's work than any of his men. The employer who is seriously trying to do his duty in the world must be a hard worker. He cannot say, "I have so many thousand men working for me." The fact of the matter is that so many thousand men have him working for them—and the better they work the busier they keep him disposing of their products. Wages and salaries are in fixed amounts, and this must be so, in order to have a basis to figure on. Wages and salaries are a sort of profit-sharing fixed in advance, but it often happens that when the business of the year is closed, it is discovered that more can be paid. And then more ought to be paid. When we are all in the business working together, we all ought to have some share in the profits—by way of a good wage, or salary, or added compensation. And that is beginning now quite generally to be recognized.

There is now a definite demand that the human side of business be elevated to a position of equal importance with the material side. And that is going to come about. It is just a question whether it is going to be brought about wisely—in a way that will conserve the material side which now sustains us, or unwisely and in such a way as shall take from us all the benefit of the work of the past years. Business represents our national livelihood, it reflects our economic progress, and gives us our place among other nations. We do not want to jeopardize that. What we want is a better recognition of the human element in business. And surely it can be achieved without dislocation, without loss to any one, indeed with an increase of benefit to every human being. And the secret of it all is in a recognition of human partnership. Until each man is absolutely sufficient unto himself, needing the services of no other human being in any capacity whatever, we shall never get beyond the need of partnership.

Such are the fundamental truths of wages. They are partnership distributions.

What Is an "Adequate Wage?"

When can a wage be considered adequate? How much of a living is reasonably to be expected from work? Have you ever considered what a wage does or ought to do? To say that it should pay the cost of living is to say almost nothing. The cost of living depends largely upon the efficiency of production and transportation; and the efficiency of these is the sum of the efficiencies of the management and the workers. Good work, well managed, ought to result in high wages and low living costs. If we attempt to regulate wages on living costs, we get nowhere. The cost of living is a result and we cannot expect to keep a result constant if we keep altering the factors which produce the result. When we try to regulate wages according to the cost of living, we are imitating a dog chasing his tail. And, anyhow, who is competent to say just what kind of living we shall base the costs on? Let us broaden our view and see what a wage is to the workmen—and what it ought to be.

The wage carries all the worker's obligations outside the shop; it carries all that is necessary in the way of service and management inside the shop. The day's productive work is the most valuable mine of wealth that has ever been opened. Certainly it ought to bear not less than all the worker's outside obligations. And certainly it ought to be made to take care of the worker's sunset days when labour is no longer possible to him—and should be no longer necessary. And if it is made to do even these, industry will have to be adjusted to a schedule of production, distribution, and reward, which will stop the leaks into the pockets of men who do not assist in production. In order to create a system which shall be as independent of the good-will of benevolent employers as of the ill-will of selfish ones, we shall have to find a basis in the actual facts of life itself.

It costs just as much physical strength to turn out a day's work when wheat is $1 a bushel, as when wheat is $2.50 a bushel. Eggs may be 12 cents a dozen or 90 cents a dozen. What difference does it make in the units of energy a man uses in a productive day's work?

If only the man himself were concerned, the cost of his maintenance and the profit he ought to have would be a simple matter. But he is not just an individual. He is a citizen, contributing to the welfare of the nation. He is a householder. He is perhaps a father with children who must be reared to usefulness on what he is able to earn. We must reckon with all these facts. How are you going to figure the contribution of the home to the day's work? You pay the man for his work, but how much does that work owe to his home? How much to his position as a citizen? How much to his position as a father? The man does the work in the shop, but his wife does the work in the home. The shop must pay them both. On what system of figuring is the home going to find its place on the cost sheets of the day's work? Is the man's own livelihood to be regarded as the "cost"? And is his ability to have a home and family the "profit"? Is the profit on a day's work to be computed on a cash basis only, measured by the amount a man has left over after his own and his family's wants are all supplied? Or are all these relationships to be considered strictly under head of cost, and the profit to be computed entirely outside of them? That is, after having supported himself and family, clothed them, housed them, educated them, given them the privileges incident to their standard of living, ought there to be provision made for still something more in the way of savings profit? And are all properly chargeable to the day's work? I think they are. Otherwise, we have the hideous prospect of little children and their mothers being forced out to work.

These are questions which call for accurate observation and computation. Perhaps there is no one item connected with our economic life that would surprise us more than a knowledge of just what burdens the day's work carries.

It is perhaps possible accurately to determine—albeit with considerable interference with the day's work itself—how much energy the day's work takes out of a man. But it is not at all possible accurately to determine how much it will require to put back that energy into him against the next day's demands. Nor is it possible to determine how much of that expended energy he will never be able to get back at all. Economics has never yet devised a sinking fund for the replacement of the strength of a worker. It is possible to set up a kind of sinking fund in the form of old-age pensions. But pensions do not attend to the profit which each day's labour ought to yield in order to take care of all of life's overhead, of all physical losses, and of the inevitable deterioration of the manual worker.

Low Wages Stem from Waste

The next paragraph elaborates on the scientific leg of the universal code. Elimination of waste or muda from the system allows the creation of more wealth and, therefore, higher wages.

* * *

The best wages that have up to date ever been paid are not nearly as high as they ought to be. Business is not yet sufficiently well organized and its objectives are not yet sufficiently clear to make it possible to pay more than a fraction of the wages that ought to be paid. That is part of the work we have before us. It does not help toward a solution to talk about abolishing the wage system and substituting communal ownership. The wage system is the only one that we have, under which contributions to production can be rewarded according to their worth. Take away the wage measure and we shall have universal injustice. Perfect the system and we may have universal justice.

THE ROLE OF WAGES IN NATIONAL PROSPERITY

Ford now makes it emphatically clear that high wages are a prerequisite for national prosperity. The peril of exporting jobs to China and similar places for cheap labor is not intuitively obvious to most businesspeople. If, however, American workers do not produce the value with which to purchase the goods in question, the goods will rightly go unsold. National prosperity, affluence, and also military security depend on the nation's ability to grow, mine, and, most importantly, manufacture wealth.

* * *

I have learned through the years a good deal about wages. I believe in the first place that, all other considerations aside, our own sales depend in a measure upon the wages we pay. If we can distribute high wages, then that money is going to be spent and it will serve to make storekeepers and distributors and manufacturers and workers in other lines more prosperous and their prosperity will be reflected in our sales. Country-wide high wages spell country-wide prosperity, provided, however, the higher wages are paid for higher production. Paying high wages and lowering production is starting down the incline toward dull business.

It took us some time to get our bearings on wages, and it was not until we had gone thoroughly into production on "Model T," that it was possible to figure out what wages ought to be. Before then we had had some profit sharing. We had at the end of each year, for some years past, divided a percentage of our earnings with the employees. For instance, as long ago as 1909 we distributed eighty thousand dollars on the basis of years of service. A one-year man received 5 per cent of his year's wages; a two-year man, 7-1/2 per cent, and a three-year man, 10 per cent. The objection to that plan was that it had no direct connection with the day's work. A man did not get his share until long after his work was done and then it came to him almost in the way of a present. It is always unfortunate to have wages tinged with charity.

Scientific Determination of Wages

And then, too, the wages were not scientifically adjusted to the jobs. The man in job "A" might get one rate and the man in job "B" a higher rate, while as a matter of fact job "A" might require more skill or exertion than job "B." A great deal of inequity creeps into wage rates unless both the employer and the employee know that the rate paid has been arrived at by something better than a guess. Therefore, starting about 1913 we had time studies made of all the thousands of operations in the shops. By a time study it is possible theoretically to determine what a man's output should be. Then, making large allowances, it is further possible to get at a satisfactory standard output for a day, and, taking into consideration the skill, to arrive at a rate which will express with fair accuracy the amount of skill and exertion that goes into a job—and how much is to be expected from the man in the job in return for the wage. Without scientific study the employer does not know why he is paying a wage and the worker does not know why he is getting it. On the time figures all of the jobs in our factory were standardized and rates set.

We do not have piece work. Some of the men are paid by the day and some are paid by the hour, but in practically every case there is a required standard output below which a man is not expected to fall. Were it otherwise, neither the workman nor ourselves would know whether or not wages were being earned. There must be a fixed day's work before a real wage can be paid. Watchmen are paid for presence. Workmen are paid for work.

The Five-Dollar Work Day

The paternalistic nature of the five-dollar work day, which included inspection of workers' homes for certain standards, is certainly not acceptable today. The mere concept of a five-dollar work day, however, was very audacious for its time. This book showed previously that Ford would not hire women whose husbands worked because he believed that a family should be able to live on one income, and this also would not be acceptable today. However, he did pay the women he hired the same wages as men in the same jobs.

* * *

Having these facts in hand we announced and put into operation in January, 1914, a kind of profit-sharing plan in which the minimum wage for any class of work and under certain conditions was five dollars a day. At the same time we reduced the working day to eight hours—it had been nine—and the week to forty-eight hours. This was entirely a voluntary act. All of our wage rates have been voluntary. It was to our way of thinking an act of social justice, and in the last analysis we did it for our own satisfaction of mind. There is a pleasure in feeling that you have made others happy—that you have lessened in some degree the burdens of your fellow-men—that you have provided a margin out of which may be had pleasure and saving. Good-will is one of the few really important assets of life. A determined man can win almost anything that he goes after, but unless, in his getting, he gains good will he has not profited much.

There was, however, no charity in any way involved. That was not generally understood. Many employers thought we were just making the announcement because we were prosperous and wanted advertising and they condemned us because we were upsetting standards—violating the custom of paying a man the smallest amount he would take. There is nothing to such standards and customs. They have to be wiped out. Some day they will be. Otherwise, we cannot abolish poverty. We made the change not merely because we wanted to pay higher wages and thought we could pay them. We wanted to pay these wages so that the business would be on a lasting foundation. We were not distributing anything—we were building for the future. A low wage business is always insecure.

Probably few industrial announcements have created a more world-wide comment than did this one, and hardly any one got the facts quite right. Workmen quite generally believed that they were going to get five dollars a day, regardless of what work they did.

The facts were somewhat different from the general impression. The plan was to distribute profits, but instead of waiting until the profits had been earned—to approximate them in advance and to add them, under certain conditions, to the wages of those persons who had been in the employ of the company for six months or more. It was classified participation among three classes of employees:

> *(1) Married men living with and taking good care of their families.*
> *(2) Single men over twenty-two years of age who are of proved thrifty habits.*
> *(3) Young men under twenty-two years of age, and women who are the sole support of some next of kin.*

A man was first to be paid his just wages—which were then on an average of about fifteen per cent above the usual market wage. He was then eligible to a certain profit. His wages plus his profit were calculated to give a minimum daily income of five dollars. The profit sharing rate was divided on an hour basis and was credited to the hourly wage rate, so as to give those receiving the lowest hourly rate the largest proportion of profits. It was paid every two weeks with the wages. For example, a man who received thirty-four cents an hour had a profit rate of twenty-eight and one half cents an hour—which would give him a daily income of five dollars. A man receiving fifty-four cents an hour would have a profit rate of twenty-one cents an hour—which would give him a daily income of six dollars.

It was a sort of prosperity-sharing plan. But on conditions. The man and his home had to come up to certain standards of cleanliness and citizenship. Nothing paternal was intended!—a certain amount of paternalism did develop, and that is one reason why the whole plan and the social welfare department were readjusted. But in the beginning the idea was that there should be a very definite incentive to better living and that the very best incentive was a money premium on proper living. A man who is living aright will do his work aright. And then, too, we wanted to avoid the possibility of lowering the standard of work through an increased wage. It was demonstrated in war time that too quickly increasing a man's pay sometimes increases only his cupidity and therefore decreases his earning power. If, in the beginning, we had simply put the increase in the pay envelopes, then very likely the work standards would have broken down. The pay of about half the men was doubled in the new plan; it might have been taken as "easy money." The thought of easy money breaks down work. There is a danger in too rapidly raising the pay of any man—whether he previously received one dollar or one hundred dollars a day. In fact, if the salary of a hundred-dollar-a-day man were increased overnight to three hundred dollars a day he would probably make a bigger fool of himself than the working man whose pay is increased from one dollar to three dollars an hour. The man with the larger amount of money has larger opportunity to make a fool of himself.

In this first plan the standards insisted upon were not petty—although sometimes they may have been administered in a petty fashion. We had about fifty investigators in the Social Department; the standard of common sense among them was very high indeed, but it is impossible to assemble fifty men equally endowed with common sense. They erred at times—one always hears about the errors. It was expected that in order to receive the bonus married men should live with and take proper care of their families. We had to break up the evil custom among many of the foreign workers of taking in boarders—of regarding their homes as something to make money out of rather than as a place to live in. Boys under eighteen received a bonus if they supported the next of kin. Single men who lived wholesomely shared. The best evidence that the plan was essentially beneficial is the record. When the plan went into effect, 60 per cent of the workers immediately qualified to share; at the end of six months 78 per cent were sharing, and at the end of one year 87 per cent. Within a year and one half only a fraction of one per cent failed to share.

High Wages Prevent Turnover

The large wage had other results. In 1914, when the first plan went into effect, we had 14,000 employees and it had been necessary to hire at the rate of about 53,000 a year in order to keep a constant force of 14,000. In 1915 we had to hire only 6,508 men and the majority of these new men were taken on because of the growth of the business. With the old turnover of labour and our present force we should have to hire at the rate of nearly 200,000 men a year—which would be pretty nearly an impossible proposition. Even with the minimum of instruction that is required to master almost any job in our place, we cannot take on a new staff each morning, or each week, or each month; for, although a man may qualify for acceptable work at an acceptable rate of speed within two or three days, he will be able to do more after a year's experience than he did at the beginning. The matter of labour turnover has not since bothered us; it is rather hard to give exact figures because when we are not running to capacity, we rotate some of the men in order to distribute the work among greatest number. This makes it hard to distinguish between the voluntary and involuntary exits. To-day we keep no figures; we now think so little of our turnover that we do not bother to keep records. As far as we know the turnover is somewhere between 3 per cent and 6 per cent a month.

We have made changes in the system, but we have not deviated from this principle:

If you expect a man to give his time and energy, fix his wages so that he will have no financial worries. It pays. Our profits, after paying good wages and a bonus—which bonus used to run around ten millions a year before we changed the system—show that paying good wages is the most profitable way of doing business.

There were objections to the bonus-on-conduct method of paying wages. It tended toward paternalism. Paternalism has no place in industry. Welfare work that consists in prying into employees' private concerns is out of date. Men need counsel and men need help, oftentimes special help; and all this ought to be rendered for decency's sake. But the broad workable plan of investment and participation will do more to solidify industry and strengthen organization than will any social work on the outside.

Without changing the principle we have changed the method of payment.

9

Why Not Always Have Good Business?

This chapter addresses the issue of cyclical and variable demand, which is specifically the kind of demand that a company that produces large volumes is ill suited to meet. Ford also addresses money as a barrier to exchange as opposed to a medium of exchange, a concept that ties in with the issue of currency exchange rates. The remedy is to guide business according to the concept of service rather than finance.

* * *

The employer has to live by the year. The workman has to live by the year. But both of them, as a rule, work by the week. They get an order or a job when they can and at the price they can. During what is called a prosperous time, orders and jobs are plentiful. During a "dull" season they are scarce. Business is always either feasting or fasting and is always either "good" or "bad." Although there is never a time when everyone has too much of this world's goods—when everyone is too comfortable or too happy—there come periods when we have the astounding spectacle of a world hungry for goods and an industrial machine hungry for work and the two—the demand and the means of satisfying it—held apart by a money barrier. Both manufacturing and employment are in-and-out affairs. Instead of a steady progression we go ahead by fits and starts—now going too fast, now stopping altogether. When a great many people want to buy, there is said to be a shortage of goods. When nobody wants to buy, there is said to be an overproduction of goods. I know that we have always had a shortage of goods, but I do not believe we have ever had an overproduction. We may have, at a particular time, too much of the wrong kind of goods. That is not overproduction—that is merely headless production. We may also have great stocks of goods at too high prices. That is not overproduction—it is either bad manufacturing or bad financing. Is business good or bad according to the dictates of fate? Must we accept the conditions as inevitable? Business is good or bad as we make it so. The only reason for growing crops, for mining, or for manufacturing, is

that people may eat, keep warm, have clothing to wear, and articles to use.
There is no other possible reason, yet that reason is forced into the back-
ground and instead we have operations carried on, not to the end of service,
but to the end of making money—and this because we have evolved a system
of money that instead of being a convenient medium of exchange, is at times
a barrier to exchange. Of this more later.

We suffer frequent periods of so-called bad luck only because we man-
age so badly. If we had a vast crop failure, I can imagine the country going
hungry, but I cannot conceive how it is that we tolerate hunger and poverty,
when they grow solely out of bad management, and especially out of the bad
management that is implicit in an unreasoned financial structure. Of course
the war upset affairs in this country. It upset the whole world. There would
have been no war had management been better. But the war alone is not
to blame. The war showed up a great number of the defects of the financial
system, but more than anything else it showed how insecure is business sup-
ported only by a money foundation. I do not know whether bad business is
the result of bad financial methods or whether the wrong motive in business
created bad financial methods, but I do know that, while it would be wholly
undesirable to try to overturn the present financial system, it is wholly desir-
able to reshape business on the basis of service. Then a better financial system
will have to come. The present system will drop out because it will have no
reason for being. The process will have to be a gradual one.

SEASONAL INDUSTRIES

The next paragraph recognizes that seasonal industries, such as agriculture, are enormously wasteful of cycle time, and that the farmers of Ford's
era spent much of their time waiting for things to grow. There is meanwhile little that farmers can do during winter. Ford's solution was to place
a valve plant in a rural area so "farmer-industrialists" could make engine
valves when they would otherwise be idle. Another solution that might
be achievable with modern technology is to farm with climate-controlled
greenhouses or hydroponic facilities that make agriculture independent of
weather, and, therefore, able to produce food year-round.

* * *

The start toward the stabilization of his own affairs may be made by any one.
One cannot achieve perfect results acting alone, but as the example begins
to sink in there will be followers, and thus in the course of time we can hope

to put inflated business and its fellow, depressed business, into a class with small-pox—that is, into the class of preventable diseases. It is perfectly possible, with the reorganization of business and finance that is bound to come about, to take the ill effect of seasons, if not the seasons, out of industry, and also the periodic depressions. Farming is already in process of reorganization. When industry and farming are fully reorganized they will be complementary; they belong together, not apart. As an indication, take our valve plant. We established it eighteen miles out in the country so that the workers could also be farmers. By the use of machinery farming need not consume more than a fraction of the time it now consumes; the time nature requires to produce is much larger than that required for the human contribution of seeding, cultivating, and harvesting; in many industries where the parts are not bulky it does not make much difference where they are made. By the aid of water power they can well be made out in farming country. Thus we can, to a much larger degree than is commonly known, have farmer-industrialists who both farm and work under the most scientific and healthful conditions. That arrangement will care for some seasonal industries; others can arrange a succession of products according to the seasons and the equipment, and still others can, with more careful management, iron out their seasons. A complete study of any specific problem will show the way.

ECONOMIC DEPRESSIONS

The following material is of particular interest because it shows that the Ford Motor Company was largely immune to economic downturns. Ford wrote explicitly that his company's ability to ride out such conditions, or even prosper despite them, was "the inevitable result of the application of a principle, which can be applied to any business." The principle in question appears to be the basic fact that there is always a market for inexpensive, high-quality goods or services, and it is up to the producer to supply them.

Ford then adds very emphatically that, if the company's product is too expensive for people to afford, it is up to the company to reduce the production cost and, therefore, the price.

* * *

The periodic depressions are more serious because they seem so vast as to be uncontrollable. Until the whole reorganization is brought about, they cannot be wholly controlled, but each man in business can easily do something for himself and while benefiting his own organization in a very material way, also help others. The Ford production has not reflected good times or bad times; it has kept right on regardless of conditions excepting from 1917 to 1919, when the factory was turned over to war work. The year 1912–1913 was supposed to be a dull one; although now some call it "normal"; we all but doubled our sales; 1913–1914 was dull; we increased our sales by more than a third. The year 1920–1921 is supposed to have been one of the most depressed in history; we sold a million and a quarter cars, or about five times as many as in 1913–1914—the "normal year." There is no particular secret in it. It is, as is everything else in our business, the inevitable result of the application of a principle which can be applied to any business.

We now have a minimum wage of six dollars a day paid without reservation. The people are sufficiently used to high wages to make supervision unnecessary. The minimum wage is paid just as soon as a worker has qualified in his production—which is a matter that depends upon his own desire to work. We have put our estimate of profits into the wage and are now paying higher wages than during the boom times after the war. But we are, as always, paying them on the basis of work. And that the men do work is evidenced by the fact that although six dollars a day is the minimum wage, about 60 per cent. of the workers receive above the minimum. The six dollars is not a flat but a minimum wage.

The Fundamentals of Prosperity

Consider first the fundamentals of prosperity. Progress is not made by pulling off a series of stunts. Each step has to be regulated. A man cannot expect to progress without thinking. Take prosperity. A truly prosperous time is when the largest number of people are getting all they can legitimately eat and wear, and are in every sense of the word comfortable. It is the degree of the comfort of the people at large—not the size of the manufacturer's bank balance—that evidences prosperity. The function of the manufacturer is to contribute to this comfort. He is an instrument of society and he can serve society only as he manages his enterprises so as to turn over to the public an increasingly better product at an ever-decreasing price, and at the same time to pay to all those who have a hand in his business an ever-increasing wage, based upon the work they do. In this way and in this way alone can a manufacturer or any one in business justify his existence.

We are not much concerned with the statistics and the theories of the economists on the recurring cycles of prosperity and depression. They call the periods when prices are high "prosperous." A really prosperous period is not to be judged on the prices that manufacturers are quoting for articles.

We are not concerned with combinations of words. If the prices of goods are above the incomes of the people, then get the prices down to the incomes.

Ordinarily, business is conceived as starting with a manufacturing process and ending with a consumer. If that consumer does not want to buy what the manufacturer has to sell him and has not the money to buy it, then the manufacturer blames the consumer and says that business is bad, and thus, hitching the cart before the horse, he goes on his way lamenting. Isn't that nonsense?

Does the manufacturer exist for the consumer or does the consumer exist for the manufacturer? If the consumer will not—says he cannot—buy what the manufacturer has to offer, is that the fault of the manufacturer or the consumer? Or is nobody at fault? If nobody is at fault then the manufacturer must go out of business.

High Quality Will Always Sell at a Low Price

But what business ever started with the manufacturer and ended with the consumer? Where does the money to make the wheels go round come from? From the consumer, of course. And success in manufacture is based solely upon an ability to serve that consumer to his liking. He may be served by quality or he may be served by price. He is best served by the highest quality at the lowest price, and any man who can give to the consumer the highest quality at the lowest price is bound to be a leader in business, whatever the kind of an article he makes. There is no getting away from this.

Then why flounder around waiting for good business? Get the costs down by better management. Get the prices down to the buying power.

Wage Cuts: Proof of Managerial Incompetence

Henry Ford would have probably fired for incompetence any manager who moved manufacturing jobs offshore for cheap labor, and the following material reflects directly on companies that have moved their operations to China. A business leader of Ford's caliber would instead look for ways to remove all forms of waste from his or her entire supply chain: "To overcome by management what other people try to overcome by wage reduction."

Anybody off the street can hire five low-wage workers in a foreign country to replace one American who spends four-fifths of his or her time on nonvalue-adding activities. Anybody who takes the time to learn Ford's common sense principles will remove the waste instead. Shigeo Shingo, for example, was particularly fond of deriding managers who assumed they needed twice as many workers to produce twice as many goods, which in turn goes back to Ford's own statement in the Introduction: "His whole idea, when there is extra work to do, is to hire extra men."

* * *

Cutting wages is the easiest and most slovenly way to handle the situation, not to speak of its being an inhuman way. It is, in effect, throwing upon labour the incompetency of the managers of the business. If we only knew it, every depression is a challenge to every manufacturer to put more brains into his business—to overcome by management what other people try to overcome by wage reduction. To tamper with wages before all else is changed, is to evade the real issue. And if the real issue is tackled first, no reduction of wages may be necessary. That has been my experience. The immediate practical point is that, in the process of adjustment, someone will have to take a loss. And who can take a loss except those who have something which they can afford to lose? But the expression, "take a loss," is rather misleading. Really no loss is taken at all. It is only a giving up of a certain part of the past profits in order to gain more in the future. I was talking not long since with a hardware merchant in a small town. He said: "I expect to take a loss of $10,000 on my stock. But of course, you know, it isn't really like losing that much. We hardware men have had pretty good times. Most of my stock was bought at high prices, but I have already sold several stocks and had the benefit of them. Besides, the ten thousand dollars which I say I will lose are not the same kind of dollars that I used to have. They are, in a way, speculative dollars. They are not the good dollars that bought 100 cents' worth. So, though my loss may sound big, it is not big. And at the same time I am making it possible for the people in my town to go on building their houses without being discouraged by the size of the hardware item."

He is a wise merchant. He would rather take less profit and keep business moving than keep his stock at high prices and bar the progress of his community. A man like that is an asset to a town. He has a clear head. He is better able to swing the adjustment through his inventory than through cutting down the wages of his delivery men—through cutting down their ability to buy.

He did not sit around holding on to his prices and waiting for something to turn up. He realized what seems to have been quite generally forgotten—that it is part of proprietorship every now and again to lose money. We had to take our loss.

Our sales eventually fell off as all other sales fell off. We had a large inventory and, taking the materials and parts in that inventory at their cost price, we could not turn out a car at a price lower than we were asking, but that was a price which on the turn of business was higher than people could or wanted *to pay. We closed down to get our bearings. We were faced with making a cut of $17,000,000 in the inventory or taking a much larger loss than that by not doing business. So there was no choice at all.*

Opportunity Cost of Not Doing Business

Accounting systems recognize the cost of what an organization does, but their design does not equip them to identify foregone revenues from the decision to do nothing: "The loss of idleness." An organization must instead be proactive, and seek to get its prices down to what customers will pay. Concentration must be on service rather than on prices.

* * *

That is always the choice that a man in business has. He can take the direct loss on his books and go ahead and do business or he can stop doing business and take the loss of idleness. The loss of not doing business is commonly a loss greater than the actual money involved, for during the period of idleness fear will consume initiative and, if the shutdown is long enough, there will be no energy left over to start up with again.

There is no use waiting around for business to improve. If a manufacturer wants to perform his function, he must get his price down to what people will pay. There is always, no matter what the condition, a price that people can and will pay for a necessity, and always, if the will is there, that price can be met.

It cannot be met by lowering quality or by shortsighted economy, which results only in a dissatisfied working force. It cannot be met by fussing or buzzing around. It can be met only by increasing the efficiency of production and, viewed in this fashion, each business depression, so-called, ought to be regarded as a challenge to the brains of the business community. Concentrating on prices instead of on service is a sure indication of the kind of business man who can give no justification for his existence as a proprietor.

This is only another way of saying that sales should be made on the natural basis of real value, which is the cost of transmuting human energy into articles of trade and commerce. But that simple formula is not considered business-like. It is not complex enough. We have "business" which takes the most honest of all human activities and makes them subject to the speculative shrewdness of men who can produce false shortages of food and other commodities, and thus excite in society anxiety of demand. We have false stimulation and then false numbness.

Economic justice is being constantly and quite often innocently violated. You may say that it is the economic condition which makes mankind what it is; or you may say that it is mankind that makes the economic condition

122 • The Expanded and Annotated My Life and Work

what it is. You will find many claiming that it is the economic system which makes men what they are. They blame our industrial system for all the faults which we behold in mankind generally. And you will find other men who say that man creates his own conditions; that if the economic, industrial, or social system is bad, it is but a reflection of what man himself is. What is wrong in our industrial system is a reflection of what is wrong in man himself. Manufacturers hesitate to admit that the mistakes of the present industrial methods are, in part at least, their own mistakes, systematized and extended. But take the question outside of a man's immediate concerns, and he sees the point readily enough.

No doubt, with a less faulty human nature a less faulty social system would have grown up. Or, if human nature were worse than it is, a worse system would have grown up—though probably a worse system would not have lasted as long as the present one has. But few will claim that mankind deliberately set out to create a faulty social system. Granting without reserve that all faults of the social system are in man himself, it does not follow that he deliberately organized his imperfections and established them. We shall have to charge a great deal up to ignorance.

Take the beginnings of our present industrial system. There was no indication of how it would grow. Every new advance was hailed with joy. No one ever thought of "capital" and "labour" as hostile interests. No one ever dreamed that the very fact of success would bring insidious dangers with it. And yet with growth every imperfection latent in the system came out. A man's business grew to such proportions that he had to have more helpers than he knew by their first names; but that fact was not regretted; it was rather hailed with joy. And yet it has since led to an impersonal system wherein the workman has become something less than a person—a mere part of the system. No one believes, of course, that this dehumanizing process was deliberately invented. It just grew. It was latent in the whole early system, but no one saw it and no one could foresee it. Only prodigious and unheard-of development could bring it to light.

WHAT IS THE "INDUSTRIAL IDEA"?

The following section reemphasizes the principle that the purpose of business is not to "make money," but rather to "express a serviceable idea" to customers who need it. The money then follows of itself. Ford then concludes that "the principles of service cannot fail to cure bad business," which is why it is possible to have good business even during bad times.

* * *

Take the industrial idea; what is it? The true industrial idea is not to make money. The industrial idea is to express a serviceable idea, to duplicate a useful idea, by as many thousands as there are people who need it.

To produce, produce; to get a system that will reduce production to a fine art; to put production on such a basis as will provide means for expansion and the building of still more shops, the production of still more thousands of useful things—that is the real industrial idea. The negation of the industrial idea is the effort to make a profit out of speculation instead of out of work. There are short-sighted men who cannot see that business is bigger than any one man's interests. Business is a process of give and take, live and let live. It is cooperation among many forces and interests. Whenever you find a man who believes that business is a river whose beneficial flow ought to stop as soon as it reaches him you find a man who thinks he can keep business alive by stopping its circulation. He would produce wealth by this stopping of the production of wealth.

The principles of service cannot fail to cure bad business. Which leads us into the practical application of the principles of service and finance.

10

How Cheaply Can Things Be Made?

This book has already shown that a business's objective should always be to lower its prices while increasing wages and profits. This chapter is especially important because it provides most of the principles with which to reconcile these seemingly contradictory goals. It begins, however, with the dangers inherent in speculation.

SPECULATION AND BUBBLES

The Introduction already warned that "speculation in things already produced—that is not business. It is just more or less respectable graft." This kind of speculation was responsible for disasters ranging from Dutch tulip mania in the seventeenth century to the more recent collapse of the dot-com stock bubble and the mortgage-backed security debacle.

* * *

No one will deny that if prices are sufficiently low, buyers will always be found, no matter what are supposed to be the business conditions. That is one of the elemental facts of business. Sometimes raw materials will not move, no matter how low the price. We have seen something of that during the last year [1921], but that is because the manufacturers and the distributors were trying to dispose of high-cost stocks before making new engagements. The markets were stagnant, but not "saturated" with goods. What is called a "saturated" market is only one in which the prices are above the purchasing power.

Unduly high prices are always a sign of unsound business, because they are always due to some abnormal condition. A healthy patient has a normal temperature; a healthy market has normal prices. High prices come about commonly by reason of speculation following the report of a shortage. Although there is never a shortage in everything, a shortage in just a few important commodities, or even in one, serves to start speculation. Or again, goods may not be short at all. An inflation of currency or credit will cause a quick bulge in apparent buying power and the consequent opportunity to speculate. There may be a combination of actual shortages and a currency inflation—as frequently happens during war. But in any condition of unduly high prices, no matter what the real cause, the people pay the high prices because they think there is going to be a shortage. They may buy bread ahead of their own needs, so as not to be left later in the lurch, or they may buy in the hope of reselling at a profit. When there was talk of a sugar shortage, housewives who had never in their lives bought more than ten pounds of sugar at once tried to get stocks of one hundred or two hundred pounds, and while they were doing this, speculators were buying sugar to store in warehouses. Nearly all our war shortages were caused by speculation or buying ahead of need.

No matter how short the supply of an article is supposed to be, no matter if the Government takes control and seizes every ounce of that article, a man who is willing to pay the money can always get whatever supply he is willing to pay for. No one ever knows actually how great or how small is the national stock of any commodity. The very best figures are not more than guesses; estimates of the world's stock of a commodity are still wilder. We may think we know how much of a commodity is produced on a certain day or in a certain month, but that does not tell us how much will be produced the next day or the next month. Likewise we do not know how much is consumed. By spending a great deal of money we might, in the course of time, get at fairly accurate figures on how much of a particular commodity was consumed over a period, but by the time those figures were compiled they would be utterly useless except for historical purposes, because in the next period the consumption might be double or half as much. People do not stay put. That is the trouble with all the framers of Socialistic and Communistic, and of all other plans for the ideal regulation of society. They all presume that people will stay put. The reactionary has the same idea. He insists that everyone ought to stay put. Nobody does, and for that I am thankful.

Consumption varies according to the price and the quality, and nobody knows or can figure out what future consumption will amount to, because every time a price is lowered a new stratum of buying power is reached. Everyone knows that, but many refuse to recognize it by their acts. When a storekeeper buys goods at a wrong price and finds they will not move, he reduces the price by degrees until they do move. If he is wise, instead of nibbling at the price and encouraging in his customers the hope of even lower prices, he takes a great big bite out of the price and gets the stuff out of his place. Everyone takes a loss on some proposition of sales. The common hope is that after the loss there may be a big profit to make up for the loss. That is usually a delusion. The profit out of which the loss has to be taken must be found in the business preceding the cut. Any one who was foolish enough to regard the high profits of the boom period as permanent profits got into financial trouble when the drop came. However, there is a belief, and a very strong one, that business consists of a series of profits and losses, and good business is one in which the profits exceed the losses. Therefore some men reason that the best price to sell at is the highest price which may be had. That is supposed to be good business practice. Is it? We have not found it so.

HOW TO ACHIEVE ZERO INVENTORY

The first part of this discussion is simply common sense because a business organization cannot achieve zero inventory if it buys ahead of its needs. The second part is particularly instructive because it shows exactly how Ford did what Goldratt and Fox's (1992) matchsticks and dice simulation shows to be impossible—run a balanced factory at close to 100% capacity without the accumulation of inventory.

Ford cited Benjamin Franklin as a major influence on his own business philosophy, and Franklin (1986, pp. 20–21) had this to say about the purchase of cheap, but unnecessary, raw materials or stock:

> You call them goods; but, if you do not take care, they will prove evils to some of you. You expect they will be sold cheap, and, perhaps, they may [be bought] for less than they cost; but, if you have no occasion for them, they must be dear to you. Remember what Poor Richard says, "Buy what thou hast no need of, and ere long thou shalt sell thy necessaries." And again, "At a great penny worth pause a while:" He means, that perhaps the cheapest is apparent only, and not real; or the bargain, by straightening thee in thy business, may do thee more harm than good. For in another place he says, "Many have been ruined by buying good penny worth."

This statement exemplifies the dysfunctional effect of "purchasing cost variances." The variance is the difference between the standard cost and the actual cost, and it is sometimes possible to get a favorable variance by buying excessive quantities of the commodity or raw material in question. An immediate effect is to tie up capital ("straighten thee in thy business" as Franklin put it), which results in cash flow problems that can destroy even a profitable business.

A legitimate purpose of inventory, however, is to serve as a buffer against variation in the process itself, and this includes transportation (both internal and external) as well as product transformation. This book has already shown that Ford worked explicitly to remove all such variation from his processes through subdivision of labor and single-unit instead of batch flow.

The following statement, "If transportation were perfect and an even flow of materials could be assured, it would not be necessary to carry any stock whatsoever," proves unequivocally that Ford recognized the benefits of eliminating all such variation. The subsequent statement, "With bad transportation one has to carry larger stocks," shows that unreliable transportation, or by implication variation in material transfer times, makes inventory buffers necessary.

* * *

We have found in buying materials that it is not worth while to buy for other than immediate needs. We buy only enough to fit into the plan of production, taking into consideration the state of transportation at the time. If transportation were perfect and an even flow of materials could be assured, it would not be necessary to carry any stock whatsoever. The carloads of raw materials would arrive on schedule and in the planned order and amounts, and go from the railway cars into production. That would save a great deal of money, for it would give a very rapid turnover and thus decrease the amount of money tied up in materials. With bad transportation one has to carry larger stocks. At the time of revaluing the inventory in 1921 the stock was unduly high because transportation had been so bad. But we learned long ago never to buy ahead for speculative purposes. When prices are going up it is considered good business to buy far ahead, and when prices are up to buy as little as possible. It needs no argument to demonstrate that, if you buy materials at ten cents a pound and the material goes later to twenty cents a pound you will have a distinct advantage over the man who is compelled to buy at twenty cents. But we have found that thus buying ahead does not pay. It is entering into a guessing contest. It is not business. If a man buys a large stock at ten cents, he is in a fine position as long as the other man is paying twenty cents. Then he later gets a chance to buy more of the material at twenty cents, and it seems to be a good buy because everything points to the price going to thirty cents. Having great satisfaction in his previous judgment, on which he made money, he of course makes the new purchase. Then the price drops and he is just where he started. We have carefully figured, over the years, that buying ahead of requirements does not pay—that the gains on one purchase will be offset by the losses on another, and in the end we have gone to a great deal of trouble without any corresponding benefit. Therefore in our buying we simply get the best price we can for the quantity that we require. We do not buy less if the price be high and we do not buy more if the price be low. We carefully avoid bargain lots in excess of requirements. It was not easy to reach that decision. But in the end speculation will kill any manufacturer. Give him a couple of good purchases on which he makes money and before long he will be thinking more about making money out of buying and selling than out of his legitimate business, and he will smash. The only way to keep out of trouble is to buy what one needs—no more and no less. That course removes one hazard from business.

This buying experience is given at length because it explains our selling policy. Instead of giving attention to competitors or to demand, our prices are based on an estimate of what the largest possible number of people will want to pay, or can pay, for what we have to sell. And what has resulted from that policy is best evidenced by comparing the price of the touring car and the production.

YEAR	PRICE	PRODUCTION
1909–10	$950	18,664 cars
1910–11	$780	34,528 "
1911–12	$690	78,440 "
1912–13	$600	168,220 "
1913–14	$550	248,307 "
1914–15	$490	308,213 "
1915–16	$440	533,921 "
1916–17	$360	785,432 "
1917–18	$450	706,584 "
1918–19	$525	533,706 "
1919–20	$575 to $440	996,660 "
1920–21	$440 to $355	1,250,000 "

Note: Years 1917 to 1919 were war years and the factory was in war work.

BENCHMARKING

Benchmarking is the study of competitors' (and other) products to identify best practices, and it was central to Ford's quality improvement efforts.

* * *

The high prices of 1921 were, considering the financial inflation, not really high. At the time of writing the price is $497. These prices are actually lower than they appear to be, because improvements in quality are being steadily made. We study every car in order to discover if it has features that might be developed and adapted. If any one has anything better than we have we want to know it, and for that reason we buy one of every new car that comes out. Usually the car is used for a while, put through a road test, taken apart, and studied as to how and of what everything is made. Scattered about Dearborn there is probably one of nearly every make of car on earth. Every little while when we buy a new car it gets into the newspapers and somebody remarks that Ford doesn't use the Ford. Last year we ordered a big Lanchester—which is supposed to be the best car in England. It lay in our Long Island factory for several months and then I decided to drive it to Detroit. There were several of us and we had a little caravan—the Lanchester, a Packard, and a Ford or two. I happened to be riding in the Lanchester passing through a New York town and when the reporters came up they wanted to know right away why I was not riding in a Ford.

"Well, you see, it is this way," I answered. "I am on a vacation now; I am in no hurry, we do not care much when we get home. That is the reason I am not in the Ford."

You know, we also have a line of "Ford stories"!

USE LOWER PRICES TO DRIVE LOWER COSTS

Ford was sufficiently confident in his Lean manufacturing program to lower his prices and expect his costs to follow. Ford and Crowther (1926, pp. 43–44) add that Ford demanded that the C.R. Wilson body company (as identified by Sorensen, 1956, p. 81) reduce its price by half. Wilson then had to increase wages to get first-class workers, but implementation of Ford's methods allowed it to earn more from the low price than it would have earned from the high one.

* * *

Our policy is to reduce the price, extend the operations, and improve the article. You will notice that the reduction of price comes first. We have never considered any costs as fixed. Therefore we first reduce the price to a point where we believe more sales will result. Then we go ahead and try to make the price. We do not bother about the costs. The new price forces the costs down.

The more usual way is to take the costs and then determine the price, and although that method may be scientific in the narrow sense, it is not scientific in the broad sense, because what earthly use is it to know the cost if it tells you you cannot manufacture at a price at which the article can be sold? But more to the point is the fact that, although one may calculate what a cost is, and of course all of our costs are carefully calculated, no one knows what a cost ought to be. One of the ways of discovering what a cost ought to be is to name a price so low as to force everybody in the place to the highest point of efficiency. The low price makes everybody dig for profits. We make more discoveries concerning manufacturing and selling under this forced method than by any method of leisurely investigation.

The payment of high wages fortunately contributes to the low costs because the men become steadily more efficient on account of being relieved of outside worries. The payment of five dollars a day for an eight-hour day was one of the finest cost-cutting moves we ever made, and the six-dollar day wage is cheaper than the five. How far this will go, we do not know.

We have always made a profit at the prices we have fixed and, just as we have no idea how high wages will go, we also have no idea how low prices will go, but there is no particular use in bothering on that point. The tractor, for instance, was first sold for $750, then at $850, then at $625, and the other day we cut it 37 per cent, to $395. The tractor is not made in connection with the automobiles. No plant is large enough to make two articles. A shop has to be devoted to exactly one product in order to get the real economies.

For most purposes a man with a machine is better than a man without a machine. By the ordering of design of product and of manufacturing process we are able to provide that kind of a machine which most multiplies the power of the hand, and therefore we give to that man a larger role of service, which means that he is entitled to a larger share of comfort.

FANCY OFFICE BUILDINGS ARE EVIDENCE OF WASTE

The following material should put into an entirely new perspective the ornate corporate headquarters in which many firms seem to "invest." Prospective customers should take these buildings not as evidence of the firm's success, but rather as a symptom of waste for which they must pay.

The same can easily be said of businesses that locate their offices in, for example, New York City for the "prestige" of a New York address. This kind of address tells the customer that he or she is paying not for value but rather for Manhattan-scale rents, taxes, and the higher salaries necessary to retain employees in an expensive city. The same applies, of course, to Los Angeles, Chicago, and other major urban centers.

Cities evolved as (1) places of safety that were defensible with walls, and later with elaborate fortresses, and (2) centers of industry and commerce. Zeppelin raids on England, and long-range artillery attacks on Paris, warned during World War I that cities were no longer places of defense and refuge. World War II then proved that a city was the most dangerous place for a British, and later a German or Japanese, civilian to live, and also the worst place for any kind of business to operate. September 11, 2001, then proved that a big skyscraper at a prestigious address can be a target even during peacetime, although a previous bomb attack on the World Trade Center should have given the tenants at least some hint that they were on somebody's list. Robert A. Heinlein's *On the Slopes of Vesuvius* (1981, originally published shortly after World War II) meanwhile discusses the means by which terrorists might deliver a nuclear weapon, and ends with a mushroom cloud over New York City.

Modern technology makes it easy to run the financial services for which large cities are known from so-called "flyover country," or at least from suburban areas in states with low taxes and low costs of living. Therefore, one can question the judgment of a firm that squanders money for a pricey location. Ford says explicitly that his company "would prefer to be advertised by our product than by where we make our product." To this we can add that the world's first "monuments of success," Egypt's pyramids, were in fact tombs.

* * *

Keeping that principle in mind we can attack waste with a definite objective. We will not put into our establishment anything that is useless. We will not put up elaborate buildings as monuments to our success. The interest on the investment and the cost of their upkeep only serve to add uselessly to the cost of what is produced—so these monuments of success are apt to end as tombs. A great administration building may be necessary. In me it arouses a suspicion that perhaps there is too much administration. We have never found a need for elaborate administration and would prefer to be advertised by our product than by where we make our product.

STANDARDIZATION AND COST REDUCTION

Ford's approach to product and process design begins with what modern practitioners would call Quality Function Deployment (QFD), which gets the voice of the customer into the procedure at a very early stage. Ford stresses that one must begin with the consumer and only then address the product design and the manufacturing process.

* * *

The standardization that effects [sic] large economies for the consumer results in profits of such gross magnitude to the producer that he can scarcely know what to do with his money. But his effort must be sincere, painstaking, and fearless. Cutting out a half-a-dozen models is not standardizing. It may be, and usually is, only the limiting of business, for if one is selling on the ordinary basis of profit—that is, on the basis of taking as much money away from the consumer as he will give up—then surely the consumer ought to have a wide range of choice.

Standardization, then, is the final stage of the process. We start with consumer, work back through the design, and finally arrive at manufacturing. The manufacturing becomes a means to the end of service.

It is important to bear this order in mind. As yet, the order is not thoroughly understood. The price relation is not understood. The notion persists that prices ought to be kept up. On the contrary, good business—large consumption—depends on their going down.

Maintainability and Reliability as Selling Points

Planned obsolescence, which includes a firm's refusal to support its older products, is not a good way to ensure that customers will continue to buy the product. Smart customers will look for ways to avoid buying a product that is not reliable, or for which customer service is discontinued or otherwise not available. Also remember that disgruntled customers can now give an unsatisfactory product a bad rating on various Internet sites where prospective customers will see it.

* * *

And here is another point. The service must be the best you can give. It is considered good manufacturing practice, and not bad ethics, occasionally to change designs so that old models will become obsolete and new ones will have to be bought either because repair parts for the old cannot be had, or because the new model offers a new sales argument which can be used to persuade a consumer to scrap what he has and buy something new. We have been told that this is good business, that it is clever business, that the object of business ought to be to get people to buy frequently and that it is bad business to try to make anything that will last forever, because when once a man is sold he will not buy again.

Our principle of business is precisely to the contrary. We cannot conceive how to serve the consumer unless we make for him something that, as far as we can provide, will last forever. We want to construct some kind of a machine that will last forever. It does not please us to have a buyer's car wear out or become obsolete. We want the man who buys one of our products never to have to buy another. We never make an improvement that renders any previous model obsolete. The parts of a specific model are not only interchangeable with all other cars of that model, but they are interchangeable with similar parts on all the cars that we have turned out. You can take a car of ten years ago and, buying to-day's parts, make it with very little expense into a car of to-day. Having these objectives the costs always come down under pressure. And since we have the firm policy of steady price reduction, there is always pressure. Sometimes it is just harder!

IDENTIFY AND ELIMINATE WASTE

The following material underscores one of Ford's success secrets, which was the ability to identify waste on sight and also apparently to teach his workforce to do the same. The statement, "The waste worried the men," which also appears more than once in Norwood (1931), underscores the fact that intolerance of all forms of waste was part of the culture as opposed to a management-driven activity.

The story about the discs of sheet metal also illustrates the concept of paying attention not only to the doughnut (the product), but also the hole (everything that is thrown away). The workers knew that the discs were recyclable, but they saw little sense in throwing them back into the blast furnace if they were usable as they were.

This section also illustrates the economy that comes from shipping parts instead of completed items (like automobiles) that occupy most of the freight train or other vehicle with predominantly air. The parts are then assembled into the complete product at the point of use. This is standard practice for many prefabricated furniture items today.

* * *

Take a few more instances of saving. The sweepings net six hundred thousand dollars a year. Experiments are constantly going on in the utilization of scrap. In one of the stamping operations six-inch circles of sheet metal are cut out. These formerly went into scrap. The waste worried the men. They worked to find uses for the discs. They found that the plates were just the right size and shape to stamp into radiator caps but the metal was not thick enough. They tried a double thickness of plates, with the result that they made a cap which tests proved to be stronger than one made out of a single sheet of metal. We get 150,000 of those discs a day. We have now found a use for about 20,000 a day and expect to find further uses for the remainder. We saved about ten dollars each by making transmissions instead of buying them. We experimented with bolts and produced a special bolt made on what is called an "upsetting machine" with a rolled thread that was stronger than any bolt we could buy, although in its making was used only about one third of the material that the outside manufacturers used. The saving on one style of bolt alone amounted to half a million dollars a year. We used to assemble our cars at Detroit, and although by special packing we managed to get five or six into a freight car, we needed many hundreds of freight cars a day. Trains were moving in and out all the time. Once a thousand freight cars were packed in a single day. A certain amount of congestion was inevitable. It is very expensive to knock down machines and crate them so that they cannot be injured in transit—to say nothing of the transportation charges. Now, we assemble only three or four hundred cars a day at Detroit—just enough for local needs. We now ship the parts to our assembling stations all over the United States and in fact pretty much all over the world, and the machines are put together there. Wherever it is possible for a branch to make a part more cheaply than we can make it in Detroit and ship it to them, then the branch makes the part.

The plant at Manchester, England, is making nearly an entire car. The tractor plant at Cork, Ireland, is making almost a complete tractor. This is an enormous saving of expense and is only an indication of what may be done throughout industry generally, when each part of a composite article is made at the exact point where it may be made most economically. We are constantly experimenting with every material that enters into the car. We cut most of our own lumber from our own forests. We are experimenting in the manufacture of artificial leather because we use about forty thousand yards of artificial leather a day. A penny here and a penny there runs into large amounts in the course of a year.

The greatest development of all, however, is the River Rouge plant, which, when it is running to its full capacity, will cut deeply and in many directions into the price of everything we make. The whole tractor plant is now there. This plant is located on the river on the outskirts of Detroit and the property covers six hundred and sixty-five acres—enough for future development. It has a large slip and a turning basin capable of accommodating any lake steamship; a short-cut canal and some dredging will give a direct lake connection by way of the Detroit River. We use a great deal of coal. This coal comes directly from our mines over the Detroit, Toledo and Ironton Railway, which we control, to the Highland Park plant and the River Rouge plant. Part of it goes for steam purposes. Another part goes to the by-product coke ovens which we have established at the River Rouge plant. Coke moves on from the ovens by mechanical transmission to the blast furnaces. The low volatile gases from the blast furnaces are piped to the power plant boilers where they are joined by the sawdust and the shavings from the body plant—the making of all our bodies has been shifted to this plant—and in addition the coke "breeze" (the dust in the making of coke) is now also being utilized for stoking. The steam power plant is thus fired almost exclusively from what would otherwise be waste products. Immense steam turbines directly coupled with dynamos transform this power into electricity, and all of the machinery in the tractor and the body plants is run by individual motors from this electricity. In the course of time it is expected that there will be sufficient electricity to run practically the whole Highland Park plant, and we shall then have cut out our coal bill.

FIND A USE FOR EVERYTHING

Ford and Crowther (1926, p. 175) elaborate on the following material with a description of the virtues of coking coal to extract the valuable coal chemicals, and only then burning the coke as fuel: "When one thinks of the precious elements which have been consumed for decades on the furnace grates, all going up in smoke and being lost to human use, it becomes clear that the new method has not come too soon." This reference (p. 106) adds that Ford paid $5 a ton for coal, from which he got $12 worth of coke and coal chemicals, such as those described below.

The following material also exemplifies how Ford could well have met the key requirements, at least in terms of results, of the ISO 14001 environmental management system standard in an era in which there were few if any environmental protection laws. The combustion of sulfur-containing coal produces sulfur dioxide, which is now a recognized pollutant that a coal user must pay to remove from its waste stream. Coking, however, allowed recovery of the sulfur as ammonium sulfate, which was then saleable as a fertilizer. Ford's intelligent approach, therefore, turned a pollutant into a useful product for which customers would pay. Ford News (1922, December 8, p. 4) elaborates as follows:

* * *

Arrangements have been made to sell Ford ammonium sulphate to anyone in need of fertilizer, within reasonable distance of the Rouge plant. It may be obtained through the regular Ford Dealer, at reasonable prices.

Ammonium sulphate is a by-product of the coke ovens at the Ford—River Rouge Plant. It is a white crystalline substance, known the world over as the best available source of nitrogen.

* * *

Note also Ford's practice of pouring molten iron from the blast furnace directly into a mold, instead of making pig iron that would later require remelting.

* * *

Among the by-products of the coke ovens is a gas. It is piped both to the Rouge and Highland Park plants where it is used for heat-treat purposes, for the enamelling ovens, for the car ovens, and the like. We formerly had to buy this gas. The ammonium sulphate is used for fertilizer. The benzol is a motor fuel. The small sizes of coke, not suitable for the blast furnaces, are sold to the employees—delivered free into their homes at much less than the ordinary market price. The large-sized coke goes to the blast furnaces. There is no manual handling. We run the melted iron directly from the blast furnaces into great ladles. These ladles travel into the shops and the iron is poured directly into the moulds without another heating. We thus not only get a uniform quality of iron according to our own specifications and directly under our control, but we save a melting of pig iron and in fact cut out a whole process in manufacturing as well as making available all our own scrap.

What all this will amount to in point of savings we do not know—that is, we do not know how great will be the saving, because the plant has not been running long enough to give more than an indication of what is ahead, and we save in so many directions—in transportation, in the generation of our power, in the generation of gas, in the expense in casting, and then over and above that is the revenue from the by-products and from the smaller sizes of coke. The investment to accomplish these objects to date amounts to something over forty million dollars.

How far we shall thus reach back to sources depends entirely on circumstances. Nobody anywhere can really do more than guess about the future costs of production. It is wiser to recognize that the future holds more than the past—that every day holds within it an improvement on the methods of the day before.

HOW TO LOSE THE LUDDITES

Ford now addresses the issue of Luddism, a problem that existed in the early days of the Industrial Revolution, if not before. The original Luddites were English workmen who destroyed textile machinery, which is why they were also called frame-breakers. They believed that mechanization would destroy their livelihoods because one person with a machine was as productive as 5 or 10 workers without one. Ford showed how, even if automation did displace workers, the same workers usually found better jobs as a result. This applies, however, to the destruction of entire industries, such as manual shoemaking, carriage driving, and so on, as opposed to layoffs by the business that has made a job more productive.

This section also reinforces the economic and behavioral legs of Ford's universal code. Consider, for example, Frank Gilbreth's nonstooping scaffold, which allowed a worker to lay 350 bricks per hour. A worker who had to bend over to pick up each brick could lay only 125 an hour, and his back was probably very sore when he finished his work day. Implementation of the nonstooping scaffold would seem to put almost two of every three bricklayers out of work, but the impartial laws of economics say that customers will not pay people to bend over 125 times an hour if they can avoid it. Luddism, therefore, would have destroyed rather than saved the jobs of the 125 brick-per-hour people. On the other hand, adoption of the new method allowed the 350 brick-per-hour workers to charge lower prices per brick while they earned higher hourly wages. The lower prices increased the demand for construction and, thus, the need for more bricks. Ford and Crowther (1926, p. 158) classify the bricklayer who deliberately limits his productivity with the executive who pays workers as little as possible while he charges customers whatever the market will bear.

Emerson (1909, p. 19) elaborates as follows, and both management and labor should pay very close attention:

What could have resulted from an elimination of this waste?

1. The product could have been cheapened.
2. The men could have worked one-third the time and have accomplished as much.
3. One man could have done all the work and have earned three times as much.

The benefits should however be distributed in all three directions. Fewer men should work less hard, receive higher wages, and deliver a cheaper product.

Emerson (1909, pp. 166–171) also addresses the issue of worker displacement, and cites examples of how efficiency improvements led to long-range growth in wages and employment.

Ford and Crowther (1930, p. 14) also address the fallacious idea that it is beneficial to have a lot of low-wage jobs instead of a few high-wage jobs. Two hundred workers who received $2 a day (in the money of 1930) could have bought little more than a subsistence existence, but 50 workers who got $8 a day could use their spending power to stimulate the economy and create more jobs. Sorensen (1956, p. 146) adds explicitly that this was the fundamental defect in Franklin Roosevelt's New Deal. The New Deal did not give unemployed people significant spending power, but the taxes necessary to support it diverted money from consumption and production that, in turn, would have created more jobs. This entire discussion is simply another example of Ford's universal code, or Kipling's Gods of the Copybook Headings, in action.

* * *

But how about production? If every necessary of life were produced so cheaply and in such quantities, would not the world shortly be surfeited with goods? Will there not come a point when, regardless of price, people simply will not want anything more than what they already have? And if in the process of manufacturing fewer and fewer men are used, what is going to become of these men—how are they going to find jobs and live?

Take the second point first. We mentioned many machines and many methods that displaced great numbers of men and then someone asks: "Yes, that is a very fine idea from the standpoint of the proprietor, but how about these poor fellows whose jobs are taken away from them?"

The question is entirely reasonable, but it is a little curious that it should be asked. For when were men ever really put out of work by the bettering of industrial processes? The stage-coach drivers lost their jobs with the coming of the railways. Should we have prohibited the railways and kept the stage-coach drivers? Were there more men working with the stage-coaches than are working on the railways? Should we have prevented the taxicab because its coming took the bread out of the mouths of the horse-cab drivers? How does the number of taxicabs compare with the number of horse-cabs when the latter were in their prime? The coming of shoe machinery closed most of the shops of those who made shoes by hand. When shoes were made by hand, only the very well-to-do could own more than a single pair of shoes, and most working people went barefooted in summer. Now, hardly any one has only one pair of shoes, and shoe making is a great industry. No, every time you can so arrange that one man will do the work of two, you so add to the wealth of the country that there will be a new and better job for the man who is displaced. If whole industries changed overnight, then disposing of the surplus men would be a problem, but these changes do not occur as rapidly as that. They come gradually. In our own experience a new place always opens for a man as soon as better processes have taken his old job. And what happens in my shops happens everywhere in industry. There are many times more men to-day employed in the steel industries than there were in the days when every operation was by hand. It has to be so. It always is so and always will be so. And if any man cannot see it, it is because he will not look beyond his own nose.

TAKE PROFITS OUT OF WASTE, NOT EMPLOYEES OR CUSTOMERS

Management experts Tom Peters and Nancy Austin (1985, p. 59) cited an encounter with a John Deere sales manager who wore a tie pin with the acronym SOQNOP: Sell On Quality, Not On Price. Ford now makes it clear that the best approach is to sell on high quality at a low price, and this chapter has shown how and why this is achievable. Ford then concludes by stressing the scientific leg of his universal code: Put brains into the business to reduce costs and thereby create more value for all stakeholders.

* * *

Now as to saturation. We are continually asked: "When will you get to the point of overproduction? When will there be more cars than people to use them?"

We believe it is possible some day to reach the point where all goods are produced so cheaply and in such quantities that overproduction will be a reality. But as far as we are concerned, we do not look forward to that condition with fear—we look forward to it with great satisfaction. Nothing could be more splendid than a world in which everybody has all that he wants. Our fear is that this condition will be too long postponed. As to our own products, that condition is very far away. We do not know how many motor cars a family will desire to use of the particular kind that we make. We know that, as the price has come down, the farmer, who at first used one car (and it must be remembered that it is not so very long ago that the farm market for motor cars was absolutely unknown—the limit of sales was at that time fixed by all the wise statistical sharps at somewhere near the number of millionaires in the country) now often uses two, and also he buys a truck. Perhaps, instead of sending workmen out to scattered jobs in a single car, it will be cheaper to send each worker out in a car of his own. That is happening with salesmen. The public finds its own consumptive needs with unerring accuracy, and since we no longer make motor cars or tractors, but merely the parts which when assembled become motor cars and tractors, the facilities as now provided would hardly be sufficient to provide replacements for ten million cars. And it would be quite the same with any business. We do not have to bother about overproduction for some years to come, provided the prices are right. It is the refusal of people to buy on account of price that really stimulates real business. Then if we want to do business we have to get the prices down without hurting the quality. Thus price reduction forces us to learn improved and less wasteful methods of production. One big part of the discovery of what is "normal" in industry depends on managerial genius discovering better ways of doing things. If a man reduces his selling price to a point where he is making no profit or incurring a loss, then he simply is forced to discover how to make as good an article by a better method—making his new method produce the profit, and not producing a profit out of reduced wages or increased prices to the public.

It is not good management to take profits out of the workers or the buyers; make management produce the profits. Don't cheapen the product; don't cheapen the wage; don't overcharge the public. Put brains into the method, and more brains, and still more brains—do things better than ever before; and by this means all parties to business are served and benefited.

And all of this can always be done.

11

Money and Goods

This chapter reiterates Ford's precept that money and finance can have seriously dysfunctional effects on any business. The sole legitimate purpose of finance is to report the company's income, assets, and liabilities as required by the Internal Revenue Service, Securities and Exchange Commission, and similar entities. It is very dangerous to use financial metrics for decision-making purposes.

The instance in which "the shop when called on raised a larger sum than any bank in this country could loan" may well relate to the material in Chapter 12, in which a cycle time reduction of one-third freed $20 million that had been tied up in inventory.

FINANCE BEGINS IN THE SHOP AND NOT THE BANK

The primary object of a manufacturing business is to produce, and if that objective is always kept, finance becomes a wholly secondary matter that has largely to do with bookkeeping. My own financial operations have been very simple. I started with the policy of buying and selling for cash, keeping a large fund of cash always on hand, taking full advantage of all discounts, and collecting interest on bank balances. I regard a bank principally as a place in which it is safe and convenient to keep money. The minutes we spend on a competitor's business we lose on our own. The minutes we spend in becoming expert in finance we lose in production. The place to finance a manufacturing business is the shop, and not the bank. I would not say that a man in business needs to know nothing at all about finance, but he is better off knowing too little than too much, for if he becomes too expert he will get into the way of thinking that he can borrow money instead of earning it and then he will borrow more money to pay back what he has borrowed, and instead of being a business man he will be a note juggler, trying to keep in the air a regular flock of bonds and notes.

If he is a really expert juggler, he may keep going quite a long time in this fashion, but some day he is bound to make a miss and the whole collection will come tumbling down around him. Manufacturing is not to be confused with banking, and I think that there is a tendency for too many business men to mix up in banking and for too many bankers to mix up in business. The tendency is to distort the true purposes of both business and banking and that hurts both of them. The money has to come out of the shop, not out of the bank, and I have found that the shop will answer every possible requirement, and in one case, when it was believed that the company was rather seriously in need of funds, the shop when called on raised a larger sum than any bank in this country could loan.

We have been thrown into finance mostly in the way of denial. Some years back we had to keep standing a denial that the Ford Motor Company was owned by the Standard Oil Company and with that denial, for convenience's sake, we coupled a denial that we were connected with any other concern or that we intended to sell cars by mail. Last year the best-liked rumour was that we were down in Wall Street hunting for money. I did not bother to deny that. It takes too much time to deny everything. Instead, we demonstrated that we did not need any money. Since then I have heard nothing more about being financed by Wall Street.

We are not against borrowing money and we are not against bankers. We are against trying to make borrowed money take the place of work. We are against the kind of banker who regards a business as a melon to be cut. The thing is to keep money and borrowing and finance generally in their proper place, and in order to do that one has to consider exactly for what the money is needed and how it is going to be paid off.

Borrowing (and Government Subsidies) Cannot Cure Bad Business

The following material is equally applicable to government bailouts and government subsidies. Solyndra's receipt of a half-billion dollar federal loan guarantee did not keep the company in business because federal support could not make up for the inadequacies of the company's product and/or processes.

The Chevy Volt also is an example of a product that cannot stand on its own feet or, in this case, wheels without government assistance. Krebs (2012) reports that the Volt requires 12 years to pay back its premium price (the difference between its price and that of an equivalent gasoline-only vehicle) if gasoline is at $4 a gallon. "The premium charged for hybrids and EVs [electric vehicles] takes time for consumers to recover in fuel savings—often a long time, maybe even longer than they intend to own the car." Note also that payback does not account for the time value of money which, despite today's relatively low interest and dividends, is still substantial for 12 years.

These observations lead us squarely back to Ford's original position. The producer must get the price down and the value up to the point where the consumer will buy the product or service. As stated below, "People buy what helps them just as naturally as they drink water."

* * *

Money is only a tool in business. It is just a part of the machinery. You might as well borrow 100,000 lathes as $100,000 if the trouble is inside your business. More lathes will not cure it; neither will more money. Only heavier doses of brains and thought and wise courage can cure. A business that misuses what it has will continue to misuse what it can get. The point is—cure the misuse. When that is done, the business will begin to make its own money, just as a repaired human body begins to make sufficient pure blood.

Borrowing may easily become an excuse for not boring into the trouble. Borrowing may easily become a sop for laziness and pride. Some business men are too lazy to get into overalls and go down to see what is the matter. Or they are too proud to permit the thought that anything they have originated could go wrong. But the laws of business are like the law of gravity, and the man who opposes them feels their power.

Borrowing for expansion is one thing; borrowing to make up for mismanagement and waste is quite another. You do not want money for the latter—for the reason that money cannot do the job. Waste is corrected by economy; mismanagement is corrected by brains. Neither of these correctives has anything to do with money. Indeed, money under certain circumstances is their enemy. And many a business man thanks his stars for the pinch which showed him that his best capital was in his own brains and not in bank loans. Borrowing under certain circumstances is just like a drunkard taking another drink to cure the effect of the last one. It does not do what it is expected to do. It simply increases the difficulty. Tightening up the loose places in a business is much more profitable than any amount of new capital at 7 per cent.

The internal ailments of business are the ones that require most attention. "Business" in the sense of trading with the people is largely a matter of filling the wants of the people. If you make what they need, and sell it at a price which makes possession a help and not a hardship, then you will do business as long as there is business to do. People buy what helps them just as naturally as they drink water.

BEWARE OF COMPLACENCY

The statement "… when business becomes a mere plantation on which to live, and not a big work which one has to do—then you may expect trouble" is consistent with Lawrence Miller's *Barbarians to Bureaucrats* (1989). This reference describes the almost inevitable life cycle of organizations and even countries whose own success leads to their takeover by bureaucrats and aristocrats; the kind of people who are temperamentally unable to respond to new threats and opportunities.

This lesson is particularly important because Ford himself fell victim to complacency even though he recognized its dangers. Ford (1922, pp. 27–29) even has a chapter entitled "Be Very Careful of Success," and it stresses explicitly that success can ruin a capable business by making it complacent. The Model T's success turned Ford himself into an aristocrat who believed that the product he had created would sustain his company forever, and all that he needed to do was to continue to reduce its price. Ford agreed only under pressure from his management team to introduce the Model A to compete with new vehicles that had more features than the Model T.

* * *

But the process of making the article will require constant care. Machinery wears out and needs to be restored. Men grow uppish, lazy, or careless. A business is men and machines united in the production of a commodity, and both the man and the machines need repairs and replacements. Sometimes it is the men "higher up" who most need revamping—and they themselves are always the last to recognize it. When a business becomes congested with bad methods; when a business becomes ill through lack of attention to one or more of its functions; when executives sit comfortably back in their chairs as if the plans they inaugurated are going to keep them going forever; when business becomes a mere plantation on which to live, and not a big work which one has to do—then you may expect trouble. You will wake up some fine morning and find yourself doing more business than you have ever done before—and getting less out of it. You find yourself short of money. You can borrow money. And you can do it, oh, so easily. People will crowd money on you. It is the most subtle temptation the young business man has. But if you do borrow money you are simply giving a stimulant to whatever may be wrong. You feed the disease. Is a man more wise with borrowed money than he is with his own? Not as a usual thing. To borrow under such conditions is to mortgage a declining property.

The time for a business man to borrow money, if ever, is when he does not need it. That is, when he does not need it as a substitute for the things he ought himself to do. If a man's business is in excellent condition and in need of expansion, it is comparatively safe to borrow. But if a business is in need of money through mismanagement, then the thing to do is to get into the business and correct the trouble from the inside—not poultice it with loans from the outside.

SEEK CONTINUOUS PRICE REDUCTIONS

My financial policy is the result of my sales policy. I hold that it is better to sell a large number of articles at a small profit than to sell a few at a large profit. This enables a larger number of people to buy and it gives a larger number of men employment at good wages. It permits the planning of production, the elimination of dull seasons, and the waste of carrying an idle plant. Thus results a suitable, continuous business, and if you will think it over, you will discover that most so-called urgent financing is made necessary because of a lack of planned, continuous business. Reducing prices is taken by the short-sighted to be the same as reducing the income of a business. It is very difficult to deal with that sort of a mind because it is so totally lacking in even the background knowledge of what business is. For instance, I was once asked, when contemplating a reduction of eighty dollars a car, whether on a production of five hundred thousand cars this would not reduce the income of the company by forty million dollars. Of course if one sold only five hundred thousand cars at the new price, the income would be reduced forty million dollars—which is an interesting mathematical calculation that has nothing whatsoever to do with business, because unless you reduce the price of an article the sales do not continuously increase and therefore the business has no stability.

If a business is not increasing, it is bound to be decreasing, and a decreasing business always needs a lot of financing. Old-time business went on the doctrine that prices should always be kept up to the highest point at which people will buy. Really modern business has to take the opposite view.

DYSFUNCTIONAL EFFECTS OF A FOCUS ON DIVIDENDS

Ford had a serious falling-out with his stockholders, which he resolved by buying them out in 1919. His position was that profits should be reinvested in the company, while they wanted high dividends. Ford now points out that people whose eye is primarily on the dollar and not on the job that delivers it should not run any business.

The Introduction already showed that the "Whiz Kids" who took over Ford after World War II based their decisions on financial metrics and, thus, proved Ford's warning accurate. It is, in fact, the same kind of people whose first thought as to how to cut labor costs is to send jobs offshore.

* * *

Bankers and lawyers can rarely appreciate this fact. They confuse inertia with stability. It is perfectly beyond their comprehension that the price should ever voluntarily be reduced. That is why putting the usual type of banker or lawyer into the management of a business is courting disaster. Reducing prices increases the volume and disposes of finance, provided one regards the inevitable profit as a trust fund with which to conduct more and better business. Our profit, because of the rapidity of the turnover in the business and the great volume of sales, has, no matter what the price at which the product was sold, always been large. We have had a small profit per article but a large aggregate profit. The profit is not constant. After cutting the prices, the profits for a time run low, but then the inevitable economies begin to get in their work and the profits go high again. But they are not distributed as dividends. I have always insisted on the payment of small dividends and the company has to-day no stockholders who wanted a different policy. I regard business profits above a small percentage as belonging more to the business than to the stockholders.

The stockholders, to my way of thinking, ought to be only those who are active in the business and who will regard the company as an instrument of service rather than as a machine for making money. If large profits are made—and working to serve forces them to be large—then they should be in part turned back into the business so that it may be still better fitted to serve, and in part passed on to the purchaser. During one year our profits were so much larger than we expected them to be that we voluntarily returned fifty dollars to each purchaser of a car. We felt that unwittingly we had overcharged the purchaser by that much. My price policy and hence my financial policy came up in a suit brought against the company several years ago to compel the payment of larger dividends. On the witness stand I gave the policy then in force and which is still in force. It is this:

> In the first place, I hold that it is better to sell a large number of cars at a reasonably small margin than to sell fewer cars at a large margin of profit.
>
> I hold this because it enables a large number of people to buy and enjoy the use of a car and because it gives a larger number of men

employment at good wages. Those are aims I have in life. But I would not be counted a success; I would be, in fact, a flat failure if I could not accomplish that and at the same time make a fair amount of profit for myself and the men associated with me in business.

This policy I hold is good business policy because it works—because with each succeeding year we have been able to put our car within the reach of greater and greater numbers, give employment to more and more men, and, at the same time, through the volume of business, increase our own profits beyond anything we had hoped for or even dreamed of when we started.

Bear in mind, every time you reduce the price of the car without reducing the quality, you increase the possible number of purchasers. There are many men who will pay $360 for a car who would not pay $440. We had in round numbers 500,000 buyers of cars on the $440 basis, and I figure that on the $360 basis we can increase the sales to possibly 800,000 cars for the year—less profit on each car, but more cars, more employment of labour, and in the end we shall get all the total profit we ought to make.

And let me say right here, that I do not believe that we should make such an awful profit on our cars. A reasonable profit is right, but not too much. So it has been my policy to force the price of the car down as fast as production would permit, and give the benefits to users and labourers—with resulting surprisingly enormous benefits to ourselves.

This policy does not agree with the general opinion that a business is to be managed to the end that the stockholders can take out the largest possible amount of cash. Therefore I do not want stockholders in the ordinary sense of the term—they do not help forward the ability to serve. My ambition is to employ more and more men and to spread, in so far as I am able, the benefits of the industrial system that we are working to found; we want to help build lives and homes. This requires that the largest share of the profits be put back into productive enterprise. Hence we have no place for the non-working stockholders. The working stockholder is more anxious to increase his opportunity to serve than to bank dividends.

Wages Come before Dividends

The following material is of particular interest to modern companies that are concerned with social responsibility. Social responsibility, as defined by Ford, consisted merely of a square deal for all participants in a supply chain including customers, suppliers, and employees. This square deal benefits all the stakeholders because, as Ford now makes clear, they are interdependent.

This discussion also reiterates the scientific element of Ford's universal code. It denounces businesses that "pass all their extra costs down the line until the whole burden is borne by the consumer," i.e., those (in business) who do not have enough basic foresight to eliminate the waste inherent in their systems.

* * *

If it at any time became a question between lowering wages or abolishing dividends, I would abolish dividends. That time is not apt to come, for, as I have pointed out, there is no economy in low wages. It is bad financial policy to reduce wages because it also reduces buying power. If one believes that leadership brings responsibility, then a part of that responsibility is in seeing that those whom one leads shall have an adequate opportunity to earn a living. Finance concerns not merely the profit or solvency of a company; it also comprehends the amount of money that the company turns back to the community through wages. There is no charity in this. There is no charity in proper wages. It is simply that no company can be said to be stable which is not so well managed that it can afford a man an opportunity to do a great deal of work and therefore to earn a good wage.

There is something sacred about wages—they represent homes and families and domestic destinies. People ought to tread very carefully when approaching wages. On the cost sheet, wages are mere figures; out in the world, wages are bread boxes and coal bins, babies' cradles and children's education— family comforts and contentment. On the other hand, there is something just as sacred about capital which is used to provide the means by which work can be made productive. Nobody is helped if our industries are sucked dry of their life-blood. There is something just as sacred about a shop that employs thousands of men as there is about a home. The shop is the mainstay of all the finer things which the home represents. If we want the home to be happy, we must contrive to keep the shop busy. The whole justification of the profits made by the shop is that they are used to make doubly secure the homes dependent on that shop, and to create more jobs for other men. If profits go to swell a personal fortune, that is one thing; if they go to provide a sounder basis for business, better working conditions, better wages, more extended employment—that is quite another thing. Capital thus employed should not be carelessly tampered with. It is for the service of all, though it may be under the direction of one.

Profits belong in three places: they belong to the business—to keep it steady, progressive, and sound. They belong to the men who helped produce them.

And they belong also, in part, to the public. A successful business is profitable to all three of these interests—planner, producer, and purchaser.

People whose profits are excessive when measured by any sound standard should be the first to cut prices. But they never are. They pass all their extra costs down the line until the whole burden is borne by the consumer; and besides doing that, they charge the consumer a percentage on the increased charges. Their whole business philosophy is: "Get while the getting is good." They are the speculators, the exploiters, the no-good element that is always injuring legitimate business. There is nothing to be expected from them. They have no vision. They cannot see beyond their own cash registers.

These people can talk more easily about a 10 or 20 per cent cut in wages than they can about a 10 or 20 per cent cut in profits. But a business man, surveying the whole community in all its interests and wishing to serve that community, ought to be able to make his contribution to stability.

It has been our policy always to keep on hand a large amount of cash—the cash balance in recent years has usually been in excess of fifty million dollars. This is deposited in banks all over the country, we do not borrow but we have established lines of credit, so that if we so cared we might raise a very large amount of money by bank borrowing. But keeping the cash reserve makes borrowing unnecessary—our provision is only to be prepared to meet an emergency. I have no prejudice against proper borrowing. It is merely that I do not want to run the danger of having the control of the business and hence the particular idea of service to which I am devoted taken into other hands.

Waste Includes the Cost of Idleness

Ford (1922, p. 329) wrote that there are exactly three kinds of waste: waste of time, waste of material, and waste of energy:

* * *

You can waste time, you can waste labor, you can waste material—and that is about all. ... Time, energy, and material are worth more than money, because they cannot be purchased by money. Not one hour of yesterday, nor one hour of today can be bought back. Not one ounce of energy can be bought back. Material wasted, is wasted beyond recovery.

* * *

Waste of time includes (1) waste of the time of people, (2) waste of the time of the product or service, as in cycle time, and (3) waste of the time of assets *for which value-adding work is available.* This does not mean that a business should produce inventory to keep equipment busy, but rather that the business should look for value-adding work to keep its assets busy. The cost of idleness is, therefore, the opportunity cost of not doing business when the resources are available to do so.

The following material also hints at an element of Goldratt's drum–buffer–rope (DBR) production control system, in which the capacity-constraining resource or constraint "beats the drum" to set the pace for the entire process or even supply chain. An information "rope" connects the constraint to production starts, while a buffer of inventory at or in transit to the constraint prevents the constraint from running out of work.

Ford used clockwork synchronization to run his operations, so there was no identifiable drum or rope. The following material suggests, however, that Ford may have treated the market itself as the constraint, which is a perfectly legitimate application of DBR. In this case, a buffer of finished goods that is actually in transit prevents stock-outs, or the external counterpart of starving the constraint. The subsequent discussion recognizes that failure to anticipate the market's needs will result either in millions of dollars of inventory or unfilled orders.

* * *

A considerable part of finance is in the overcoming of seasonal operation. The flow of money ought to be nearly continuous. One must work steadily in order to work profitably. Shutting down involves great waste. It brings the waste of unemployment of men, the waste of unemployment of equipment, and the waste of restricted future sales through the higher prices of interrupted production. That has been one of the problems we had to meet. We could not manufacture cars to stock during the winter months when purchases are less than in spring or summer. Where or how could any one store half a million cars? And if stored, how could they be shipped in the rush season? And who would find the money to carry such a stock of cars even if they could be stored?

Seasonal work is hard on the working force. Good mechanics will not accept jobs that are good for only part of the year. To work in full force twelve months of the year guarantees workmen of ability, builds up a permanent manufacturing organization, and continually improves the product—the men in the factory, through uninterrupted service, become more familiar with the operations.

The factory must build, the sales department must sell, and the dealer must buy cars all the year through, if each would enjoy the maximum profit to be derived from the business. If the retail buyer will not consider purchasing except in "seasons," a campaign of education needs to be waged, proving the all-the-year-around value of a car rather than the limited-season value. And while the educating is being done, the manufacturer must build, and the dealer must buy, in anticipation of business.

We were the first to meet the problem in the automobile business. The selling of Ford cars is a merchandising proposition. In the days when every car was built to order and 50 cars a month a big output, it was reasonable to wait for the sale before ordering. The manufacturer waited for the order before building.

We very shortly found that we could not do business on order. The factory could not be built large enough—even were it desirable—to make between March and August all the cars that were ordered during those months. Therefore, years ago began the campaign of education to demonstrate that a Ford was not a summer luxury but a year-round necessity. Coupled with that came the education of the dealer into the knowledge that even if he could not sell so many cars in winter as in summer it would pay him to stock in winter for the summer and thus be able to make instant delivery. Both plans have worked out; in most parts of the country cars are used almost as much in winter as in summer. It has been found that they will run in snow, ice, or mud—in anything. Hence the winter sales are constantly growing larger and the seasonal demand is in part lifted from the dealer. And he finds it profitable to buy ahead in anticipation of needs. Thus we have no seasons in the plant; the production, up until the last couple of years, has been continuous excepting for the annual shut downs for inventory. We have had an interruption during the period of extreme depression but it was an interruption made necessary in the process of readjusting ourselves to the market conditions.

In order to attain continuous production and hence a continuous turning over of money we have had to plan our operations with extreme care. The plan of production is worked out very carefully each month between the sales and production departments, with the object of producing enough cars so that those in transit will take care of the orders in hand. Formerly, when we assembled and shipped cars, this was of the highest importance because we had no place in which to store finished cars. Now we ship parts instead of cars and assemble only those required for the Detroit district. That makes the planning no less important, for if the production stream and the order stream are not approximately equal we should be either jammed with unsold parts or behind in our orders. When you are turning out the parts to make 4,000 cars a day, just a very little carelessness in overestimating orders will pile up a finished inventory running into the millions. That makes the balancing of operations an exceedingly delicate matter.

Inventory: "Everything Has to Move In and Move Out."

Ford reiterates the need to avoid inventories of raw or finished material, but adds that a company must be able to deal quickly with supply chain interruptions. A shortage of radiator parts, for example, prevented his company from shipping cars for more than a week. It was to his company's credit that it got the supplier up and running again in less than three weeks.

* * *

In order to earn the proper profit on our narrow margin we must have a rapid turnover. We make cars to sell, not to store, and a month's unsold production would turn into a sum the interest on which alone would be enormous. The production is planned a year ahead and the number of cars to be made in each month of the year is scheduled, for of course it is a big problem to have the raw materials and such parts as we still buy from the outside flowing in consonance with production. We can no more afford to carry large stocks of finished than we can of raw material. Everything has to move in and move out. And we have had some narrow escapes. Some years ago the plant of the Diamond Manufacturing Company burned down. They were making radiator parts for us and the brass parts—tubings and castings. We had to move quickly or take a big loss. We got together the heads of all our departments, the pattern-makers and the draughtsmen. They worked from twenty-four to forty-eight hours on a stretch. They made new patterns; the Diamond Company leased a plant and got some machinery in by express. We furnished the other equipment for them and in twenty days they were shipping again. We had enough stock on hand to carry us over, say, for seven or eight days, but that fire prevented us shipping cars for ten or fifteen days. Except for our having stock ahead it would have held us up for twenty days—and our expenses would have gone right on.

To repeat. The place in which to finance is the shop. It has never failed us, and once, when it was thought that we were hard up for money, it served rather conclusively to demonstrate how much better finance can be conducted from the inside than from the outside.

12

Money: Master or Servant?

The concept that money is the servant (i.e., a medium of exchange with which to do business) is vitally important. Ford has already described how, if money becomes the master, it then drives extremely dysfunctional behavior. Examples include excessive material purchases to get favorable price variances, and the manufacture of inventory to "absorb overhead."

* * *

In December 1920, business the country over was marking time. More automobile plants were closed than were open and quite a number of those which were closed were completely in the charge of bankers. Rumours of bad financial condition were afloat concerning nearly every industrial company, and I became interested when the reports persisted that the Ford Motor Company not only needed money but could not get it. I have become accustomed to all kinds of rumours about our company—so much so, that nowadays I rarely deny any sort of rumour. But these reports differed from all previous ones. They were so exact and circumstantial. I learned that I had overcome my prejudice against borrowing and that I might be found almost any day down in Wall Street, hat in hand, asking for money. And rumour went even further and said that no one would give me money and that I might have to break up and go out of business.

It is true that we did have a problem. In 1919 we had borrowed $70,000,000 on notes to buy the full stock interest in the Ford Motor Company. On this we had $33,000,000 left to pay. We had $18,000,000 in income taxes due or shortly to become due to the Government, and also we intended to pay our usual bonus for the year to the workmen, which amounted to $7,000,000. Altogether, between January 1st and April 18, 1921, we had payments ahead totaling $58,000,000. We had only $20,000,000 in bank. Our balance sheet was more or less common knowledge and I suppose it was taken for granted that we could not raise the $38,000,000 needed without borrowing. For that is quite a large sum of money. Without the aid of Wall Street such a sum could *not easily and quickly be raised. We were perfectly good for the money. Two years before we had borrowed $70,000,000. And since our whole property was unencumbered and we had no commercial debts, the matter of lending a large sum to us would not ordinarily have been a matter of moment. In fact, it would have been good banking business.*

However, I began to see that our need for money was being industriously circulated as an evidence of impending failure. Then I began to suspect that, although the rumours came in news dispatches from all over the country, they might perhaps be traced to a single source. This belief was further strengthened when we were informed that a very fat financial editor was at Battle Creek sending out bulletins concerning the acuteness of our financial condition. Therefore, I took care not to deny a single rumour. We had made our financial plans and they did not include borrowing money.

I cannot too greatly emphasize that the very worst time to borrow money is when the banking people think that you need money. In the last chapter I outlined our financial principles. We simply applied those principles. We planned a thorough house-cleaning.

Go back a bit and see what the conditions were. Along in the early part of 1920 came the first indications that the feverish speculative business engendered by the war was not going to continue. A few concerns that had sprung out of the war and had no real reason for existence failed. People slowed down in their buying. Our own sales kept right along, but we knew that sooner or later they would drop off. I thought seriously of cutting prices, but the costs of manufacturing everywhere were out of control. Labour gave less and less in return for high wages. The suppliers of raw material refused even to think of coming back to earth. The very plain warnings of the storm went quite unheeded.

In June our own sales began to be affected. They grew less and less each month from June on until September. We had to do something to bring our product within the purchasing power of the public, and not only that, we had to do something drastic enough to demonstrate to the public that we were actually playing the game and not just shamming. Therefore in September we cut the price of the touring car from $575 to $440. We cut the price far below the cost of production, for we were still making from stock bought at boom prices. The cut created a considerable sensation. We received a deal of criticism. It was said that we were disturbing conditions. That is exactly what we were trying to do. We wanted to do our part in bringing prices from an artificial to a natural level. I am firmly of the opinion that if at this time or earlier manufacturers and distributors had all made drastic cuts in their prices and had put through thorough house-cleanings we should not have so long a business depression. Hanging on in the hope of getting higher prices simply delayed adjustment. Nobody got the higher prices they hoped for, and *if the losses had been taken all at once, not only would the productive and the buying powers of the country have become harmonized, but we should have been saved this long period of general idleness. Hanging on in the hope of higher prices merely made the losses greater, because those who hung on had to pay interest on their high-priced stocks and also lost the profits they might have made by working on a sensible basis. Unemployment cut down wage distribution and thus the buyer and the seller became more and more separated. There was a lot of flurried talk of arranging to give vast credits to Europe—the idea being that thereby the high-priced stocks might be palmed off. Of course the proposals were not put in any such crude fashion, and I think that quite a lot of people sincerely believed that if large credits were extended abroad even without a hope of the payment of either principal or interest, American business would somehow be benefited. It is true that if these credits were taken by American banks, those who had high-priced stocks might have gotten rid of them at a profit, but the banks would have acquired so much frozen credit that they would have more nearly resembled ice houses than banks. I suppose it is natural to hang on to the possibility of profits until the very last moment, but it is not good business.*

Our own sales, after the cut, increased, but soon they began to fall off again. We were not sufficiently within the purchasing power of the country to make buying easy. Retail prices generally had not touched bottom. The public distrusted all prices. We laid our plans for another cut and we kept our production around one hundred thousand cars a month. This production was not justified by our sales but we wanted to have as much as possible of our raw material transformed into finished product before we shut down. We knew that we would have to shut down in order to take an inventory and clean house. We wanted to open with another big cut and to have cars on hand to supply the demand. Then the new cars could be built out of material bought at lower prices. We determined that we were going to get lower prices.

We shut down in December with the intention of opening again in about two weeks. We found so much to do that actually we did not open for nearly six weeks. The moment that we shut down the rumours concerning our financial condition became more and more active. I know that a great many people hoped that we should have to go out after money—for, were we seeking money, then we should have to come to terms. We did not ask for money. We did not want money. We had one offer of money. An officer of a New York bank called on me with a financial plan which included a large loan and in which also was an arrangement by which a representative of the bankers would act as treasurer and take charge of the finance of the company. Those people meant well enough, I am quite sure. We did not want to borrow money but it so happened that at the moment we were without a treasurer. To that extent the bankers had envisaged our condition correctly. I asked my son Edsel to be treasurer as well as president of the company. That fixed us up as to a treasurer, so there was really nothing at all that the bankers could do for us.

Then we began our house-cleaning. During the war we had gone into many kinds of war work and had thus been forced to depart from our principle of a single product. This had caused many new departments to be added. The office force had expanded and much of the wastefulness of scattered production had crept in. War work is rush work and is wasteful work. We began throwing out everything that did not contribute to the production of cars.

The only immediate payment scheduled was the purely voluntary one of a seven-million-dollar bonus to our workmen. There was no obligation to pay, but we wanted to pay on the first of January. That we paid out of our cash on hand.

Throughout the country we have thirty-five branches. These are all assembling plants, but in twenty-two of them parts are also manufactured. They had stopped the making of parts but they went on assembling cars. At the time of shutting down we had practically no cars in Detroit. We had shipped out all the parts, and during January the Detroit dealers actually had to go as far afield as Chicago and Columbus to get cars for local needs. The branches shipped to each dealer, under his yearly quota, enough cars to cover about a month's sales. The dealers worked hard on sales. During the latter part of January we called in a skeleton organization of about ten thousand men, mostly foremen, sub-foremen, and straw bosses, and we started Highland Park into production. We collected our foreign accounts and sold our by-products.

"HOUSECLEANING" DOES NOT MEAN LAYOFFS

Reassignment of workers from nonvalue-adding work to value-adding work will correct most financial problems. Note also the virtues of flat organizations in which supervisors have relatively wide spans of control; one foreman was adequate for 20 line workers. Ford emphasizes specifically that elimination of all forms of waste is the key to low costs and low prices. This includes the waste of time, and an increase in turnover equates to reduction of cycle time and also inventory.

* * *

Then we were ready for full production. And gradually into full production we went—on a profitable basis. The house-cleaning swept out the waste that had both made the prices high and absorbed the profit. We sold off the useless stuff. Before we had employed fifteen men per car per day. Afterward we employed nine per car per day. This did not mean that six out of fifteen men lost their jobs. They only ceased being unproductive. We made that cut by applying the rule that everything and everybody must produce or get out.

We cut our office forces in halves and offered the office workers better jobs in the shops. Most of them took the jobs. We abolished every order blank and every form of statistics that did not directly aid in the production of a car. We had been collecting tons of statistics because they were interesting. But statistics will not construct automobiles—so out they went.

We took out 60 per cent of our telephone extensions. Only a comparatively few men in any organization need telephones. We formerly had a foreman for every five men; now we have a foreman for every twenty men. The other foremen are working on machines.

We cut the overhead charge from $146 a car to $93 a car, and when you realize what this means on more than four thousand cars a day you will have an idea how, not by economy, not by wage-cutting, but by the elimination of waste, it is possible to make an "impossible" price.

Most important of all, we found out how to use less money in our business by speeding up the turnover. And in increasing the turnover rate, one of the most important factors was the Detroit, Toledo, & Ironton Railroad—which we purchased. The railroad took a large place in the scheme of economy. To the road itself I have given another chapter.

TRANSPORTATION AND CYCLE TIME

Ford described previously how elimination of variation in transportation time removes the need to carry protective inventory. The following material shows very explicitly how a superior logistics system could reduce cycle time by a third and, thus, release $20 million (in the money of the early 1920s) in cash. The lesson is that it is often possible to find cash within the business, which eliminates the need to borrow.

* * *

We discovered, after a little experimenting, that freight service could be improved sufficiently to reduce the cycle of manufacture from twenty-two to fourteen days. That is, raw material could be bought, manufactured, and the finished product put into the hands of the distributor in (roughly) 33 per cent less time than before. We had been carrying an inventory of around

$60,000,000 to insure [sic] uninterrupted production. Cutting down
the time one third released $20,000,000, or $1,200,000 a year in interest. Counting the finished inventory, we saved approximately $8,000,000
more—that is, we were able to release $28,000,000 in capital and save the
interest on that sum.

On January 1st we had $20,000,000. On April 1st we had $87,300,000, or
$27,300,000 more than we needed to wipe out all our indebtedness. That is
what boring into the business did for us! This amount came to us in these
items:

Cash on hand, January	$20,000,000
Stock on hand turned into cash, January 1 to April 1	24,700,000
Speeding up transit of goods released	28,000,000
Collected from agents in foreign countries	3,000,000
Sale of by-products	3,700,000
Sale of Liberty Bonds	7,900,000
TOTAL	$87,300,000

Now I have told about all this not in the way of an exploit, but to point out
how a business may find resources within itself instead of borrowing, and
also to start a little thinking as to whether the form of our money may not
put a premium on borrowing and thus give far too great a place in life to the
bankers.

Borrowing Cures the Symptoms But Not the Disease

Ford now reiterates his position that borrowing may fix the symptoms
of an underlying problem, but does not correct the problem itself. Ford
proved on the other hand that attention to the job, and particularly any
wasteful aspects of the job, will address most monetary concerns.

* * *

We could have borrowed $40,000,000—more had we wanted to. Suppose we
had borrowed, what would have happened? Should we have been better fitted to go on with our business? Or worse fitted? If we had borrowed we should
not have been under the necessity of finding methods to cheapen production.
Had we been able to obtain the money at 6 per cent flat—and we should
in commissions and the like have had to pay more than that—the interest
charge alone on a yearly production of 500,000 cars would have amounted
to about four dollars a car. Therefore we should now be without the benefit

of better production and loaded with a heavy debt. Our cars would probably cost about one hundred dollars more than they do; hence we should have a smaller production, for we could not have so many buyers; we should employ fewer men, and in short, should not be able to serve to the utmost. You will note that the financiers proposed to cure by lending money and not by bettering methods. They did not suggest putting in an engineer; they wanted to put in a treasurer.

And that is the danger of having bankers in business. They think solely in terms of money. They think of a factory as making money, not goods. They want to watch the money, not the efficiency of production. They cannot comprehend that a business never stands still, it must go forward or go back. They regard a reduction in prices as a throwing away of profit instead of as a building of business.

Bankers play far too great a part in the conduct of industry. Most business men will privately admit that fact. They will seldom publicly admit it because they are afraid of their bankers. It required less skill to make a fortune dealing in money than dealing in production. The average successful banker is by no means so intelligent and resourceful a man as is the average successful business man. Yet the banker through his control of credit practically controls the average business man.

There has been a great reaching out by bankers in the last fifteen or twenty years—and especially since the war—and the Federal Reserve System for a time put into their hands an almost limitless supply of credit. The banker is, as I have noted, by training and because of his position, totally unsuited to the conduct of industry. If, therefore, the controllers of credit have lately acquired this very large power, is it not to be taken as a sign that there is something wrong with the financial system that gives to finance instead of to service the predominant power in industry? It was not the industrial acumen of the bankers that brought them into the management of industry. Everyone will admit that. They were pushed there, willy-nilly, by the system itself. Therefore, I personally want to discover whether we are operating under the best financial system.

THE ROLE OF THE NATIONAL FINANCIAL SYSTEM

The following material is not particularly important to a thorough understanding of Henry Ford's business and management system, but it is noteworthy that Ford published it about seven years before the 1929 stock market crash. Fluctuation and, even worse, speculation on currency exchange rates leads to dysfunctional effects that are totally unrelated to the creation of actual wealth.

* * *

Now, let me say at once that my objection to bankers has nothing to do with personalities. I am not against bankers as such. We stand very much in need of thoughtful men, skilled in finance. The world cannot go on without banking facilities. We have to have money. We have to have credit. Otherwise the fruits of production could not be exchanged. We have to have capital. Without it there could be no production. But whether we have based our banking and our credit on the right foundation is quite another matter.

It is no part of my thought to attack our financial system. I am not in the position of one who has been beaten by the system and wants revenge. It does not make the least difference to me personally what bankers do because we have been able to manage our affairs without outside financial aid. My inquiry is prompted by no personal motive whatsoever. I only want to know whether the greatest good is being rendered to the greatest number.

No financial system is good which favors one class of producers over another. We want to discover whether it is not possible to take away power which is not based on wealth creation. Any sort of class legislation is pernicious. I think that the country's production has become so changed in its methods that gold is not the best medium with which it may be measured, and that the gold standard as a control of credit gives, as it is now (and I believe inevitably) administered, class advantage. The ultimate check on credit is the amount of gold in the country, regardless of the amount of wealth in the country.

I am not prepared to dogmatize on the subject of money or credit. As far as money and credit are concerned, no one as yet knows enough about them to dogmatize. The whole question will have to be settled as all other questions of real importance have to be settled, and that is by cautious, well-founded experiment. And I am not inclined to go beyond cautious experiments. We have to proceed step by step and very carefully. The question is not political, it is economic, and I am perfectly certain that helping the people to think on the question is wholly advantageous. They will not act without adequate knowledge, and thus cause disaster, if a sincere effort is made to provide them with knowledge. The money question has first place in multitudes of minds of all degrees or power. But a glance at most of the cure-all systems shows how contradictory they are. The majority of them make the assumption of honesty among mankind, to begin with, and that, of course, is a prime defect. Even our present system would work splendidly if all men were honest. As a matter of fact, the whole money question is 95 per cent human nature; and your successful system must check human nature, not depend upon it.

The people are thinking about the money question; and if the money masters have any information which they think the people ought to have to prevent them going astray, now is the time to give it. The days are fast slipping away when the fear of credit curtailment will avail, or when wordy slogans will affright. The people are naturally conservative. They are more conservative than the financiers. Those who believe that the people are so easily led that they would permit printing presses to run off money like milk tickets do not understand them. It is the innate conservation of the people that has kept our money good in spite of the fantastic tricks which the financiers play—and which they cover up with high technical terms.

The people are on the side of sound money. They are so unalterably on the side of sound money that it is a serious question how they would regard the system under which they live, if they once knew what the initiated can do with it.

The present money system is not going to be changed by speech-making or political sensationalism or economic experiment. It is going to change under the pressure of conditions—conditions that we cannot control and pressure that we cannot control. These conditions are now with us; that pressure is now upon us.

The people must be helped to think naturally about money. They must be told what it is, and what makes it money, and what are the possible tricks of the present system which put nations and peoples under control of the few.

Money, after all, is extremely simple. It is a part of our transportation system. It is a simple and direct method of conveying goods from one person to another. Money is in itself most admirable. It is essential. It is not intrinsically evil. It is one of the most useful devices in social life. And when it does what it was intended to do, it is all help and no hindrance.

But money should always be money. A foot is always twelve inches, but when is a dollar a dollar? If ton weights changed in the coal yard, and peck measures changed in the grocery, and yard sticks were to-day 42 inches and to-morrow 33 inches (by some occult process called "exchange") the people would mighty soon remedy that. When a dollar is not always a dollar, when the 100-cent dollar becomes the 65-cent dollar, and then the 50-cent dollar, and then the 47-cent dollar, as the good old American gold and silver dollars did, what is the use of yelling about "cheap money," "depreciated money"? A dollar that stays 100 cents is as necessary as a pound that stays 16 ounces and a yard that stays 36 inches.

The bankers who do straight banking should regard themselves as naturally the first men to probe and understand our monetary system—instead of being content with the mastery of local banking-house methods; and if they would deprive the gamblers in bank balances of the name of "banker" and oust them once for all from the place of influence which that name gives them, banking would be restored and established as the public service it ought to be, and the iniquities of the present monetary system and financial devices would be lifted from the shoulders of the people.

There is an "if" here, of course. But it is not insurmountable. Affairs are coming to a jam as it is, and if those who possess technical facility do not engage to remedy the case, those who lack that facility may attempt it. Nothing is more foolish than for any class to assume that progress is an attack upon it. Progress is only a call made upon it to lend its experience for the general advancement. It is only those who are unwise who will attempt to obstruct progress and thereby become its victims. All of us are here together, all of us must go forward together; it is perfectly silly for any man or class to take umbrage at the stirring of progress. If financiers feel that progress is only the restlessness of weak-minded persons, if they regard all suggestions of betterment as a personal slap, then they are taking the part which proves more than anything else could their unfitness to continue in their leadership.

Finance Should Serve Industry

Many problems arise today when, as Ford puts it, the financial sector becomes the master of industry as opposed to its servant.

* * *

If the present faulty system is more profitable to a financier than a more perfect system would be, and if that financier values his few remaining years of personal profits more highly than he would value the honour of making a contribution to the life of the world by helping to erect a better system, then there is no way of preventing a clash of interests. But it is fair to say to the selfish financial interests that, if their fight is waged to perpetuate a system just because it profits them, then their fight is already lost. Why should finance fear? The world will still be here. Men will do business with one another. There will be money and there will be need of masters of the mechanism of money. Nothing is going to depart but the knots and tangles. There will be some readjustments, of course. Banks will no longer be the masters of industry. They will be the servants of industry. Business will control money instead of money controlling business. The ruinous interest system will be greatly modified. Banking will not be a risk, but a service. Banks will begin to do much more for the people than they do now, and instead of being the most expensive businesses in the world to manage, and the most highly profitable in the matter of dividends, they will become less costly, and the profits of their operation will go to the community which they serve.

Two facts of the old order are fundamental. First: that within the nation itself the tendency of financial control is toward its largest centralized banking institutions—either a government bank or a closely allied group of private financiers. There is always in every nation a definite control of credit by private or semi-public interests. Second: in the world as a whole the same centralizing tendency is operative. An American credit is under control of New York interests, as before the war world credit was controlled in London—the British pound sterling was the standard of exchange for the world's trade.

Two methods of reform are open to us, one beginning at the bottom and one beginning at the top. The latter is the more orderly way, the former is being tried in Russia. If our reform should begin at the top it will require a social vision and an altruistic fervour of a sincerity and intensity which is wholly inconsistent with selfish shrewdness.

Money Is Not Wealth

Money should be a lubricant and not an obstacle to the creation and distribution of genuine wealth. Speculation in money, including currency speculation, levies a tax on the production of actual wealth and, therefore, promotes hardship and poverty.

Ford (1922, p. 31) elaborates that wealth consists not of money, but rather of "things in use" and then adds (p. 329) that "use is better than economy." The context of economy indicates not prudent thrift, but rather nonuse of an asset to the point where it might as well not exist. Ford and Crowther (1926, p. 93) cite the example of coal in the ground, which does not become wealth until somebody mines it and puts it to use.

The stereotypical miser who hides money under a mattress or buries it in the ground is another example. He may have access to the money during time of need, but it gains him nothing in the meantime. Chapter 13 of this book shows further that Ford speaks almost as badly of those who hoard resources as he does of those who waste them, and for the same reason.

* * *

The wealth of the world neither consists in nor is adequately represented by the money of the world. Gold itself is not a valuable commodity. It is no more wealth than hat checks are hats. But it can be so manipulated, as the sign of wealth, as to give its owners or controllers the whip-hand over the credit which producers of real wealth require. Dealing in money, the commodity of exchange, is a very lucrative business. When money itself becomes an article of commerce to be bought and sold before real wealth can be moved

166 • The Expanded and Annotated My Life and Work

or exchanged, the usurers and speculators are thereby permitted to lay a tax on production. The hold which controllers of money are able to maintain on productive forces is seen to be more powerful when it is remembered that, although money is supposed to represent the real wealth of the world, there is always much more wealth than there is money, and real wealth is often compelled to wait upon money, thus leading to that most paradoxical situation—a world filled with wealth but suffering want.

These facts are not merely fiscal, to be cast into figures and left there. They are instinct with human destiny and they bleed. The poverty of the world is seldom caused by lack of goods but by a "money stringency." Commercial competition between nations, which leads to international rivalry and ill-will, which in their turn breed wars—these are some of the human significations of these facts. Thus poverty and war, two great preventable evils, grow on a single stem.

Let us see if a beginning toward a better method cannot be made.

13

Why Be Poor?

This chapter contends very accurately that industry offers the only certain solution to poverty. Attempts to legislate poverty out of existence violate the impartial economic aspect of Ford's universal code, and this is why Lyndon Johnson's "war on poverty" was as much a failure as the Vietnam War.

"Leveling down," or taxing producers for well-meaning social welfare programs, spreads poverty instead of relieving it. Consider, for example, the provision of the Affordable Care Act that assesses a $2,000 per worker penalty on businesses that employ 50 or more people, but do not provide healthcare benefits. A business that employs 49 people, therefore, can save $100,000 a year by not hiring a 50th person. A business that employs 50 people can do the same by discharging at least one. A financial incentive to eliminate or not create jobs is hardly the way to fight poverty.

This is not to say that employers that can afford to do so should not offer health benefits regardless of the size of their workforces, and the tax code makes their cost every bit as deductible as wages. The jobs, however, must create enough value to support these benefits. In contrast, well-meaning efforts to legislate poverty out of existence make the dangerous assumption that there is, in fact, such a thing as a free lunch.

* * *

Poverty springs from a number of sources, the more important of which are controllable. So does special privilege. I think it is entirely feasible to abolish both poverty and special privilege—and there can be no question but that their abolition is desirable. Both are unnatural, but it is work, not law, to which we must look for results.

By poverty I mean the lack of reasonably sufficient food, housing, and clothing for an individual or a family. There will have to be differences in the grades of sustenance. Men are not equal in mentality or in physique. Any plan which starts with the assumption that men are or ought to be equal is unnatural and therefore unworkable. There can be no feasible or desirable process of leveling down. Such a course only promotes poverty by making it universal instead of exceptional. Forcing the efficient producer to become inefficient does not make the inefficient producer more efficient. Poverty can be done away with only by plenty, and we have now gone far enough along in the science of production to be able to see, as a natural development, the day when production and distribution will be so scientific that all may have according to ability and industry.

The extreme Socialists went wide of the mark in their reasoning that industry would inevitably crush the worker. Modern industry is gradually lifting the worker and the world. We only need to know more about planning and methods. The best results can and will be brought about by individual initiative and ingenuity—by intelligent individual leadership. The government, because it is essentially negative, cannot give positive aid to any really constructive programme. It can give negative aid—by removing obstructions to progress and by ceasing to be a burden upon the community.

PUT THE JOB FIRST AND MONEY SECOND

The economic leg of Ford's universal code has already stated unequivocally that money has to come from work, and that it cannot come from any other source. The following material explores the role of the scientific leg, the removal of waste from every activity, in the abolition of poverty.

* * *

The underlying causes of poverty, as I can see them, are essentially due to the bad adjustment between production and distribution, in both industry and agriculture—between the source of power and its application. The wastes due to lack of adjustment are stupendous. All of these wastes must fall before intelligent leadership consecrated to service. So long as leadership thinks more of money than it does of service, the wastes will continue. Waste is prevented by far-sighted not by short-sighted men. Short-sighted men think first of money. They cannot see waste. They think of service as altruistic instead of as the most practical thing in the world. They cannot get far enough away from the little things to see the big things—to see the biggest thing of all, which is that opportunist production from a purely money standpoint is the least profitable.

Service can be based upon altruism, but that sort of service is not usually the best. The sentimental trips up the practical.

Waste Is the Primary Barrier to Production and Service

It is important to recognize all forms of waste, and Ford cites the example of the cost of transporting coal to the Mississippi Valley. In this case, use of readily available hydroelectric power for heat is more cost-efficient. The most important lesson is, however, the need to identify and remove all forms of waste.

* * *

It is not that the industrial enterprises are unable fairly to distribute a share of the wealth which they create. It is simply that the waste is so great that there is not a sufficient share for everyone engaged, notwithstanding the fact that the product is usually sold at so high a price as to restrict its fullest consumption.

Take some of the wastes. Take the wastes of power. The Mississippi Valley is without coal. Through its centre pour many millions of potential horsepower—the Mississippi River. But if the people by its banks want power or heat they buy coal that has been hauled hundreds of miles and consequently has to be sold at far above its worth as heat or power. Or if they cannot afford to buy this expensive coal, they go out and cut down trees, thereby depriving themselves of one of the great conservers of water power. Until recently they never thought of the power at hand which, at next to nothing beyond the initial cost, could heat, light, cook, and work for the huge population which that valley is destined to support.

HOARDING AS A FORM OF WASTE

It is interesting to note that Dante's *Inferno* assigns a place to those who hoard things as well as waste them, and Ford depicts both practices as aspects of the same economic sin of misuse. An idle or unused asset is little better than one whose owner squanders it.

* * *

The cure of poverty is not in personal economy but in better production. The "thrift" and "economy" ideas have been overworked. The word "economy" represents a fear. The great and tragic fact of waste is impressed on a mind by some circumstance, usually of a most materialistic kind. There comes a violent reaction against extravagance—the mind catches hold of the idea of "economy." But it only flies from a greater to a lesser evil; it does not make the full journey from error to truth.

Economy is the rule of half-alive minds. There can be no doubt that it is better than waste; neither can there be any doubt that it is not as good as use. People who pride themselves on their economy take it as a virtue. But what is more pitiable than a poor, pinched mind spending the rich days and years clutching a few bits of metal? What can be fine about paring the necessities of life to the very quick? We all know "economical people" who seem to be niggardly even about the amount of air they breathe and the amount of appreciation they will allow themselves to give to anything. They shrivel—body and soul. Economy is waste: it is waste of the juices of life, the sap of living. For there are two kinds of waste—that of the prodigal who throws his substance away in riotous living, and that of the sluggard who allows his substance to rot from non-use. The rigid economizer is in danger of being classed with the sluggard. Extravagance is usually a reaction from suppression of expenditure. Economy is likely to be a reaction from extravagance.

Everything was given us to use. There is no evil from which we suffer that did not come about through misuse. The worst sin we can commit against the things of our common life is to misuse them. "Misuse" is the wider term. We like to say "waste," but waste is only one phase of misuse. All waste is misuse; all misuse is waste.

It is possible even to overemphasize the saving habit. It is proper and desirable that everyone have a margin; it is really wasteful not to have one—if you can have one. But it can be overdone. We teach children to save their money. As an attempt to counteract thoughtless and selfish expenditure, that has a value. But it is not positive; it does not lead the child out into the safe and useful avenues of self-expression or self-expenditure. To teach a child to invest and use is better than to teach him to save. Most men who are laboriously saving a few dollars would do better to invest those few dollars—first in themselves, and then in some useful work. Eventually they would have more to save. Young men ought to invest rather than save. They ought to invest in themselves to increase creative value; after they have taken themselves to the peak of usefulness, then will be time enough to think of laying aside, as a fixed policy, a certain substantial share of income. You are not "saving" when you prevent yourself from becoming more productive. You are really taking away from your ultimate capital; you are reducing the value of one of nature's investments. The principle of use is the true guide. Use is positive, active, life-giving. Use is alive. Use adds to the sum of good.

Personal want may be avoided without changing the general condition. Wage increases, price increases, profit increases, other kinds of increases designed to bring more money here or money there, are only attempts of this or that class to get out of the fire—regardless of what may happen to everyone else. There is a foolish belief that if only the money can be gotten, somehow the storm can be weathered. Labour believes that if it can get more wages, it can weather the storm. Capital thinks that if it can get more profits, it can weather the storm. There is a pathetic faith in what money can do. Money is very useful in normal times, but money has no more value than the people put into it by production, and it can be so misused. It can be so superstitiously worshipped as a substitute for real wealth as to destroy its value altogether.

SEASONAL WORK AND CYCLICAL INDUSTRIES

The following material is not particularly important to a thorough understanding of Ford's system, but it was more relevant in an era during which farmers might have worked in industry to occupy themselves productively in winter. The underlying concept still applies, however, to the potential virtues of greenhouse and hydroponic farms: "food factories" that are independent of the seasons. The issue of seasonal work for builders is meanwhile as applicable today as it was in 1922.

* * *

The idea persists that there exists an essential conflict between industry and the farm. There is no such conflict. It is nonsense to say that because the cities are overcrowded everybody ought to go back to the farm. If everybody did so farming would soon decline as a satisfactory occupation. It is not more sensible for everyone to flock to the manufacturing towns. If the farms be deserted, of what use are manufacturers? A reciprocity can exist between farming and manufacturing. The manufacturer can give the farmer what he needs to be a good farmer, and the farmer and other producers of raw materials can give the manufacturer what he needs to be a good manufacturer. Then with transportation as a messenger, we shall have a stable and a sound system built on service. If we live in smaller communities where the tension of living is not so high, and where the products of the fields and gardens can be had without the interference of so many profiteers, there will be little poverty or unrest.

Look at this whole matter of seasonal work. Take building as an example of a seasonal trade. What a waste of power it is to allow builders to hibernate through the winter, waiting for the building season to come around! And what an equal waste of skill it is to force experienced artisans who have gone into factories to escape the loss of the winter season to stay in the factory jobs through the building season because they are afraid they may not get their factory places back in the winter. What a waste this all-year system has been! If the farmer could get away from the shop to till his farm in the planting, growing, and harvesting seasons (they are only a small part of the year, after all), and if the builder could get away from the shop to ply his useful trade in its season, how much better they would be, and how much more smoothly the world would proceed.

Suppose we all moved outdoors every spring and summer and lived the wholesome life of the outdoors for three or four months! We could not have "slack times."

The farm has its dull season. That is the time for the farmer to come into the factory and help produce the things he needs to till the farm. The factory also has its dull season. That is the time for the workmen to go out to the land to help produce food. Thus we might take the slack out of work and restore the balance between the artificial and the natural.

But not the least benefit would be the more balanced view of life we should thus obtain. The mixing of the arts is not only beneficial in a material way, but it makes for breadth of mind and fairness of judgment. A great deal of our unrest to-day is the result of narrow, prejudiced judgment. If our work were more diversified, if we saw more sides of life, if we saw how necessary was one factor to another, we should be more balanced. Every man is better for a period of work under the open sky.

It is not at all impossible. What is desirable and right is never impossible. It would only mean a little teamwork—a little less attention to greedy ambition and a little more attention to life.

Those who are rich find it desirable to go away for three or four months a year and dawdle in idleness around some fancy winter or summer resort. The rank and file of the American people would not waste their time that way even if they could. But they would provide the team-work necessary for an outdoor, seasonal employment.

It is hardly possible to doubt that much of the unrest we see about us is the result of unnatural modes of life. Men who do the same thing continuously the year around and are shut away from the health of the sun and the spacious-ness of the great out of doors are hardly to be blamed if they see matters in a distorted light. And that applies equally to the capitalist and the worker.

What is there in life that should hamper normal and wholesome modes of living? And what is there in industry incompatible with all the arts receiv-ing in their turn the attention of those qualified to serve in them? It may be objected that if the forces of industry were withdrawn from the shops every summer it would impede production. But we must look at the matter from a universal point of view. We must consider the increased energy of the indus-trial forces after three or four months in outdoor work. We must also con-

sider the effect on the cost of living which would result from a general return to the fields.

We have, as I indicated in a previous chapter, been working toward this combination of farm and factory and with entirely satisfactory results. At Northville, not far from Detroit, we have a little factory making valves. It is a little factory, but it makes a great many valves. Both the management and the mechanism of the plant are comparatively simple because it makes but one thing. We do not have to search for skilled employees. The skill is in the machine. The people of the countryside can work in the plant part of the time and on the farm part of the time, for mechanical farming is not very laborious. The plant power is derived from water.

Another plant on a somewhat larger scale is in building at Flat Rock, about fifteen miles from Detroit. We have dammed the river. The dam also serves as a bridge for the Detroit, Toledo & Ironton Railway, which was in need of a new bridge at that point, and a road for the public—all in one construction. We are going to make our glass at this point. The damming of the river gives sufficient water for the floating to us of most of our raw material. It also gives us our power through a hydroelectric plant. And, being well out in the midst of the farming country, there can be no possibility of crowding or any of the ills incident to too great a concentration of population. The men will have plots of ground or farms as well as their jobs in the factory, and these can be scattered over fifteen or twenty miles surrounding—for of course nowadays the workingman can come to the shop in an automobile. There we shall have the combination of agriculture and industrialism and the entire absence of all the evils of concentration.

The belief that an industrial country has to concentrate its industries is not, in my opinion, well-founded. That is only a stage in industrial development. As we learn more about manufacturing and learn to make articles with interchangeable parts, then those parts can be made under the best possible conditions. And these best possible conditions, as far as the employees are concerned, are also the best possible conditions from the manufacturing standpoint. One could not put a great plant on a little stream. One can put a small plant on a little stream, and the combination of little plants, each making a single part, will make the whole cheaper than a vast factory would. There are exceptions, as where casting has to be done. In such case, as at River Rouge, we want to combine the making of the metal and the casting of it and also we want to use all of the waste power. This requires a large investment and a considerable force of men in one place. But such combinations are the exception rather than the rule, and there would not be enough of them seriously to interfere with the process of breaking down the concentration of industry.

THE OBSOLESCENCE OF THE CITY

The following material should be of particular interest to businesses that feel a compulsion, perhaps bred from long-obsolete habits, to locate themselves in large cities. We have previously observed that cities evolved (1) as places of communal defense and (2) centers of commerce.

The airplane and the ballistic missile made cities into attractive and indefensible targets more than 65 years ago. Cantor Fitzgerald's reward for its presence in New York was the loss of two-thirds of its workforce on 9/11, and its neighbor Marsh & McLennan also lost hundreds of employees. The Internet has meanwhile made obsolete the function of a city as a center of commerce.

There was a time, namely decades ago, that members of the Chicago Board of Trade exchanged commodities in person. The author's uncle commuted more than an hour each way from a North Shore suburb for this purpose. There was also a time when all stocks had to be sold on the floor of the New York Stock Exchange or American Stock Exchange. It now possible to buy or sell a stock in literally seconds, and for a nominal commission, over the Internet. The server that processes the exchange, and the employees who manage it, can be anywhere in the country. There is no need to pay for big city taxes, big city office space, or premium salaries to cover the extra cost of living in a big city. Intelligent managers will realize the wisdom of Ford's words: "The modern city has been prodigal, it is to-day bankrupt, and to-morrow it will cease to be." Ford (1922, pp. 118–122) elaborates on this considerably with a chapter called "The City: A Pestiferous Growth."

* * *

Industry will decentralize. There is no city that would be rebuilt as it is, were it destroyed—which fact is in itself a confession of our real estimate of our cities. The city had a place to fill, a work to do. Doubtless the country places would not have approximated their livableness had it not been for the cities. By crowding together, men have learned some secrets. They would never have learned them alone in the country. Sanitation, lighting, social organization—all these are products of men's experience in the city. But also every social ailment from which we to-day suffer originated and centres in the big cities. You will find the smaller communities living along in unison with the seasons, having neither extreme poverty nor wealth—none of the violent plagues of upheave and unrest which afflict our great populations. There is something about a city of a million people which is untamed and threatening. Thirty miles away, happy and contented villages read of the ravings of the city! A great city is really a helpless mass. Everything it uses is carried to it. Stop transport and the city stops. It lives off the shelves of stores. The shelves produce nothing. The city cannot feed, clothe, warm, or house itself. City conditions of work and living are so artificial that instincts sometimes rebel against their unnaturalness.

And finally, the overhead expense of living or doing business in the great cities is becoming so large as to be unbearable. It places so great a tax upon life that there is no surplus over to live on. The politicians have found it easy to borrow money and they have borrowed to the limit. Within the last decade the expense of running every city in the country has tremendously increased. A good part of that expense is for interest upon money borrowed; the money has gone either into non-productive brick, stone, and mortar, or into necessities of city life, such as water supplies and sewage systems at far above a reasonable cost. The cost of maintaining these works, the cost of keeping in order great masses of people and traffic is greater than the advantages derived from community life. The modern city has been prodigal, it is to-day bankrupt, and to-morrow it will cease to be.

THE ROLE OF ENERGY IN WEALTH CREATION

Ford and Crowther (1926, p. 165) state explicitly the role of "developed power" in the creation of material wealth. The fact that the United States' 4% of the world's population once used more than a quarter of its energy is why it also produced at least this share of the world's wealth. The fact that China is surpassing the United States as the world's biggest user of energy, therefore, should be nothing less than alarming.

* * *

The provision of a great amount of cheap and convenient power—not all at once, but as it may be used—will do more than anything else to bring about the balancing of life and the cutting of the waste which breeds poverty. There is no single source of power. It may be that generating electricity by a steam plant at the mine mouth will be the most economical method for one community. Hydro-electric power may be best for another community. But certainly in every community there ought to be a central station to furnish cheap power—it ought to be held as essential as a railway or a water supply. And we could have every great source of power harnessed and working for the common good were it not that the expense of obtaining capital stands in the way. I think that we shall have to revise some of our notions about capital.

THE PROPER ROLE OF CAPITAL

The concept of holding capital in trust is consistent with the idea of stewardship, or "responsibility for." The Indo-European root dher, which appears in Persian names like Darius and in Indian titles like Jemadar and Sirdar, means to hold in trust. The idea of the leader as a steward of the organization's welfare is a common theme in Ford's business system.

* * *

Capital that a business makes for itself, that is employed to expand the workman's opportunity and increase his comfort and prosperity, and that is used to give more and more men work, at the same time reducing the cost of service to the public—that sort of capital, even though it be under single control, is not a menace to humanity. It is a working surplus held in trust and daily use for the benefit of all. The holder of such capital can scarcely regard it as a personal reward. No man can view such a surplus as his own, for he did not create it alone. It is the joint product of his whole organization. The owner's idea may have released all the energy and direction, but certainly it did not supply all the energy and direction. Every workman was a partner in the creation. No business can possibly be considered only with reference to today and to the individuals engaged in it. It must have the means to carry on. The best wages ought to be paid. A proper living ought to be assured every participant in the business—no matter what his part. But, for the sake of that business's ability to support those who work in it, a surplus has to be held somewhere. The truly honest manufacturer holds his surplus profits in that trust. Ultimately it does not matter where this surplus be held nor who controls it; it is its use that matters.

Capital that is not constantly creating more and better jobs is more useless than sand. Capital that is not constantly making conditions of daily labour better and the reward of daily labour more just, is not fulfilling its highest function. The highest use of capital is not to make more money, but to make money do more service for the betterment of life. Unless we in our industries are helping to solve the social problem, we are not doing our principal work. We are not fully serving.

14

The Tractor and Power Farming

This chapter, which is primarily of historical interest, shows the effect of mechanization on agricultural productivity. Ford contended, and proved very conclusively on his own farms, that tractors could increase agricultural output enormously.

It is particularly impressive, however, that when the United Kingdom offered the Ford Motor Company $1,500 per tractor during the World War I, Ford's production chief Charles Sorensen declared the offer unreasonable—because the tractors could be delivered for $700 apiece. It is quite likely that the rapid delivery of these tractors saved the United Kingdom from starvation during the war.

* * *

It is not generally known that our tractor, which we call the "Fordson," was put into production about a year before we had intended, because of the Allies' war-time food emergency, and that all of our early production (aside, of course, from the trial and experimental machines) went directly to England. We sent in all five thousand tractors across the sea in the critical 1917–18 period when the submarines were busiest. Every one of them arrived safely, and officers of the British Government have been good enough to say that without their aid England could scarcely have met its food crisis.

It was these tractors, run mostly by women, that ploughed up the old estates and golf courses and let all England be planted and cultivated without taking away from the fighting man power or crippling the forces in the munitions factories.

It came about in this way: The English food administration, about the time that we entered the war in 1917, saw that, with the German submarines torpedoing a freighter almost every day, the already low supply of shipping was going to be totally inadequate to carry the American troops across the seas, to carry the essential munitions for these troops and the Allies, to carry the food for the fighting forces, and at the same time carry enough food for the home population of England. It was then that they began shipping out of England the wives and families of the colonials and made plans for the growing of crops at home. The situation was a grave one. There were not enough draft animals in all England to plough and cultivate land to raise crops in sufficient volume to make even a dent in the food imports. Power farming was scarcely known, for the English farms were not, before the war, big enough to warrant the purchase of heavy, expensive farm machinery, and especially with agricultural labour so cheap and plentiful. Various concerns in England made tractors, but they were heavy affairs and mostly run by steam. There were not enough of them to go around. More could not easily be made, for all the factories were working on munitions, and even if they had been made they were too big and clumsy for the average field and in addition required the management of engineers.

We had put together several tractors at our Manchester plant for demonstration purposes. They had been made in the United States and merely assembled in England. The Board of Agriculture requested the Royal Agricultural Society to make a test of these tractors and report. This is what they reported:

> At the request of the Royal Agricultural Society of England, we have examined two Ford tractors, rated at 25 h. p., at work ploughing:—
>
> First, cross-ploughing a fallow of strong land in a dirty condition, and subsequently in a field of lighter land which had seeded itself down into rough grass, and which afforded every opportunity of testing the motor on the level and on a steep hill.
>
> In the first trial, a 2-furrow Oliver plough was used, ploughing on an average 5 inches deep with a 16-inch wide furrow; a 3-furrow Cockshutt plough was also used at the same depth with the breast pitched 10 inches.
>
> In the second trial, the 3-furrow plough was used, ploughing an average of 6 inches deep.
>
> In both cases the motor did its work with ease, and on a measured acre the time occupied was 1 hour 30 minutes, with a consumption of 2 gallons of paraffin per acre.
>
> These results we consider very satisfactory.
>
> The ploughs were not quite suitable to the land, and the tractors, consequently, were working at some disadvantage.
>
> The total weight of the tractor fully loaded with fuel and water, as weighed by us, was 23 1/4 cwts [hundred weights; the tractor weighed somewhat more than a ton].
>
> The tractor is light for its power, and, consequently, light on the land, is easily handled, turns in a small circle, and leaves a very narrow headland.

The motor is quickly started up from cold on a small supply of petrol.

After these trials we proceeded to Messrs. Ford's works at Trafford Park, Manchester, where one of the motors had been sent to be dismantled and inspected in detail.

We find the design of ample strength, and the work of first-rate quality. We consider the driving-wheels rather light, and we understand that a new and stronger pattern is to be supplied in future.

The tractor is designed purely for working on the land, and the wheels, which are fitted with spuds, should be provided with some protection to enable them to travel on the road when moving from farm to farm.

Bearing the above points in mind, we recommend, under existing circumstances, that steps be taken to construct immediately as many of these tractors as possible.

The report was signed by Prof. W. E. Dalby and F. S. Courtney, engineering; R. N. Greaves, engineering and agriculture; Robert W. Hobbs and Henry Overman, agriculture; Gilbert Greenall, honorary directors, and John E. Cross, steward.

Almost immediately after the filing of that report we received the following wire:

Have not received anything definite concerning shipment necessary steel and plant for Cork factory. Under best circumstances however Cork factory production could not be available before next spring. The need for food production in England is imperative and large quantity of tractors must be available at earliest possible date for purpose breaking up existing grass land and ploughing for Fall wheat. Am requested by high authorities to appeal to Mr. Ford for help. Would you be willing to send Sorensen and others with drawings of everything necessary, loaning them to British Government so that parts can be manufactured over here and assembled in Government factories under Sorensen's guidance? Can assure you positively this suggestion is made in national interest and if carried out will be done by the Government for the people with no manufacturing or capitalist interest invested and no profit being made by any interests whatever. The matter is very urgent. Impossible to ship anything adequate from America because many thousand tractors must be provided. Ford Tractor considered best and only suitable design. Consequently national necessity entirely dependent Mr. Ford's design. My work prevents me coming [to] America to present the proposal personally. Urge favorable consideration and immediate decision because every day is of vital importance. You may rely on manufacturing facility for production here under strictest impartial Government control. Would welcome Sorensen and any and every other assistance and guidance you can furnish from America. Cable reply, Perry, Care of Harding "Prodome," London.

PRODOME.

I understand that its sending was directed by the British Cabinet. We at once cabled our entire willingness to lend the drawings, the benefit of what experience we had to date, and whatever men might be necessary to get production under way, and on the next ship sent Charles E. Sorensen with full drawings. Mr. Sorensen had opened the Manchester plant and was familiar with English conditions. He was in charge of the manufacture of tractors in this country.

Mr. Sorensen started at work with the British officials to the end of having the parts made and assembled in England. Many of the materials which we used were special and could not be obtained in England. All of their factories equipped for doing casting and machine work were filled with munition orders. It proved to be exceedingly difficult for the Ministry to get tenders of any kind. Then came June and a series of destructive air raids on London. There was a crisis. Something had to be done, and finally, after passing to and fro among half the factories of England, our men succeeded in getting the tenders lodged with the Ministry.

Lord Milner exhibited these tenders to Mr. Sorensen. Taking the best of them the price per tractor came to about $1,500 without any guarantee of delivery.

"That price is out of all reason," said Mr. Sorensen. "These should not cost more than $700 apiece."

"Can you make five thousand at that price?" asked Lord Milner.

"Yes," answered Mr. Sorensen.

"How long will it take you to deliver them?"

"We will start shipping within sixty days."

They signed a contract on the spot, which, among other things, provided for an advance payment of 25 per cent of the total sum. Mr. Sorensen cabled us what he had done and took the next boat home. The 25 five per cent payment was, by the way, not touched by us until after the entire contract was completed: we deposited it in a kind of trust fund.

The tractor works was not ready to go into production. The Highland Park plant might have been adapted, but every machine in it was going day and night on essential war work. There was only one thing to do. We ran up an emergency extension to our plant at Dearborn, equipped it with machinery that was ordered by telegraph and mostly came by express, and in less than sixty days the first tractors were on the docks in New York in the hands of the

British authorities. They delayed in getting cargo space, but on December 6, 1917, we received this cable:

> London, December 5, 1917.
> SORENSEN,
> Fordson, F. R. Dearborn.
> First tractors arrived, when will Smith and others leave? Cable.
> PERRY.

The entire shipment of five thousand tractors went through within three months and that is why the tractors were being used in England long before they were really known in the United States.

THE DEVELOPMENT OF THE TRACTOR

The planning of the tractor really antedated that of the motor car. Out on the farm my first experiments were with tractors, and it will be remembered that I was employed for some time by a manufacturer of steam tractors—the big heavy road and thresher engines. But I did not see any future for the large tractors. They were too expensive for the small farm, required too much skill to operate, and were much too heavy as compared with the pull they exerted. And anyway, the public was more interested in being carried than in being pulled; the horseless carriage made a greater appeal to the imagination. And so it was that I practically dropped work upon a tractor until the automobile was in production. With the automobile on the farms, the tractor became a necessity. For then the farmers had been introduced to power.

The farmer does not stand so much in need of new tools as of power to run the tools that he has. I have followed many a weary mile behind a plough and I know all the drudgery of it. What a waste it is for a human being to spend hours and days behind a slowly moving team of horses when in the same time a tractor could do six times as much work! It is no wonder that, doing everything slowly and by hand, the average farmer has not been able to earn more than a bare living while farm products are never as plentiful and cheap as they ought to be.

As in the automobile, we wanted power—not weight. The weight idea was firmly fixed in the minds of tractor makers. It was thought that excess weight meant excess pulling power—that the machine could not grip unless it were heavy. And this in spite of the fact that a cat has not much weight and is a pretty good climber. I have already set out my ideas on weight. The only kind of tractor that I thought worth working on was one that would be light, strong, and so simple that any one could run it. Also it had to be so cheap that any one could buy it.

With these ends in view, we worked for nearly fifteen years on a design and spent some millions of dollars in experiments. We followed exactly the same course as with the automobile. Each part had to be as strong as it was possible to make it, the parts had to be few in number, and the whole had to admit of quantity production. We had some thought that perhaps the automobile engine might be used and we conducted a few experiments with it. But finally we became convinced that the kind of tractor we wanted and the automobile had practically nothing in common. It was the intention from the beginning that the tractor should be made as a separate undertaking from the automobile and in a distinct plant. No plant is big enough to make two articles.

The automobile is designed to carry; the tractor is designed to pull—to climb. And that difference in function made all the difference in the world in construction. The hard problem was to get bearings that would stand up against the heavy pull. We finally got them and a construction which seems to give the best average performance under all conditions. We fixed upon a four-cylinder engine that is started by gasoline but runs thereafter on kerosene. The lightest weight that we could attain with strength was 2,425 pounds. The grip is in the lugs on the driving wheels—as in the claws of the cat.

In addition to its strictly pulling functions, the tractor, to be of the greatest service, had also to be designed for work as a stationary engine so that when it was not out on the road or in the fields it might be hitched up with a belt to run machinery. In short, it had to be a compact, versatile power plant. And that it has been. It has not only ploughed, harrowed, cultivated, and reaped, but it has also threshed, run grist mills, saw mills, and various other sorts of mills, pulled stumps, ploughed snow, and done about everything that a plant of moderate power could do from sheep-shearing to printing a newspaper. It has been fitted with heavy tires to haul on roads, with sledge runners for the woods and ice, and with rimmed wheels to run on rails. When the shops in Detroit were shut down by coal shortage, we got out the Dearborn Independent by sending a tractor to the electro-typing factory—stationing the tractor in the alley, sending up a belt four stories, and making the plates by tractor power. Its use in ninety-five distinct lines of service has been called to our attention, and probably we know only a fraction of the uses.

The mechanism of the tractor is even more simple than that of the automobile and it is manufactured in exactly the same fashion. Until the present year, the production has been held back by the lack of a suitable factory. The first tractors had been made in the plant at Dearborn which is now used as an experimental station. That was not large enough to affect the economies of large-scale production and it could not well be enlarged because the design was to make the tractors at the River Rouge plant, and that, until this year, was not in full operation.

Now that plant is completed for the making of tractors. The work flows exactly as with the automobiles. Each part is a separate departmental undertaking and each part as it is finished joins the conveyor system which leads it to its proper initial assembly and eventually into the final assembly. Everything moves and there is no skilled work. The capacity of the present plant is one million tractors a year. That is the number we expect to make— for the world needs inexpensive, general-utility power plants more now than ever before—and also it now knows enough about machinery to want such plants.

The first tractors, as I have said, went to England. They were first offered in the United States in 1918 at $750. In the next year, with the higher costs, the price had to be made $885; in the middle of the year it was possible again to make the introductory price of $750. In 1920 we charged $790; in the next year we were sufficiently familiar with the production to begin cutting. The price came down to $625 and then in 1922 with the River Rouge plant functioning we were able to cut to $395. All of which shows what getting into scientific production will do to a price. Just as I have no idea how cheaply the Ford automobile can eventually be made, I have no idea how cheaply the tractor can eventually be made.

THE MECHANIZATION OF AGRICULTURE

The following material shows why one American farmer is now able to feed more than a hundred people. Ford and Crowther (1926, pp. 164–165) add that 10 tractors plowed 1,000 acres in Armenia in the space of 11 days. This task would have otherwise required 1,000 oxen and 500 laborers. The same reference adds that, in French Morocco, a threshing machine could process as much grain as 135 men.

Soviet Russia also was eager to buy Ford's tractors. *Ford News* (1922, December 15, p. 3) adds, "'Fifty thousand American tractors,' said Mr. [David A.] Brown, 'will do more than $100,000,000 in foodstuffs to save the Russian people from starvation and put them back on the road to economic liberty.'" Brown, a relief and construction worker, added that he had seen Russian children in loin cloths while the exchange rate was 17 million rubles to the dollar. The catastrophic effects of the Communist system had done to the ruble what would later happen to the Weimar Deutschmark and the currency of Zimbabwe.

* * *

It is important that it shall be cheap. Otherwise power will not go to all the farms. And they must all of them have power. Within a few years a farm depending solely on horse and hand power will be as much of a curiosity as a factory run by a treadmill. The farmer must either take up power or go out of business. The cost figures make this inevitable. During the war the Government made a test of a Fordson tractor to see how it's costs compared with doing the work with horses. The figures on the tractor were taken at the high price plus freight. The depreciation and repair items are not so great as the report sets them forth, and even if they were, the prices are cut in halves which would therefore cut the depreciation and repair charge in halves. These are the figures:

COST, FORDSON, $880. WEARING LIFE, 4,800 HOURS AT 4/5 ACRES PER HOUR, 3,840 ACRES

3,840 acres at $880; depreciation per acre	$0.221
Repairs for 3,840 acres, $100; per acre	0.026
Fuel cost, kerosene at 19 cents; 2 gal. per acre	0.38
1 gal. oil per 8 acres; per acre	0.075
Driver, $2 per day, 8 acres; per acre	0.25
Cost of ploughing with Fordson; per acre.	0.95

8 HORSES COST, $1,200. WORKING LIFE, 5,000 HOURS AT 4/5 ACRE PER HOUR, 4,000 ACRES

4,000 acres at $1,200, depreciation of horses, per acre	$0.30
Feed per horse, 40 cents (100 working days) per acre	0.40
Feed per horse, 10 cents a day (265 idle days) per acre	0.265
Two drivers, two gang ploughs, at $2 each per day, per acre	0.50
Cost of ploughing with horses; per acre	1.46

At present costs, an acre would run about 40 cents only two cents representing depreciation and repairs. But this does not take account of the time element. The ploughing is done in about one fourth the time, with only the physical energy used to steer the tractor. Ploughing has become a matter of motoring across a field.

Farming in the old style is rapidly fading into a picturesque memory. This does not mean that work is going to [be] remove[d] from the farm. Work cannot be removed from any life that is productive. But power-farming does mean this—drudgery is going to be removed from the farm. Power-farming is simply taking the burden from flesh and blood and putting it on steel. We are in the opening years of power-farming. The motor car wrought a revolution in modern farm life, not because it was a vehicle, but because it had power. Farming ought to be something more than a rural occupation. It ought to be the business of raising food. And when it does become a business the actual work of farming the average sort of farm can be done in twenty-four days a year. The other days can be given over to other kinds of business. Farming is too seasonal an occupation to engage all of a man's time.

As a food business, farming will justify itself as a business if it raises food in sufficient quantity and distributes it under such conditions as will enable every family to have enough food for its reasonable needs. There could not be a food trust if we were to raise such overwhelming quantities of all kinds of food as to make manipulation and exploitation impossible. The farmer who limits his planting plays into the hands of the speculators.

Wasteful Transportation in Agriculture

The following material challenges the merits of food distribution systems that may spend more on transportation than on actual production. Ford cites the example of the shipment of steers from Texas to Chicago stock-yards to be processed into beef for consumption in Boston.

There is an obvious extra cost to the shipment of foods that consist primarily of water. Most fruits and vegetables are in fact more than 80% water by weight. The "Henry Ford thought process," therefore, would ask whether they should be produced in greenhouses relatively close to where they are to be eaten despite the up-front capital cost of the greenhouses.

* * *

And then, perhaps, we shall witness a revival of the small flour-milling business. It was an evil day when the village flour mill disappeared. Cooperative farming will become so developed that we shall see associations of farmers with their own packing houses in which their own hogs will be turned into ham and bacon, and with their own flour mills in which their grain will be turned into commercial foodstuffs.

Why a steer raised in Texas should be brought to Chicago and then served in Boston is a question that cannot be answered as long as all the steers the city needs could be raised near Boston. The centraliza-tion of food manufacturing industries, entailing enormous costs for transportation and organization, is too wasteful[ly] long to continue in a developed community.

We shall have as great a development in farming during the next twenty years as we have had in manufacturing during the last twenty.

15

Why Charity?

This chapter challenges the fundamental concept of philanthropy, and it does so very credibly. Ford did not object to charity for immediate needs (such as food for people who would otherwise starve in the streets), but his goal was to make charity unnecessary. His industries eradicated most poverty from the communities in which they appeared, which again makes his principles proven methods as opposed to mere theories.

Ford's condemnation of traditional charity also applies to the failure of Lyndon Johnson's War on Poverty. Programs that address the immediate symptoms of poverty, but fail to address its underlying causes, foster a "state of expectant, child-like helplessness" among their beneficiaries. Ford reminds his readers that people with physical disabilities could fill many jobs in his factories, and perform them every bit as well as people with no physical impairments.

* * *

Why should there be any necessity for almsgiving in a civilized community? It is not the charitable mind to which I object. Heaven forbid that we should ever grow cold toward a fellow creature in need. Human sympathy is too fine for the cool, calculating attitude to take its place. One can name very few great advances that did not have human sympathy behind them. It is in order to help people that every notable service is undertaken.

The trouble is that we have been using this great, fine motive force for ends too small. If human sympathy prompts us to feed the hungry, why should it not give the larger desire—to make hunger in our midst impossible? If we have sympathy enough for people to help them out of their troubles, surely we ought to have sympathy enough to keep them out.

It is easy to give; it is harder to make giving unnecessary. To make the giving unnecessary we must look beyond the individual to the cause of his misery—not hesitating, of course, to relieve him in the meantime, but not stopping with mere temporary relief. The difficulty seems to be in getting to

look beyond to the causes. More people can be moved to help a poor fam-
ily than can be moved to give their minds toward the removal of poverty
altogether.

I have no patience with professional charity, or with any sort of commer-
cialized humanitarianism. The moment human helpfulness is systematized,
organized, commercialized, and professionalized, the heart of it is extin-
guished, and it becomes a cold and clammy thing.

Real human helpfulness is never card-catalogued or advertised. There are
more orphan children being cared for in the private homes of people who
love them than in the institutions. There are more old people being sheltered
by friends than you can find in the old people's homes. There is more aid by
loans from family to family than by the loan societies. That is, human society
on a humane basis looks out for itself. It is a grave question how far we ought
to countenance the commercialization of the natural instinct of charity.

Professional charity is not only cold but it hurts more than it helps. It
degrades the recipients and drugs their self-respect. Akin to it is sentimental
idealism. The idea went abroad not so many years ago that "service" was
something that we should expect to have done for us. Untold numbers of
people became the recipients of well-meant "social service." Whole sections
of our population were coddled into a state of expectant, child-like helpless-
ness. There grew up a regular profession of doing things for people, which
gave an outlet for a laudable desire for service, but which contributed noth-
ing whatever to the self-reliance of the people nor to the correction of the
conditions out of which the supposed need for such service grew.

Worse than this encouragement of childish wistfulness, instead of training
for self-reliance and self-sufficiency, was the creation of a feeling of resent-
ment which nearly always overtakes the objects of charity. People often com-
plain of the "ingratitude" of those whom they help. Nothing is more natural.
In the first place, precious little of our so-called charity is ever real charity,
offered out of a heart full of interest and sympathy. In the second place, no
person ever relishes being in a position where he is forced to take favors.

Such "social work" creates a strained relation—the recipient of bounty
feels that he has been belittled in the taking, and it is a question whether
the giver should not also feel that he has been belittled in the giving. Charity
never led to a settled state of affairs. The charitable system that does not aim
to make itself unnecessary is not performing service. It is simply making a job
for itself and is an added item to the record of non-production.

INDUSTRY CAN MAKE CHARITY UNNECESSARY

Ford's industries proved that there were places for a wide variety of workers, including those without traditional skills. Readers of Charles Dickens' *Oliver Twist* will be familiar with the workhouse (and prison) occupation of picking hemp or oakum. This involved picking apart discarded ropes for conversion into tarred fiber; an activity that was quite consistent with Ford's subsequent view that waste materials ought to be put to use. It, however, was so labor-intensive as to be economical only for prison or, in the previous century, workhouse labor. Ford's position on this was that prison labor should produce enough value to allow an inmate to support his family, and also that the economic world had enough work available that prison labor would not take jobs from free workers.

* * *

Charity becomes unnecessary as those who seem to be unable to earn livings are taken out of the non-productive class and put into the productive. In a previous chapter I have set out how experiments in our shops have demonstrated that in sufficiently subdivided industry there are places which can be filled by the maimed, the halt, and the blind. Scientific industry need not be a monster devouring all who come near it. When it is, then it is not fulfilling its place in life. In and out of industry there must be jobs that take the full strength of a powerful man; there are other jobs, and plenty of them, that require more skill than the artisans of the Middle Ages ever had. The minute subdivision of industry permits a strong man or a skilled man always to use his strength or skill. In the old hand industry, a skilled man spent a good part of his time at unskilled work. That was a waste. But since in those days every task required both skilled and unskilled labour to be performed by the one man, there was little room for either the man who was too stupid ever to be skilled or the man who did not have the opportunity to learn a trade.

No mechanic working with only his hands can earn more than a bare sustenance. He cannot have a surplus. It has been taken for granted that, coming into old age, a mechanic must be supported by his children or, if he has no children, that he will be a public charge. All of that is quite unnecessary. The subdivision of industry opens places that can be filled by practically any one. There are more places in subdivision industry that can be filled by blind men than there are blind men. There are more places that can be filled by cripples than there are cripples. And in each of these places the man who short-sightedly might be considered as an object of charity can earn just as adequate a living as the keenest and most able-bodied. It is waste to put an able-bodied man in a job that might be just as well cared for by a cripple. It is a frightful waste to put the blind at weaving baskets. It is waste to have convicts breaking stone or picking hemp or doing any sort of petty, useless task.

A well-conducted jail should not only be self-supporting, but a man in jail ought to be able to support his family or, if he has no family, he should be able to accumulate a sum of money sufficient to put him on his feet when he gets out of jail. I am not advocating convict labour or the farming out of men practically as slaves. Such a plan is too detestable for words. We have greatly overdone the prison business, anyway; we begin at the wrong end. But as long as we have prisons they can be fitted into, the general scheme of production so neatly that a prison may become a productive unit working for the relief of the public and the benefit of the prisoners. I know that there are laws—foolish laws passed by unthinking men—that restrict the industrial activities of prisons. Those laws were passed mostly at the behest of what is called Labour. They are not for the benefit of the workingman. Increasing the charges upon a community does not benefit any one in the community. If the idea of service be kept in mind, then there is always in every community more work to do than there are men who can do it.

Industry Removes the Need for Charity

Remember that *My Life and Work* is not a theory or idea, but a proven set of synergistic methods. Ford did not merely say that industry ought to make charity unnecessary; he proved that a hospital and a trade school could support themselves while they rendered world-class service.

* * *

Industry organized for service removes the need for philanthropy. Philanthropy, no matter how noble its motive, does not make for self-reliance. We must have self-reliance. A community is the better for being discontented, for being dissatisfied with what it has. I do not mean the petty, daily, nagging, gnawing sort of discontent, but a broad, courageous sort of discontent which believes that everything which is done can and ought to be eventually done better. Industry organized for service—and the workingman as well as the leader must serve—can pay wages sufficiently large to permit every family to be both self-reliant and self-supporting. A philanthropy that spends its time and money in helping the world to do more for itself is far better than the sort which merely gives and thus encourages idleness. Philanthropy, like everything else, ought to be productive, and I believe that it can be. I have personally been experimenting with a trade school and a hospital to discover if such institutions, which are commonly regarded as benevolent, cannot be made to stand on their own feet. I have found that they can be.

THE HENRY FORD TRADE SCHOOL

The Henry Ford Trade School (Highland Park, Michigan) offered an outstanding model that could easily apply to modern secondary schools. It was not merely a vocational school, as one might conclude from the phrase "trade school," but a college preparatory school. Its graduates could command wages higher than those of many college graduates or, if they chose, go on to college themselves. Additional information is available from the Henry Ford Trade School Alumni Association at http://www.hftsaa.org.

The production of useful articles was among the key aspects of the Ford trade school. This not only made the school self-supporting, it also applied the motivation concept of task identity. The students' realization that they were actually making parts for Ford cars, as opposed to producing items that would simply be thrown away, doubtlessly helped to hold their attention.

* * *

I am not in sympathy with the trade school as it is commonly organized—the boys get only a smattering of knowledge and they do not learn how to use that knowledge. The trade school should not be a cross between a technical college and a school; it should be a means of teaching boys to be productive. If they are put at useless tasks—at making articles and then throwing them away— they cannot have the interest or acquire the knowledge which is their right. And during the period of schooling the boy is not productive; the schools— unless by charity—make no provision for the support of the boy. Many boys need support; they must work at the first thing which comes to hand. They have no chance to pick and choose.

When the boy thus enters life untrained, he but adds to the already great scarcity of competent labour. Modern industry requires a degree of ability and skill which neither early quitting of school nor long continuance at school provides. It is true that, in order to retain the interest of the boy and train him in handicraft, manual training departments have been introduced in the more progressive school systems, but even these are confessedly make- shifts because they only cater to, without satisfying, the normal boy's creative instincts.

To meet this condition—to fulfill the boy's educational possibilities and at the same time begin his industrial training along constructive lines—the Henry Ford Trade School was incorporated in 1916. We do not use the word philanthropy in connection with this effort. It grew out of a desire to aid the boy whose circumstances compelled him to leave school early. This desire to aid fitted in conveniently with the necessity of providing trained tool-makers in the shops. From the beginning we have held to three cardinal principles: first, that the boy was to be kept a boy and not changed into a premature working-man; second, that the academic training was to go hand in hand with the industrial instruction; third, that the boy was to be given a sense of pride and responsibility in his work by being trained on articles which were to be used. He works on objects of recognized industrial worth. The school is incorporated as a private school and is open to boys between the ages of twelve and eighteen. It is organized on the basis of scholarships and each boy is awarded an annual cash scholarship of four hundred dollars at his entrance. This is gradually increased to a maximum of six hundred dollars if his record is satisfactory.

A record of the class and shop work is kept and also of the industry the boy displays in each. It is the marks in industry which are used in making subsequent adjustments of his scholarship. In addition to his scholarship each boy is given a small amount each month which must be deposited in his savings account. This thrift fund must be left in the bank as long as the boy remains in the school unless he is given permission by the authorities to use it for an emergency.

One by one the problems of managing the school are being solved and better ways of accomplishing its objects are being discovered. At the beginning it was the custom to give the boy one third of the day in class work and two thirds in shop work. This daily adjustment was found to be a hindrance to progress, and now the boy takes his training in blocks of weeks—one week in the class and two weeks in the shop. Classes are continuous, the various groups taking their weeks in turn.

The best instructors obtainable are on the staff, and the text-book is the Ford plant. It offers more resources for practical education than most universities. The arithmetic lessons come in concrete shop problems. No longer is the boy's mind tortured with the mysterious A who can row four miles while B is rowing two. The actual processes and actual conditions are exhibited to him—he is taught to observe. Cities are no longer black specks on maps and continents are not just pages of a book. The shop shipments to Singapore, the shop receipts of material from Africa and South America are shown to him, and the world becomes an inhabited planet instead of a coloured globe on the teacher's desk. In physics and chemistry the industrial plant provides a laboratory in which theory becomes practice and the lesson becomes actual experience. Suppose the action of a pump is being taught. The teacher explains the parts and their functions, answers questions, and then they all troop away to the engine rooms to see a great pump. The school has a regular factory workshop with the finest equipment. The boys work up from one machine to the next. They work solely on parts or articles needed by the company, but our needs are so vast that this list comprehends nearly everything. The inspected work is purchased by the Ford Motor Company, and, of course, the work that does not pass inspection is a loss to the school.

The boys who have progressed furthest do fine micrometer work, and they do every operation with a clear understanding of the purposes and principles involved. They repair their own machines; they learn how to take care of themselves around machinery; they study pattern-making and in clean, well-lighted rooms with their instructors they lay the foundation for successful careers.

When they graduate, places are always open for them in the shops at good wages. The social and moral well-being of the boys is given an unobtrusive care. The supervision is not of authority but of friendly interest. The home conditions of every boy are pretty well known, and his tendencies are observed. And no attempt is made to coddle him. No attempt is made to render him namby-pamby. One day when two boys came to the point of a fight, they were not lectured on the wickedness of fighting. They were counseled to make up their differences in a better way, but when, boy-like, they preferred the more primitive mode of settlement, they were given gloves and made to fight it out in a corner of the shop. The only prohibition laid upon them was that they were to finish it there, and not to be caught fighting outside the shop. The result was a short encounter and—friendship.

They are handled as boys; their better boyish instincts are encouraged; and when one sees them in the shops and classes one cannot easily miss the light of dawning mastery in their eyes. They have a sense of "belonging." They feel they are doing something worth while. They learn readily and eagerly because they are learning the things which every active boy wants to learn and about which he is constantly asking questions that none of his home-folks can answer.

Beginning with six boys the school now has two hundred and is possessed of so practical a system that it may expand to seven hundred. It began with a deficit, but as it is one of my basic ideas that anything worth while in itself can be made self-sustaining, it has so developed its processes that it is now paying its way.

We have been able to let the boy have his boyhood. These boys learn to be workmen but they do not forget how to be boys. That is of the first importance. They earn from 19 to 35 cents an hour—which is more than they could earn as boys in the sort of job open to a youngster. They can better help support their families by staying in school than by going out to work. When they are through, they have a good general education, the beginning of a technical education, and they are so skilled as workmen that they can earn wages which will give them the liberty to continue their education if they like. If they do not want more education, they have at least the skill to command high wages anywhere. They do not have to go into our factories; most of them do because they do not know where better jobs are to be had—we want all our jobs to be good for the men who take them. But there is no string tied to the boys. They have earned their own way and are under obligations to no one. There is no charity. The place pays for itself.

THE HENRY AND CLARA FORD HOSPITAL

The following material has profound implications for twenty-first century healthcare and its skyrocketing costs. Godfrey (2000) estimates that the cost of poor quality in healthcare wastes 30 to 50 cents of every healthcare dollar, while Panchak (2003) cites an estimate of up to 60% waste.

Ford set up a hospital along industrial lines, including a design that eliminated as much as possible the need for nurses to walk: a nonvalue-adding activity for which they could not be paid. Doctors and nurses worked on a salary basis, and each patient was evaluated for overall health by a multidisciplinary team as opposed to receiving treatment for a specific ailment. The result was that the hospital delivered very high quality of care, and at a very low cost. The daily charge was $4.50 (less than the daily wage at the Ford plants), and a major operation cost $125 in the money of the early 1920s.

It is also noteworthy that the hospital had private rooms, and only private rooms. This doubtlessly helped prevent the spread of the hospital-acquired infections that claim thousands of lives even today. The semiprivate room, although nominally cheaper, therefore, is a false economy.

Anand (2009) reports meanwhile how an Indian surgeon, Dr. Devi Shetty, has revived Ford's healthcare model very successfully. His Narayana Hrudayalaya Hospital performs open heart surgery for $2,000, in comparison to $20,000 to $100,000 for similar procedures in American hospitals. The article reports a 30-day mortality rate of 1.4% for coronary artery bypass graft surgery versus the United States average of 1.9%. The hospital's keys to success include economy of scale, extensive experience among the doctors, and a focus on continuous cost reduction.

Shetty, like Ford, speaks explicitly about the need to pay attention to every aspect of cost: "In healthcare, you can't do one big thing and reduce the price. We have to do 1,000 small things." The article adds that he plans to open a hospital in the Cayman Islands for medical tourism purposes, which suggests that American hospitals need to pay attention to his methods and copy them if they do not wish to be left behind. Ford and Crowther (1926, p. 193) also identified the role of diet, a role that the United States only now seems to be rediscovering, in overall health.

It is also particularly telling that Ford was more than 40 years ahead of the Surgeon General in declaring that tobacco was a major cause of preventable illnesses. *Ford News* (August 1, 1923, pp. 2–3) carried an article by Luther Burbank that said, among other things, that tobacco caused President Grant's throat cancer. Burbank also depicted nicotine as toxic to the heart, and added that money squandered on tobacco could instead pay for a house or a farm. Only in 1964 did the Surgeon General's office finally publish similar conclusions, and tobacco use remains a major problem almost 60 years later.

* * *

The Ford Hospital is being worked out on somewhat similar lines, but because of the interruption of the war—when it was given to the Government and became General Hospital No. 36, housing some fifteen hundred patients—the work has not yet advanced to the point of absolutely definite results. I did not deliberately set out to build this hospital. It began in 1914 as the Detroit General Hospital and was designed to be erected by popular subscription. With others, I made a subscription, and the building began. Long before the first buildings were done, the funds became exhausted and I was asked to make another subscription. I refused because I thought that the managers should have known how much the building was going to cost before they started. And that sort of a beginning did not give great confidence as to how the place would be managed after it was finished. However, I did offer to take the whole hospital, paying back all the subscriptions that had been made. This was accomplished, and we were going forward with the work when, on August 1, 1918, the whole institution was turned over to the Government. It was returned to us in October, 1919, and on the tenth day of November of the same year the first private patient was admitted.

The hospital is on West Grand Boulevard in Detroit and the plot embraces twenty acres, so that there will be ample room for expansion. It is our thought to extend the facilities as they justify themselves. The original design of the hospital has been quite abandoned and we have endeavoured to work out a new kind of hospital, both in design and management. There are plenty of hospitals for the rich. There are plenty of hospitals for the poor. There are no hospitals for those who can afford to pay only a moderate amount and yet desire to pay without a feeling that they are recipients of charity. It has been taken for granted that a hospital cannot both serve and be self-supporting— that it has to be either an institution kept going by private contributions or pass into the class of private sanitariums managed for profit. This hospital is designed to be self-supporting—to give a maximum of service at a minimum of cost and without the slightest colouring of charity.

In the new buildings that we have erected there are no wards. All of the rooms are private and each one is provided with a bath. The rooms—which are in groups of twenty-four—are all identical in size, in fittings, and in furnishings. There is no choice of rooms. It is planned that there shall be no choice of anything within the hospital. Every patient is on an equal footing with every other patient.

It is not at all certain whether hospitals as they are now managed exist for patients or for doctors. I am not unmindful of the large amount of time which a capable physician or surgeon gives to charity, but also I am not convinced that the fees of surgeons should be regulated according to the wealth of the patient, and I am entirely convinced that what is known as "professional etiquette" is a curse to mankind and to the development of medicine. Diagnosis is not very much developed. I should not care to be among the proprietors of a hospital in which every step had not been taken to insure [sic] that the patients were being treated for what actually was the matter with them, instead of for something that one doctor had decided they had. Professional etiquette makes it very difficult for a wrong diagnosis to be corrected. The consulting physician, unless he be a man of great tact, will not change a diagnosis or a treatment unless the physician who has called him in is in thorough agreement, and then if a change be made, it is usually without the knowledge of the patient. There seems to be a notion that a patient, and especially when in a hospital, becomes the property of the doctor. A conscientious practitioner does not exploit the patient. A less conscientious one does. Many physicians seem to regard the sustaining of their own diagnoses as of as great [a] moment as the recovery of the patient.

It has been an aim of our hospital to cut away from all of these practices and to put the interest of the patient first. Therefore, it is what is known as a "closed" hospital. All of the physicians and all of the nurses are employed by the year and they can have no practice outside of the hospital. Including the interns, twenty-one physicians and surgeons are on the staff. These men have been selected with great care and they are paid salaries that amount to at least as much as they would ordinarily earn in successful private practice. They have, none of them, any financial interest whatsoever in any patient, and a patient may not be treated by a doctor from the outside. We gladly acknowledge the place and the use of the family physician. We do not seek to supplant him. We take the case where he leaves off, and return the patient as quickly as possible. Our system makes it undesirable for us to keep patients longer than necessary—we do not need that kind of business. And we will share with the family physician our knowledge of the case, but while the patient is in the hospital we assume full responsibility. It is "closed" to out-side physicians' practice, though it is not closed to our cooperation with any family physician who desires it.

The admission of a patient is interesting. The incoming patient is first examined by the senior physician and then is routed for examination through three, four, or whatever number of doctors seems necessary. This routing takes place regardless of what the patient came to the hospital for, because, as we are gradually learning, it is the complete health rather than a single ailment which is important. Each of the doctors makes a complete examina-tion, and each sends in his written findings to the head physician without any opportunity whatsoever to consult with any of the other examining phy-sicians. At least three, and sometimes six or seven, absolutely complete and absolutely independent diagnoses are thus in the hands of the head of the hospital. They constitute a complete record of the case. These precautions are taken in order to insure [sic], within the limits of present-day knowledge, a correct diagnosis.

At the present time, there are about six hundred beds available. Every patient pays according to a fixed schedule that includes the hospital room, board, medical and surgical attendance, and nursing. There are no extras. There are no private nurses. If a case requires more attention than the nurses assigned to the wing can give, then another nurse is put on, but without any additional expense to the patient. This, however, is rarely nec-essary because the patients are grouped according to the amount of nursing that they will need. There may be one nurse for two patients, or one nurse for five patients, as the type of cases may require. No one nurse ever has more than seven patients to care for, and because of the arrangements it is easily possible for a nurse to care for seven patients who are not desperately ill. In the ordinary hospital the nurses must make many useless steps. More of their time is spent in walking than in caring for the patient. This hospi-tal is designed to save steps. Each floor is complete in itself, and just as in the factories we have tried to eliminate the necessity for waste motion, so *have we also tried to eliminate waste motion in the hospital. The charge to patients for a room, nursing, and medical attendance is $4.50 a day. This will be lowered as the size of the hospital increases. The charge for a major operation is $125. The charge for minor operations is according to a fixed scale. All of the charges are tentative. The hospital has a cost system just like a factory. The charges will be regulated to make ends just meet.*

There seems to be no good reason why the experiment should not be successful. Its success is purely a matter of management and mathematics. The same kind of management which permits a factory to give the fullest service will permit a hospital to give the fullest service, and at a price so low as to be within the reach of everyone. The only difference between hospital and factory accounting is that I do not expect the hospital to return a profit; we do expect it to cover depreciation. The investment in this hospital to date is about $9,000,000.

NO FREE LUNCH

This section is merely a restatement of the economic aspect of Ford's universal code. The concept of no such thing as a free lunch seems like common sense, but it is far too uncommon even in the twenty-first century. The United States cannot maintain an affluent and prosperous society by exporting jobs to China, or by trading in carbon credits as recommended by Senator Kirsten Gillibrand (2009). The United States can no more deliver high quality healthcare to all its citizens through government mandates than Shakespeare's Jack Cade could decree that a penny was to buy seven half-penny loaves of bread.

The idea that governments can mandate free lunches, or that unions can negotiate them, exemplifies what Ford calls "the unreasonable demands of irresponsible labour." To this Ford (1922, p. 177) adds: "If everybody does less work and everybody gets more of the product of work, how long can it last?"

This is not to say that a penny could not have conceivably bought seven half-penny loaves of bread during the fifteenth century. A contemporary Henry Ford, however, would have had to get the production and distribution cost below an eighth of a penny so the baker could earn a reasonable profit. Jack Cade could not do this by decree, and neither could the King, whether Lancastrian or Yorkist. If Henry VI or Edward IV had issued such a decree, there would have been no bread at all because farmers and millers would not have sold their product at a loss. If Medicare emulates Jack Cade by "controlling" healthcare costs through cuts to physician reimbursements, senior citizens will be unable to find doctors who are willing to treat them. The government-run healthcare systems in the United Kingdom and Canada sometimes deliver long waiting times for elective and even mandatory medical procedures.

* * *

If we can get away from charity, the funds that now go into charitable enterprises can be turned to furthering production—to making goods cheaply and in great plenty. And then we shall not only be removing the burden of taxes from the community and freeing men but also we can be adding to the general wealth. We leave for private interest too many things we ought to do for ourselves as a collective interest. We need more constructive thinking in public service. We need a kind of "universal training" in economic facts. The over-reaching ambitions of speculative capital, as well as the unreasonable demands of irresponsible labour, are due to ignorance of the economic basis of life. Nobody can get more out of life than life can produce—yet nearly everybody thinks he can. Speculative capital wants more; labour wants more; the source of raw material wants more; and the purchasing public wants more. A family knows that it cannot live beyond its income; even the children know that. But the public never seems to learn that it cannot live beyond its income—have more than it produces.

THE ROLE OF SELF-RELIANCE

Modern management practitioners use the term *internal locus of control* for the characteristic that Ford now describes. The value of persistence cannot be overemphasized. Ford himself did not succeed in his original car business, and he had to try more than once before it finally worked.

* * *

In clearing out the need for charity we must keep in mind not only the economic facts of existence, but also that lack of knowledge of these facts encourages fear. Banish fear and we can have self-reliance. Charity is not present where self-reliance dwells.

Fear is the offspring of a reliance placed on something outside—on a fore-man's good-will, perhaps, on a shop's prosperity, on a market's steadiness. That is just another way of saying that fear is the portion of the man who acknowledges his career to be in the keeping of earthly circumstances. Fear is the result of the body assuming ascendancy over the soul.

The habit of failure is purely mental and is the mother of fear. This habit gets itself fixed on men because they lack vision. They start out to do some-thing that reaches from A to Z. At A they fail, at B they stumble, and at C they meet with what seems to be an insuperable difficulty. They then cry "Beaten" and throw the whole task down. They have not even given them-selves a chance really to fail; they have not given their vision a chance to be proved or disproved. They have simply let themselves be beaten by the natu-ral difficulties that attend every kind of effort.

More men are beaten than fail. It is not wisdom they need or money, or brilliance, or "pull," but just plain gristle and bone. This rude, simple, primi-tive power which we call "stick-to-it-iveness" is the uncrowned king of the world of endeavour. People are utterly wrong in their slant upon things. They see the successes that men have made and somehow they appear to be easy. But that is a world away from the facts. It is failure that is easy. Success is always hard. A man can fail in ease; he can succeed only by paying out all that he has and is. It is this which makes success so pitiable a thing if it be in lines that are not useful and uplifting.

If a man is in constant fear of the industrial situation he ought to change his life so as not to be dependent upon it. There is always the land, and fewer people are on the land now than ever before. If a man lives in fear of an employer's favor changing toward him, he ought to extricate himself from dependence on any employer. He can become his own boss. It may be that he will be a poorer boss than the one he leaves, and that his returns will be much less, but at least he will have rid himself of the shadow of his pet fear, and that is worth a great deal in money and position. Better still is for the man to come through himself and exceed himself by getting rid of his fears in the midst of the circumstances where his daily lot is cast. Become a freeman in the place where you first surrendered your freedom. Win your battle where you lost it. And you will come to see that, although there was much outside of you that was not right, there was more inside of you that was not right. Thus you will learn that the wrong inside of you spoils even the right that is outside of you.

A man is still the superior being of the earth. Whatever happens, he is still a man. Business may slacken tomorrow—he is still a man. He goes through the changes of circumstances, as he goes through the variations of tempera-ture—still a man. If he can only get this thought reborn in him, it opens new wells and mines in his own being. There is no security outside of himself.

There is no wealth outside of himself. The elimination of fear is the bringing in of security and supply.

Let every American become steeled against coddling. Americans ought to resent coddling. It is a drug. Stand up and stand out; let weaklings take charity.

16

The Railroads

"Making a Railroad Pay" (Ford and Crowther, 1926, Chapter 17) goes into greater detail on how Ford turned the decrepit Detroit, Toledo, & Ironton (DTI) Railroad into a highly profitable operation. This reference (p. 199) cites the Ford principles of management:

(1) The overriding goal is to get the job done. Job definitions, red tape, and departmental boundaries are irrelevant to this objective.
(2) Pay high wages, and limit the work week to 48 hours.
(3) Keep all equipment in good condition, which includes preventive maintenance and the utmost cleanliness. This principle contains the major elements of 5S-CANDO (Clearing up, Arranging, Neatness, Discipline, Ongoing Improvement. 5S stands for the corresponding Japanese words Seiri, Seitori, Seiso, Shitsuke, and Seiketsu.) Ford and Crowther (1926, p. 201) add explicitly that there were standard racks for tools and materials, which is another aspect of 5S: a place for everything, and everything in its place.

Ford adds to these principles the rule of the situation: Everybody takes direction from the needs of the job as opposed to a superior. There were also no restrictive job classifications that prevented anybody from doing work that he or she could do.

Some of this chapter's lessons could easily be applicable to passenger rail service in the United States. The airlines' history of unreliable service has, during the past 15 years, included stranding passengers on runways in unsanitary conditions. Airlines are adding fees for luggage, whose carriage was once part of the ticket price. This is a perfect opportunity for safer, cheaper, and more reliable trains to compete with them.

* * *

Nothing in this country furnishes a better example of how a business may be turned from its function of service than do the railroads. We have a railroad problem, and much learned thought and discussion have been devoted to the solution of that problem. Everyone is dissatisfied with the railways. The public is dissatisfied because both the passenger and freight rates are too high. The railroad employees are dissatisfied because they say their wages are too low and their hours too long. The owners of the railways are dissatisfied because it is claimed that no adequate return is realized upon the money invested. All of the contacts of a properly managed undertaking ought to be satisfactory. If the public, the employees, and the owners do not find themselves better off because of the undertaking, then there must be something very wrong indeed with the manner in which the undertaking is carried through.

I am entirely without any disposition to pose as a railroad authority. There may be railroad authorities, but if the service as rendered by the American railroad to-day is the result of accumulated railway knowledge, then I cannot say that my respect for the usefulness of that knowledge is at all profound. I have not the slightest doubt in the world that the active managers of the railways, the men who really do the work, are entirely capable of conducting the railways of the country to the satisfaction of every one, and I have equally no doubt that these active managers have, by force of a chain of circumstances, all but ceased to manage. And right there is the source of most of the trouble. The men who know railroading have not been allowed to manage railroads.

In a previous chapter on finance were set forth the dangers attendant upon the indiscriminate borrowing of money. It is inevitable that any one who can borrow freely to cover errors of management will borrow rather than correct the errors. Our railway managers have been practically forced to borrow, for since the very inception of the railways they have not been free agents. The guiding hand of the railway has been, not the railroad man, but the banker. When railroad credit was high, more money was to be made out of floating bond issues and speculating in the securities than out of service to the public. A very small fraction of the money earned by the railways has gone back into the rehabilitation of the properties. When by skilled management the net revenue became large enough to pay a considerable dividend upon the stock, then that dividend was used first by the speculators on the inside and controlling the railroad fiscal policy to boom the stock and unload their holdings, and then to float a bond issue on the strength of the credit gained through the earnings. When the earnings dropped or were artificially depressed, then the speculators bought back the stock and in the course of time staged another advance and unloading. There is scarcely a railroad in the United States that has not been through one or more receiverships, due to the fact that the financial interests piled on load after load of securities until the structures grew *top heavy and fell over. Then they got in on the receiverships, made money at the expense of gullible security holders, and started the same old pyramiding game all over again.*

The natural ally of the banker is the lawyer. Such games as have been played on the railroads have needed expert legal advice. Lawyers, like bankers, know absolutely nothing about business. They imagine that a business is properly conducted if it keeps within the law or if the law can be altered or interpreted to suit the purpose in hand. They live on rules. The bankers took finance out of the hands of the managers. They put in lawyers to see that the railroads violated the law only in legal fashion, and thus grew up immense legal departments. Instead of operating under the rules of common sense and according to circumstances, every railroad had to operate on the advice of counsel. Rules spread through every part of the organization. Then came the avalanche of state and federal regulations, until to-day we find the railways hog-tied in a mass of rules and regulations. With the lawyers and the financiers on the inside and various state commissions on the outside, the railway manager has little chance. That is the trouble with the railways. Business cannot be conducted by law.

We have had the opportunity of demonstrating to ourselves what a freedom from the banker-legal mortmain means, in our experience with the Detroit, Toledo & Ironton Railway. We bought the railway because its right of way interfered with some of our improvements on the River Rouge. We did not buy it as an investment, or as an adjunct to our industries, or because of its strategic position. The extraordinarily good situation of the railway seems to have become universally apparent only since we bought it. That, however, is beside the point. We bought the railway because it interfered with our plans. Then we had to do something with it. The only thing to do was to run it as a productive enterprise, applying to it exactly the same principles as are applied in every department of our industries. We have as yet made no special efforts of any kind and the railway has not been set up as a demonstration of how every railway should be run. It is true that applying the rule of maximum service at minimum cost has caused the income of the road to exceed the outgo—which, for that road, represents a most unusual condition. It has been represented that the changes we have made—and remember they have been made simply as part of the day's work—are peculiarly revolutionary and quite without application to railway management in general. Personally, it would seem to me that our little line does not differ much from the big lines. In our own work we have always found that, if our principles were right, the area over which they were applied did not matter. The principles that we use in the big Highland Park plant seem to work equally well in every plant that we establish. It has never made any difference with us whether we multiplied what we were doing by five or five hundred. Size is only a matter of the multiplication table, anyway.

The Detroit, Toledo & Ironton Railway was organized some twenty-odd years ago and has been reorganized every few years since then. The last reorganization was in 1914. The war and the federal control of the railways interrupted the cycle of reorganization. The road owns 343 miles of track, has 52 miles of branches, and 45 miles of trackage rights over other roads. It goes from Detroit almost due south to Ironton on the Ohio River, thus tapping the West Virginia coal deposits. It crosses most of the large trunk lines and it is a road which, from a general business standpoint, ought to pay. It has paid. It seems to have paid the bankers. In 1913 the net capitalization per mile of road was $105,000. In the next receivership this was cut down to $47,000 per mile. I do not know how much money in all has been raised on the strength of the road. I do know that in the reorganization of 1914 the bondholders were assessed and forced to turn into the treasury nearly five million dollars— which is the amount that we paid for the entire road. We paid sixty cents on the dollar for the outstanding mortgage bonds, although the ruling price just before the time of purchase was between thirty and forty cents on the dollar. We paid a dollar a share for the common stock and five dollars a share for the preferred stock—which seemed to be a fair price considering that no interest had ever been paid upon the bonds and a dividend on the stock was a most remote possibility. The rolling stock of the road consisted of about seventy locomotives, twenty-seven passenger cars, and around twenty-eight hundred freight cars. All of the rolling stock was in extremely bad condition and a good part of it would not run at all. All of the buildings were dirty, unpainted, and generally run down. The roadbed was something more than a streak of rust and something less than a railway. The repair shops were over-manned and under-machined. Practically everything connected with operation was conducted with a maximum of waste. There was, however, an exceedingly ample executive and administration department, and of course a legal department. The legal department alone cost in one month nearly $18,000.

HOW FORD TURNED DT&I AROUND

Application of Ford's basic principle that the objective is simply to get the job done without regard to bureaucracy, titles, and red tape changed DT&I's fortunes drastically. Ford's statement "… a message has to go up through a certain line of authority and no man is expected to do anything without explicit orders from his superior," reinforces his commentary about bureaucracies and departmental barriers in Chapter 6.

* * *

We took over the road in March, 1921. We began to apply industrial principles. There had been an executive office in Detroit. We closed that up and put the administration into the charge of one man and gave him half of the flat-topped desk out in the freight office. The legal department went with the executive offices. There is no reason for so much litigation in connection with railroading. Our people quickly settled all the mass of outstanding claims, some of which had been hanging on for years. As new claims arise, they are settled at once and on the facts, so that the legal expense seldom exceeds $200 a month. All of the unnecessary accounting and red tape were thrown out and the payroll of the road was reduced from 2,700 to 1,650 men.

Following our general policy, all titles and offices other than those required by law were abolished. The ordinary railway organization is rigid; a message has to go up through a certain line of authority and no man is expected to do anything without explicit orders from his superior. One morning I went out to the road very early and found a wrecking train with steam up, a crew aboard and all ready to start. It had been "awaiting orders" for half an hour. We went down and cleared the wreck before the orders came through; that was before the idea of personal responsibility had soaked in. It was a little hard to break the "orders" habit; the men at first were afraid to take responsibility. But as we went on, they seemed to like the plan more and more and now no man limits his duties. A man is paid for a day's work of eight hours and he is expected to work during those eight hours. If he is an engineer and finishes a run in four hours then he works at whatever else may be in demand for the next four hours. If a man works more than eight hours he is not paid for overtime—he deducts his overtime from the next working day or saves it up and gets a whole day off with pay. Our eight-hour day is a day of eight hours and not a basis for computing pay.

The minimum wage is six dollars a day. There are no extra men. We have cut down in the offices, in the shops, and on the roads. In one shop 20 men are now doing more work than 59 did before. Not long ago one of our track gangs, consisting of a foreman and 15 men, was working beside a parallel road on which was a gang of 40 men doing exactly the same sort of track repairing and ballasting. In five days our gang did two telegraph poles more than the competing gang!

The road is being rehabilitated; nearly the whole track has been reballasted and many miles of new rails have been laid. The locomotives and rolling stock are being overhauled in our own shops and at a very slight expense. We found that the supplies bought previously were of poor quality or unfitted for the use; we are saving money on supplies by buying better qualities and seeing that nothing is wasted. The men seem entirely willing to cooperate in saving. They do not discard that which might be used. We ask a man, "What can you get out of an engine?" and he answers with an economy record. And we are not pouring in great amounts of money. Everything is being done out of earnings. That is our policy.

Lesson in Waste Recognition

Recall that Ford (1922, p. 329) defined exactly three kinds of waste: waste of time, waste of materials, and waste of energy. Waste of time includes that of the time of people, time of the product or service (as in cycle or lead time), and time of assets for which value-adding work is available.

The following statements that: "A car on a siding is … a great big question mark" and "a delay is a criticism of our work and is something at once to be investigated," underscores the Ford business culture that taught the entire workforce to recognize waste on sight. Most people would take the idle rail car for granted, and then simply ignore it. A Ford worker would on the other hand ask why the car was not in use: "Someone has to know why it is there."

The same thought process applies, for example, to a truck caught in rush-hour traffic. Most observers probably take this for granted, and so does the driver if he is being paid by the hour. The truth, of course, is that the truck is burning fuel while going nowhere, a cargo that may easily be worth five figures is piling up cycle time, and the driver is meanwhile being paid to sit in traffic. The trucking firm that learns to think like Henry Ford, and there is no reason why the thought process cannot originate with a driver who recognizes the enormous wastefulness of this situation, will act on it quickly. Solutions may include driving the route in off hours (even if drivers get a shift premium) and use of navigation devices to go around traffic jams.

Ford's statement: "… a delay is a criticism of our work and is something at once to be investigated," also applies directly to airlines that have, and on more than one occasion, stranded passengers on runways for eight or more hours. The Ford business culture would have challenged a delay of even 15 minutes; the attitude was that transportation ought to be on schedule. The recurrence of this kind of problem in the airline industry exemplifies a lack of investigation and closed-loop corrective action. This should encourage people to look for alternative forms of transportation, and it should encourage railroads and bus lines to develop them.

* * *

The trains must go through and on time. The time of freight movements has been cut down about two thirds. A car on a siding is not just a car on a siding. It is a great big question mark. Someone has to know why it is there. It used to take 8 or 9 days to get freight through to Philadelphia or New York; now it takes three and a half days. The organization is serving.

All sorts of explanations are put forward, of why a deficit was turned into a surplus. I am told that it is all due to diverting the freight of the Ford industries. If we had diverted all of our business to this road, that would not explain why we manage at so much lower an operating cost than before. We are routing as much as we can of our own business over the road, but only because we there get the best service. For years past we had been trying to send freight over this road because it was conveniently located, but we had never been able to use it to any extent because of the delayed deliveries. We could not count on a shipment to within five or six weeks; that tied up too much money and also broke into our production schedule. There was no reason why the road should not have had a schedule; but it did not. The delays became legal matters to be taken up in due legal course; that is not the way of business. We think that a delay is a criticism of our work and is something at once to be investigated. That is business.

The railroads in general have broken down, and if the former conduct of the Detroit, Toledo & Ironton is any criterion of management in general there is no reason in the world why they should not have broken down. Too many railroads are run, not from the offices of practical men, but from banking offices, and the principles of procedure, the whole outlook, are financial—not transportational, but financial. There has been a breakdown simply because more attention has been paid to railroads as factors in the stock market than as servants of the people. Outworn ideas have been retained, development has been practically stopped, and railroad men with vision have not been set free to grow.

Will a billion dollars solve that sort of trouble? No, a billion dollars will only make the difficulty one billion dollars worse. The purpose of the billion is simply to continue the present methods of railroad management, and it is because of the present methods that we have any railroad difficulties at all.

Waste Was Built in by Design

The mistaken and foolish things we did years ago are just overtaking us. At the beginning of railway transportation in the United States, the people had to be taught its use, just as they had to be taught the use of the telephone. Also, the new railroads had to make business in order to keep themselves solvent. And because railway financing began in one of the rottenest periods of our business history, a number of practices were established as precedents which have influenced railway work ever since. One of the first things the railways did was to throttle all other methods of transportation. There was the beginning of a splendid canal system in this country and a great move-ment for canalization was at its height. The railroad companies bought out the canal companies and let the canals fill up and choke with weeds and refuse. All over the Eastern and in parts of the Middle Western states are the remains of this network of internal waterways. They are being restored now as rapidly as possible; they are being linked together; various commissions, public and private, have seen the vision of a complete system of waterways serving all parts of the country, and thanks to their efforts, persistence, and faith, progress is being made.

But there was another. This was the system of making the haul as long as possible. Any one who is familiar with the exposures which resulted in the formation of the Interstate Commerce Commission knows what is meant by this. There was a period when rail transport was not regarded as the servant of the traveling, manufacturing, and commercial publics. Business was treated as if it existed for the benefit of the railways. During this period of folly, it was not good railroading to get goods from their shipping point to their destination by the most direct line possible, but to keep them on the road as long as possible, send them around the longest way, give as many connecting lines as possible a piece of the profit, and let the public stand the resulting loss of time and money. That was once counted good railroading. It has not entirely passed out of practice to-day.

Avoid Wasteful Transportation

Transportation is essentially a necessary evil that adds no value to the product. Ford cites grain as a product that should be processed into flour prior to shipment to eliminate wasteful transportation. It also was his practice to ship dry wood instead of green (wet) wood from his lumber operations because the water in the wood carried weight but no value. Supply chain managers should pay particular attention to Ford's state-ment, "One angle of the transportation problem to which too few men are paying attention is this useless hauling of material."

Ford and Crowther (1930, p. 273) add that it would be ideal, although it is not practical, to process iron ore at its mine to avoid transportation of what would eventually become slag.

* * *

One of the great changes in our economic life to which this railroad policy contributed was the centralization of certain activities, not because centralization was necessary, nor because it contributed to the well-being of the people, but because, among other things, it made double business for the railroads. Take two staples—meat and grain. If you look at the maps which the packing houses put out, and see where the cattle are drawn from; and then if you consider that the cattle, when converted into food, are hauled again by the same railways right back to the place where they came from, you will get some sidelight on the transportation problem and the price of meat. Take also grain. Every reader of advertisements knows where the great flour mills of the country are located. And they probably know also that these great mills are not located in the sections where the grain of the United States is raised. There are staggering quantities of grain, thousands of trainloads, hauled uselessly long distances, and then in the form of flour hauled back again long distances to the states and sections where the grain was raised—a burdening of the railroads which is of no benefit to the communities where the grain originated, nor to any one else except the monopolistic mills and the railroads. The railroads can always do a big business without helping the business of the country at all; they can always be engaged in just such useless hauling. On meat and grain and perhaps on cotton, too, the transportation burden could be reduced by more than half, by the preparation of the product for use before it is shipped. If a coal community mined coal in Pennsylvania, and then sent it by railway to Michigan or Wisconsin to be screened, and then hauled it back again to Pennsylvania for use, it would not be much sillier than the hauling of Texas beef alive to Chicago, there to be killed, and then shipped back dead to Texas; or the hauling of Kansas grain to Minnesota, there to be ground in the mills and hauled back again as flour. It is good business for the railroads, but it is bad business for business. One angle of the transportation problem to which too few men are paying attention is this useless hauling of material. If the problem were tackled from the point of ridding the railroads of their useless hauls, we might discover that we are in better shape than we think to take care of the legitimate transportation business of the country.

In commodities like coal it is necessary that they be hauled from where they are to where they are needed. The same is true of the raw materials of industry—they must be hauled from the place where nature has stored them to the place where there are people ready to work them. And as these raw materials are not often found assembled in one section, a considerable amount of transportation to a central assembling place is necessary. The coal comes from one section, the copper from another, the iron from another, the wood from another—they must all be brought together.

But wherever it is possible a policy of decentralization ought to be adopted. We need, instead of mammoth flour mills, a multitude of smaller mills distributed through all the sections where grain is grown. Wherever it is possible, the section that produces the raw material ought to produce also the finished product. Grain should be ground to flour where it is grown. A hog-growing country should not export hogs, but pork, hams, and bacon. The cotton mills ought to be near the cotton fields. This is not a revolutionary idea. In a sense it is a reactionary one. It does not suggest anything new; it suggests something that is very old. This is the way the country did things before we fell into the habit of carting everything around a few thousand miles and adding the cartage to the consumer's bill. Our communities ought to be more complete in themselves. They ought not to be unnecessarily dependent on railway transportation. Out of what they produce they should supply their own needs and ship the surplus. And how can they do this unless they have the means of taking their raw materials, like grain and cattle, and changing them into finished products? If private enterprise does not yield these means, the cooperation of farmers can. The chief injustice sustained by the farmer to-day is that, being the greatest producer, he is prevented from being also the greatest merchandiser, because he is compelled to sell to those who put his products into merchantable form. If he could change his grain into flour, his cattle into beef, and his hogs into hams and bacon, not only would he receive the fuller profit of his product, but he would render his near-by communities more independent of railway exigencies, and thereby improve the transportation system by relieving it of the burden of his unfinished product. The thing is not only reasonable and practicable, but it is becoming absolutely necessary. More than that, it is being done in many places. But it will not register its full effect on the transportation situation and upon the cost of living until it is done more widely and in more kinds of materials.

It is one of nature's compensations to withdraw prosperity from the business which does not serve.

We have found that on the Detroit, Toledo & Ironton we could, following our universal policy, reduce our rates and get more business. We made some cuts, but the Interstate Commerce Commission refused to allow them! Under such conditions why discuss the railroads as a business? Or as a service?

17

Things in General

The first part of this chapter describes Ford's relationship with inventor Thomas Edison and naturalist John Burroughs. These three men, along with Harvey Firestone, constituted the "Vagabonds" who often took road trips together. However, it is not particularly important to a thorough understanding of Ford's management system, and we have omitted it in the interests of conserving space. The next section shows how industry can abolish the root causes of war, and then it provides a very valuable warning against the role of propaganda in fomenting war.

MANUFACTURING AN END TO WAR

George S. Patton Jr.'s "The End of War" condemns the naïve belief that treaties, pacifism, and so on can prevent war. The poem concludes (Nye, 1993, 49):

> They will return to futileness,
> As quickly as before,
> Though Truth and History vainly shout,
> "THERE IS NO END TO WAR."

Historians have depicted Henry Ford as a pacifist, but he was actually a pragmatic realist. Per Ford and Crowther (1926, pp. 258–259), Ford opposed unilateral disarmament on a national scale, along with restrictive gun control laws on an individual level. He said explicitly that it is worse than futile to arm the world's bandits while disarming the world's honest nations and citizens. The fact that Ford opposed war (as do most professional soldiers) did not mean he was against possession of the means of finishing a conflict that somebody else started. His industries meanwhile played major and decisive roles in both World Wars.

Ford's achievement, however, was to describe an economic model that might make war obsolete. Ford and Crowther (1930, p. 270) apply the same model to crime with the statement that a typical criminal actually works harder, and for less remuneration, than an honest worker. Somebody who can earn a higher wage than he can steal will obviously prefer the honest job that entails no chance of trouble with the police. It is reasonable to expand this common sense observation to argue that a nation that can produce more wealth than it can rob from its neighbors will do the former and not the latter.

This vision became realistic only with the advent of the Industrial Revolution. Land was the human species' predominant source of wealth well into the mid-nineteenth century, and land and armies have shared a close connection throughout history. The most prestigious Greek soldiers (hoplites) were landowners who could afford costly bronze armor, and they were willing to fight in ranks with other landowners to protect this source of immovable wealth. They also were frequently the only people who had the right to vote in Greece's democracies, which was eminently reasonable because they had the biggest stakes in their communities. Those without land could simply flee from an invader, while landowners had to stand and fight if they wanted to keep their property.

Medieval feudal systems also centered on land. A king would typically grant land to a vassal in return for the vassal's fealty. The vassal used the land as a source of wealth, and also to support armed retainers upon whom the king could call in time of war. The Ottoman Empire's timariot system granted a fief of land to a spahi (cavalryman) who then had to make himself and his retainers available for military service.

There was meanwhile a clear class distinction in the British Army between officers who owned land or were heirs to land, and those who had no land. The former often purchased commissions, i.e., paid for the privilege of fighting, which demonstrated to upper-class society their willingness to defend the nation's land. This social class tended to look down on those who earned money from any kind of trade, and might show more respect to a debt-ridden landowner than to a prosperous industrialist. In George MacDonald Fraser's *Flashman* (1969), Lord Cardigan expels the protagonist from his regiment after the latter's shotgun marriage to the daughter of a wealthy factory owner.

The ability of the factory to transform raw material into enormous wealth, however, should have begun to change the "land = wealth" paradigm in the late nineteenth century. Industrialization provides a nation with the ability to create far more material wealth than it is likely to seize from its neighbors. Ford and Crowther (1926, p. 268) conclude that world peace will come from a working class whose men can afford collared shirts instead of kerchiefs, and whose women can buy hats instead of shawls.

* * *

Today I am more opposed to war than ever I was, and I think the people of the world know—even if the politicians do not—that war never settles anything. It was war that made the orderly and profitable processes of the world what they are to-day—a loose, disjointed mass. Of course, some men get rich out of war; others get poor. But the men who get rich are not those who fought or who really helped behind the lines. No patriot makes money out of war. No man with true patriotism could make money out of war—out of the sacrifice of other men's lives. Until the soldier makes money by fighting, until mothers make money by giving their sons to death—not until then should any citizen make money out of providing his country with the means to preserve its life.

If wars are to continue, it will be harder and harder for the upright business man to regard war as a legitimate means of high and speedy profits. War fortunes are losing caste every day. Even greed will some day hesitate before the overwhelming unpopularity and opposition which will meet the war profiteer. Business should be on the side of peace, because peace is business's best asset. And, by the way, was inventive genius ever so sterile as it was during the war?

THE DANGER OF PROPAGANDA

The following material is particularly important because propaganda fomented the Spanish-American War and both World Wars. Ford (1922, p. 203) was actually somewhat ahead of Linebarger's (1954) *Psychological Warfare* in the identification of honest and dishonest uses of propaganda:

There has been too much of this kind of psychological crime committed in the world these past few years—the crime of bringing men to act from the highest and sincerest motives of self-sacrifice, and then using that high spirit for the lowest purposes.

Ford was doubtlessly familiar with the role of the "yellow press," the competing newspapers of William Randolph Hearst and Joseph Pulitzer, in fomenting the Spanish-American War. There was and is no evidence that Spain sabotaged the battleship *Maine*, but the yellow press proclaimed immediately that Spain had murdered American sailors with a perfidious attack. *Judge Magazine* (July 9, 1898) had on its cover Grant Hamilton's "The Spanish Brute: Adds Mutilation to Murder." This may well have been the first widely circulated cartoon that depicted the enemy as a subhuman monster; in this case, a fanged ape in a Spanish uniform with blood dripping from his knife.

Ford's statement, "Make the nation suspicious; make the other nation suspicious," applied to Spanish newspapers almost as much as to the yellow press. One Spanish cartoon portrayed the United States as a pig, and the implication was clearly that the Spanish people were spoiling for a fight. An intelligent Spanish propagandist would have instead attempted to derail a war by portraying Hearst and Pulitzer as using the blood of Spanish and American soldiers as ink for their newspapers.

Propagandists of World War I transformed Grant Hamilton's creation into a fanged ape in a spiked helmet, with a terrified woman in one paw and a bloody club labeled *kultur* (German for "culture") in the other. The cartoonist W. A. Rogers meanwhile created images of dead American children after the sinking of the *Lusitania* in 1915. The sensationalistic portrayal of Germany as the murderer of American civilians overcame all inquiries as to whether Germany had a legal right to sink the *Lusitania*, which it did. Greenhill (2008) reported that a diving team found 4 million rounds of 0.303 caliber rifle ammunition, that of Britain's Short Magazine Lee-Enfield Rifle, on the sunken wreck. This kind of propaganda, and Germany's failure to respond effectively, drew the United States into a war in which more than 100,000 American soldiers died and more than 200,000 were wounded.

The German who learned the most from Germany's propaganda failures and the Triple Entente's (Great Britain, France, and Russia) success was unfortunately Adolf Hitler. His successful application of the lessons in question then enabled him to take over Germany and perpetrate World War II.

If this is not enough reason for citizens and national leaders to beware of dishonest propaganda, it is necessary to add that *Ford himself fell victim to it despite his explicit knowledge of its dangers.* His publication of the infamous *International Jew* was the direct result of his interaction with the

Czarist propagandist Boris Brasol, who presented him with a copy of the *Protocols of the Elders of Zion*. The copy was sufficiently authoritative that Ford believed its contents to be accurate. Sinclair (1937, p. 55) cites Ford's meeting with Brasol, as does the Jewish Virtual Library.* The result was the promotion of anti-Semitism along with enormous damage to Ford's reputation. This, along with the role of propaganda in drawing the United States into at least two conflicts (Spanish-American War and World War I) in which it had no business, reinforces the need for every citizen to educate himself or herself on the subject of propaganda and psychological warfare.

Ford's description of a "group of men with vast powers of control" applies to what President Eisenhower would later call the military-industrial complex. Eisenhower's observation meanwhile echoes that of Niccolò Machiavelli (1965, pp. 17–21), who warned that no country should allow anybody to make war his only profession. A company that can make only military products is in roughly the same position, and it requires either a war or the threat of one to prosper. It also is quite possible that Ford knew the reputation of Basil Zaharoff, the arms trader known as the Merchant of Death.

The needs of twenty-first century armies admittedly require specialized defense contractors, but it is in these companies' interest to be able to make peacetime products to avoid dependence on government contracts. Ford's industries were obviously capable of doing this.

* * *

An impartial investigation of the last war, of what preceded it and what has come out of it, would show beyond a doubt that there is in the world a group of men with vast powers of control, that prefers to remain unknown, that does not seek office or any of the tokens of power, that belongs to no nation whatever but is international—a force that uses every government, every widespread business organization, every agency of publicity, every resource of national psychology, to throw the world into a panic for the sake of getting still more power over the world. An old gambling trick used to be for the gambler to cry "Police!" when a lot of money was on the table, and, in the panic that followed, to seize the money and run off with it. There is a power within the world which cries "War!" and in the confusion of the nations, the unrestrained sacrifice which people make for safety and peace runs off with the spoils of the panic.

---

* http://www.jewishvirtuallibrary.org/jsource/anti-semitism/protocols1.html (accessed July 2 2012).

The point to keep in mind is that, though we won the military contest, the world has not yet quite succeeded in winning a complete victory over the promoters of war. We ought not to forget that wars are a purely manufactured evil and are made according to a definite technique. A campaign for war is made upon as definite lines as a campaign for any other purpose. First, the people are worked upon. By clever tales the people's suspicions are aroused toward the nation against whom war is desired. Make the nation suspicious; make the other nation suspicious. All you need for this is a few agents with some cleverness and no conscience and a press whose interest is locked up with the interests that will be benefited by war. Then the "overt act" will soon appear. It is no trick at all to get an "overt act" once you work the hatred of two nations up to the proper pitch.

There were men in every country who were glad to see the World War begin and sorry to see it stop. Hundreds of American fortunes date from the Civil War; thousands of new fortunes date from the World War. Nobody can deny that war is a profitable business for those who like that kind of money. War is an orgy of money, just as it is an orgy of blood.

And we should not so easily be led into war if we considered what it is that makes a nation really great. It is not the amount of trade that makes a nation great. The creation of private fortunes, like the creation of an autocracy, does not make any country great. Nor does the mere change of an agricultural population into a factory population. A country becomes great when, by the wise development of its resources and the skill of its people, property is widely and fairly distributed.

INTERNATIONAL PROSPERITY PROMOTES PEACE

Foreign trade is full of delusions. We ought to wish for every nation as large a degree of self-support as possible. Instead of wishing to keep them dependent on us for what we manufacture, we should wish them to learn to manufacture themselves and build up a solidly founded civilization. When every nation learns to produce the things which it can produce, we shall be able to get down to a basis of serving each other along those special lines in which there can be no competition. The North Temperate Zone will never be able to compete with the tropics in the special products of the tropics. Our country will never be a competitor with the Orient in the production of tea, nor with the South in the production of rubber.

A large proportion of our foreign trade is based on the backwardness of our foreign customers. Selfishness is a motive that would preserve that backwardness. Humanity is a motive that would help the backward nations to a self-supporting basis. Take Mexico, for example. We have heard a great deal about the "development" of Mexico. Exploitation is the word that ought instead to be used. When its rich natural resources are exploited for the increase of the private fortunes of foreign capitalists, that is not development, it is ravishment. You can never develop Mexico until you develop the Mexican. And yet how much of the "development" of Mexico by foreign exploiters ever took account of the development of its people? The Mexican peon has been regarded as mere fuel for the foreign money-makers. Foreign trade has been his degradation.

Short-sighted people are afraid of such counsel. They say: "What would become of our foreign trade?"

When the natives of Africa begin raising their own cotton and the natives of Russia begin making their own farming implements and the natives of China begin supplying their own wants, it will make a difference, to be sure, but does any thoughtful man imagine that the world can long continue on the present basis of a few nations supplying the needs of the world? We must think in terms of what the world will be when civilization becomes general, when all the peoples have learned to help themselves.

When a country goes mad about foreign trade it usually depends on other countries for its raw material, turns its population into factory fodder, creates a private rich class, and lets its own immediate interest lie neglected. Here in the United States we have enough work to do developing our own country to relieve us of the necessity of looking for foreign trade for a long time. We have agriculture enough to feed us while we are doing it, and money enough to carry the job through. Is there anything more stupid than the United States standing idle because Japan or France or any other country has not sent us an order when there is a hundred-year job awaiting us in developing our own country?

Commerce began in service. Men carried off their surplus to people who had none. The country that raised corn carried it to the country that could raise no corn. The lumber country brought wood to the treeless plain. The vine country brought fruit to cold northern climes. The pasture country brought meat to the grassless region. It was all service. When all the peoples of the world become developed in the art of self-support, commerce will get back to that basis. Business will once more become service. There will be no competition, because the basis of competition will have vanished. The varied peoples will develop skills which will be in the nature of monopolies and not competitive. From the beginning, the races have exhibited distinct strains of genius: this one for government; another for colonization; another for the sea; another for art and music; another for agriculture; another for business, and so on. Lincoln said that this nation could not survive half-slave and half-free. The human race cannot forever exist half-exploiter and half-exploited. Until we become buyers and sellers alike, producers and consumers alike, keeping the balance not for profit but for service, we are going to have topsy-turvy conditions.

France has something to give the world of which no competition can cheat her. So has Italy. So has Russia. So have the countries of South America. So has Japan. So has Britain. So has the United States. The sooner we get back to a basis of natural specialties and drop this free-for-all system of grab, the sooner we shall be sure of international self-respect—and international peace. Trying to take the trade of the world can promote war. It cannot promote prosperity. Some day even the international bankers will learn this.

I have never been able to discover any honourable reasons for the beginning of the World War. It seems to have grown out of a very complicated situation created largely by those who thought they could profit by war. I believed, on the information that was given to me in 1916, that some of the nations were anxious for peace and would welcome a demonstration for peace. It was in the hope that this was true that I financed the expedition to Stockholm in what has since been called the "Peace Ship." I do not regret the attempt. The mere fact that it failed is not, to me, conclusive proof that it was not worth trying. We learn more from our failures than from our successes. What I learned on that trip was worth the time and the money expended. I do not now know whether the information as conveyed to me was true or false. I do not care. But I think everyone will agree that if it had been possible to end the war in 1916 the world would be better off than it is today.

For the victors wasted themselves in winning, and the vanquished in resisting. Nobody got an advantage, honourable or dishonourable, out of that war. I had hoped, finally, when the United States entered the war, that it might be a war to end wars, but now I know that wars do not end wars any more than an extraordinarily large conflagration does away with the fire hazard. When our country entered the war, it became the duty of every citizen to do his utmost toward seeing through to the end that which we had undertaken. I believe that it is the duty of the man who opposes war to oppose going to war up until the time of its actual declaration.

My opposition to war is not based upon pacifist or non-resistant principles. It may be that the present state of civilization is such that certain international questions cannot be discussed; it may be that they have to be fought out. But the fighting never settles the question. It only gets the participants around to a frame of mind where they will agree to discuss what they were fighting about.

Once we were in the war, every facility of the Ford industries was put at the disposal of the Government. We had, up to the time of the declaration of war, absolutely refused to take war orders from the foreign belligerents. It is entirely out of keeping with the principles of our business to disturb the routine of our production unless in an emergency. It is at variance with our human principles to aid either side in a war in which our country was not involved. These principles had no application, once the United States entered the war. From April, 1917, until November, 1918, our factory worked practically exclusively for the Government. Of course we made cars and parts and special delivery trucks and ambulances as a part of our general production, but we also made many other articles that were more or less new to us. We made 2 1/2-ton and 6-ton trucks. We made Liberty motors in great quantities, aero cylinders, 1.55 Mm. and 4.7 Mm. caissons. We made listening devices, steel helmets (both at Highland Park and Philadelphia), and Eagle Boats, and we did a large amount of experimental work on armour plate, compensators, and body armour. For the Eagle Boats we put up a special plant on the River Rouge site. These boats were designed to combat the submarines. They were 204 feet long, made of steel, and one of the conditions precedent to their building was that their construction should not interfere with any other line of war production and also that they be delivered quickly. The design was worked out by the Navy Department. On December 22, 1917, I offered to build the boats for the Navy. The discussion terminated on January 15, 1918, when the Navy Department awarded the contract to the Ford Company. On July 11th, the first completed boat was launched. We made both the hulls and the engines, and not a forging or a rolled beam entered into the construction of other than the engine. We stamped the hulls entirely out of sheet steel. They were built indoors. In four months we ran up a building at the River Rouge a third of a mile long, 350 feet wide, and 100 feet high, covering more than thirteen acres. These boats were not built by marine engineers. They were built simply by applying our production principles to a new product.

With the Armistice, we at once dropped the war and went back to peace.

EDUCATION MUST BE PRACTICAL

Several corporations use the phrase "tools not toys" to describe their products, and the same concept applies to education. There should always be a connection between what a student learns in a classroom and what he or she can do with the knowledge in the real world. The Henry Ford Trade School implemented this approach by interspersing classroom instruction and the production of usable products in the shop.

Ford warns, as he did in previous chapters, that education becomes a liability when its sole function is to tell its owner why something cannot be done. Ford (1922, p. 146) adds that, had Christopher Columbus relied on his education in contemporary geography, he would have never discovered America. "Columbus did not study geography; he made it."

* * *

An able man is a man who can do things, and his ability to do things is dependent on what he has in him. What he has in him depends on what he started with and what he has done to increase and discipline it.

An educated man is not one whose memory is trained to carry a few dates in history—he is one who can accomplish things. A man who cannot think is not an educated man however many college degrees he may have acquired. Thinking is the hardest work any one can do—which is probably the reason why we have so few thinkers. There are two extremes to be avoided: one is the attitude of contempt toward education, the other is the tragic snobbery of assuming that marching through an educational system is a sure cure for ignorance and mediocrity. You cannot learn in any school what the world is going to do next year, but you can learn some of the things which the world has tried to do in former years, and where it failed and where it succeeded. If education consisted in warning the young student away from some of the false theories on which men have tried to build, so that he may be saved the loss of the time in finding out by bitter experience, its good would be unquestioned. An education which consists of signposts indicating the failure and the fallacies of the past doubtless would be very useful. It is not education just to possess the theories of a lot of professors. Speculation is very interesting, and sometimes profitable, but it is not education. To be learned in science to-day is merely to be aware of a hundred theories that have not been proved. And not to know what those theories are is to be "uneducated," "ignorant," and so forth. If knowledge of guesses is learning, then one may become learned by the simple expedient of making his own guesses. And by the same token he can dub the rest of the world "ignorant" because it does not know what his guesses are. But the best that education can do for a man is to put him in possession of his powers, give him control of the tools with which destiny has endowed him, and teach him how to think. The college renders its best service as an intellectual gymnasium, in which mental muscle is developed and the student strengthened to do what he can. To say, however, that mental gymnastics can be had only in college is not true, as every educator knows. A man's real education begins after he has left school. True education is gained through the discipline of life.

There are many kinds of knowledge, and it depends on what crowd you happen to be in, or how the fashions of the day happen to run, which kind of knowledge, is most respected at the moment. There are fashions in knowledge, just as there are in everything else. When some of us were lads, knowledge used to be limited to the Bible. There were certain men in the neighbourhood who knew the Book thoroughly, and they were looked up to and respected. Biblical knowledge was highly valued then. But nowadays it is doubtful whether deep acquaintance with the Bible would be sufficient to win a man a name for learning.

Knowledge, to my mind, is something that in the past somebody knew and left in a form which enables all who will to obtain it. If a man is born with normal human faculties, if he is equipped with enough ability to use the tools which we call "letters" in reading or writing, there is no knowledge within the possession of the race that he cannot have—if he wants it! The only reason why every man does not know everything that the human mind has ever learned is that no one has ever yet found it worth while to know that much. Men satisfy their minds more by finding out things for themselves than by heaping together the things which somebody else has found out. You can go out and gather knowledge all your life, and with all your gathering you will not catch up even with your own times. You may fill your head with all the "facts" of all the ages, and your head may be just an overloaded fact-box when you get through. The point is this: Great piles of knowledge in the head are not the same as mental activity. A man may be very learned and very useless. And then again, a man may be unlearned and very useful.

The object of education is not to fill a man's mind with facts; it is to teach him how to use his mind in thinking. And it often happens that a man can think better if he is not hampered by the knowledge of the past.

It is a very human tendency to think that what mankind does not yet know no one can learn. And yet it must be perfectly clear to everyone that the past learning of mankind cannot be allowed to hinder our future learning. Mankind has not gone so very far when you measure its progress against the knowledge that is yet to be gained—the secrets that are yet to be learned.

One good way to hinder progress is to fill a man's head with all the learning of the past; it makes him feel that because his head is full, there is nothing more to learn. Merely gathering knowledge may become the most useless work a man can do. What can you do to help and heal the world? That is the educational test. If a man can hold up his own end, he counts for one. If he can help ten or a hundred or a thousand other men hold up their ends, he counts for more. He may be quite rusty on many things that inhabit the realm of print, but he is a learned man just the same. When a man is master of his own sphere, whatever it may be, he has won his degree—he has entered the realm of wisdom.

18

Democracy and Industry

This chapter exposes the fallacies of class warfare and then, more importantly, addresses industrial and labor relations. Ford denounced equally managers who tried to pay their workers as little as possible, and demagogues who fomented labor unrest for their own benefit.

THE FALLACIES OF CLASS WARFARE

Today's alleged conflict between "1%" and "the 99%" is simply the latest incarnation of the primarily self-serving agenda of the fomenters of class warfare. Ford was a member of both these classes during his lifetime and, even after he became perhaps the wealthiest person on Earth, he still counted himself as a member of the working class. This is probably why he could look at wages from the perspective of both the employer and the worker, and conclude that a square deal for both was a prerequisite for organizational prosperity. Ford (1922, p. 179) elaborates on this as follows, and the reference also uses the phrase "industrial justice."

> And if so be an employer, having been once a workingman himself, sees the need of adjustments and makes them before his men ask him, so much the better—his act means a great increase in confidence and a new feeling that the world still has a square deal left in it.

* * *

> *Perhaps no word is more overworked nowadays than the word "democracy," and those who shout loudest about it, I think, as a rule, want it least. I am always suspicious of men who speak glibly of democracy. I wonder if they want to set up some kind of a despotism or if they want to have somebody do*

for them what they ought to do for themselves. I am for the kind of democracy that gives to each an equal chance according to his ability. I think if we give more attention to serving our fellows we shall have less concern with the empty forms of government and more concern with the things to be done. Thinking of service, we shall not bother about good feeling in industry or life; we shall not bother about masses and classes, or closed and open shops, and such matters as have nothing at all to do with the real business of living. We can get down to facts. We stand in need of facts.

It is a shock when the mind awakens to the fact that not all of humanity is human—that whole groups of people do not regard others with humane feelings. Great efforts have been made to have this appear as the attitude of a class, but it is really the attitude of all "classes," in so far as they are swayed by the false notion of "classes." Before, when it was the constant effort of propaganda to make the people believe that it was only the "rich" who were without humane feelings, the opinion became general that among the "poor" the humane virtues flourished.

But the "rich" and the "poor" are both very small minorities, and you cannot classify society under such heads. There are not enough "rich" and there are not enough "poor" to serve the purpose of such classification. Rich men have become poor without changing their natures, and poor men have become rich, and the problem has not been affected by it.

Between the rich and the poor is the great mass of the people who are neither rich nor poor. A society made up exclusively of millionaires would not be different from our present society; some of the millionaires would have to raise wheat and bake bread and make machinery and run trains—else they would all starve to death. Someone must do the work. Really we have no fixed classes. We have men who will work and men who will not. Most of the "classes" that one reads about are purely fictional. Take certain capitalist papers. You will be amazed by some of the statements about the labouring class. We who have been and still are a part of the labouring class know that the statements are untrue. Take certain of the labour papers. You are equally amazed by some of the statements they make about "capitalists." And yet on both sides there is a grain of truth. The man who is a capitalist and nothing else, who gambles with the fruits of other men's labours, deserves all that is said against him. He is in precisely the same class as the cheap gambler who cheats workingmen out of their wages. The statements we read about the labouring class in the capitalistic press are seldom written by managers of great industries, but by a class of writers who are writing what they think will please their employers. They write what they imagine will please. Examine the labour press and you will find another class of writers who similarly seek to tickle the prejudices which they conceive the labouring man to have. Both kinds of writers are mere propagandists. And propaganda that

*does not spread facts is self-destructive. And it should be. You cannot preach
patriotism to men for the purpose of getting them to stand still while you
rob them—and get away with that kind of preaching very long. You cannot
preach the duty of working hard and producing plentifully, and make that a
screen for an additional profit to yourself. And neither can the worker con-
ceal the lack of a day's work by a phrase.*

*Undoubtedly the employing class possesses facts which the employed
ought to have in order to construct sound opinions and pass fair judgments.
Undoubtedly the employed possess facts which are equally important to the
employer. It is extremely doubtful, however, if either side has all the facts.
And this is where propaganda, even if it were possible for it to be entirely successful, is defective. It is not desirable that one set of ideas be "put over" on a
class holding another set of ideas. What we really need is to get all the ideas
together and construct from them.*

*Take, for instance, this whole matter of union labour and the right to
strike.*

LABOR UNREST AND STRIKES
SHOULD BE UNNECESSARY

Ford (1922, p. 250) warned against the kind of union organizer who is

> A spokesman who does not work in the shop, who does not work in any
> shop, whose sole ambition perhaps is never again to have to work in a shop,
> is usually the "bargainer," and it is from what he says or does that many
> employers draw their opinion of the men in the shop.

Furthermore:

> It is a truth which every American workman ought to know is that 95 per-
> cent of the agitation which they see around them does not grow up out of
> the working people, but it comes down through hired agitators from the
> would-be capitalistic rulers who want to use the workmen themselves to
> break down the very industries on which the workmen depend, in order
> that then the workmen may be thrown on their tender mercies (Ford,
> 1922, p. 252).

Ford says instead in this section that "the only true labour leader is the
one who leads labour to work and to wages, and not the leader who leads

labour to strikes, sabotage, and starvation." Management has the unequivocal obligation to provide the fair wages, and Ford lays equal blame for labor unrest on "bosses who never did a decent thing for their employees until they were compelled."

How does a labor leader lead workers to high wages? It is not, as the United Auto Workers did prior to General Motors' bankruptcy, by negotiating with management over who would pay what percentage of employee healthcare benefits. The UAW could have instead urged management to demand that providers of healthcare to GM employees implement the kind of quality management systems that GM already demands of its part suppliers. GM's own industry association, the Automotive Industry Action Group (AIAG), in fact, had worked with the American Society for Quality and other organizations to develop a healthcare-specific version of the ISO 9001 quality system standard. The result would have been lower healthcare premiums along with better care for GM's workers and retirees. Levinson (2006) recommended this very explicitly, although GM and the UAW should have been independently aware of the AIAG's off-the-shelf solution.

The statement about leading labor to jobs and wages also applies to the Luddism of the International Longshore and Warehouse Union (ILWU), which resisted data entry automation out of fear that this might eliminate jobs (Levinson, 2002). The truth is, of course, that a worker can receive a higher wage for automated instead of manual data entry, just as a mason who used Frank Gilbreth's nonstooping scaffold could receive higher pay than a mason who bent over to pick up each brick. Taylor (1911b, pp. 187–188) said of Luddism and soldiering (marking time and limiting production) in general, "If their employers are in a competitive business, sooner or later those competitors whose workmen do not limit the output will take the trade away from them, and they will be thrown out of work."

Ford's statement below about a "whole set of false theories and promises which can never be fulfilled as long as the earth remains what it is" is simply a restatement of the economic aspect of his universal code. No amount of labor negotiations will allow the business to pay wages that its productivity cannot support. An honest partnership between management and labor, however, can apply the scientific leg of the universal code to make higher wages possible.

* * *

The only strong group of union men in the country is the group that draws salaries from the unions. Some of them are very rich. Some of them are interested in influencing the affairs of our large institutions of finance. Others are so extreme in their so-called socialism that they border on Bolshevism and anarchism—their union salaries liberating them from the necessity of work so that they can devote their energies to subversive propaganda. All of them enjoy a certain prestige and power which, in the natural course of competition, they could not otherwise have won.

If the official personnel of the labour unions were as strong, as honest, as decent, and as plainly wise as the bulk of the men who make up the membership, the whole movement would have taken on a different complexion these last few years. But this official personnel, in the main—there are notable exceptions—has not devoted itself to an alliance with the naturally strong qualities of the workingman; it has rather devoted itself to playing upon his weaknesses, principally upon the weaknesses of that newly arrived portion of the population which does not yet know what Americanism is, and which never will know if left to the tutelage of their local union leaders.

The workingmen, except those few who have been inoculated with the fallacious doctrine of "the class war" and who have accepted the philosophy that progress consists in fomenting discord in industry ("When you get your $12 a day, don't stop at that. Agitate for $14. When you get your eight hours a day, don't be a fool and grow contented; agitate for six hours. Start something! Always start something!"), have the plain sense which enables them to recognize that with principles accepted and observed, conditions change. The union leaders have never seen that. They wish conditions to remain as they are, conditions of injustice, provocation, strikes, bad feeling, and crippled national life. Else where would be the need for union officers? Every strike is a new argument for them; they point to it and say, "You see! You still need us."

The only true labour leader is the one who leads labour to work and to wages, and not the leader who leads labour to strikes, sabotage, and starvation. The union of labour which is coming to the fore in this country is the union of all whose interests are interdependent—whose interests are altogether dependent on the usefulness and efficiency of the service they render.

There is a change coming. When the union of "union leaders" disappears, with it will go the union of blind bosses—bosses who never did a decent thing for their employees until they were compelled. If the blind boss was a disease, the selfish union leader was the antidote. When the union leader became the disease, the blind boss became the antidote. Both are misfits, both are out of place in well-organized society. And they are both disappearing together.

It is the blind boss whose voice is heard to-day saying, "Now is the time to smash labour, we've got them on the run." That voice is going down to silence with the voice that preaches "class war." The producers—from the men at the drawing board to the men on the moulding floor—have gotten together in a real union, and they will handle their own affairs henceforth.

The exploitation of dissatisfaction is an established business to-day. Its object is not to settle anything, nor to get anything done, but to keep dissatisfaction in existence. And the instruments used to do this are a whole set of false theories and promises which can never be fulfilled as long as the earth remains what it is.

I am not opposed to labour organization. I am not opposed to any sort of organization that makes for progress. It is organizing to limit production—whether by employers or by workers—that matters.

Productivity Creates High-Wage Jobs

The following material addresses the issue of the restrictive work rules that unions often demand to "protect" jobs. Automation does not, contrary to the belief of the Luddites, destroy jobs, it creates more and better jobs. This section's statement that "we cannot play fast and loose with economic laws, because if we do they handle us in very hard ways," is meanwhile simply another restatement of the impartial economic leg of Ford's triad. Customers will simply not pay two workers to do a job that can and should be performed by one.

The behavioral leg meanwhile requires employers to remember Taylor's warning (1911a, p. 8) against cutting piece rates, or by implication discharging workers when efficiency improvements make them unnecessary. If either of these things happen, the worker "is likely entirely to lose sight of his employer's side of the case and become imbued with a grim determination to have no more cuts if soldiering can prevent it."

This section then adds the scientific leg of Ford's triad with the statement: " An industrial concern which is wide enough awake to reorganize for efficiency, and honest enough with the public to charge it necessary costs and no more, is usually such an enterprising concern that it has plenty of jobs at which to employ the tenth man." Once again, application of the synergistic union of impartial economic, behavioral, and management science creates and protects high-wage jobs, while violation of any of these considerations can only destroy jobs.

The last paragraph of this section, which also appears in *Ford Ideals* (1922, p. 17) reiterates the need for a square deal in all economic transactions: "When the man gives more than he receives, or receives more than he gives—it is not long before serious dislocation will be manifest. Extend that condition throughout the country, and you have a complete upset of business."

* * *

The workingman himself must be on guard against some very dangerous notions—dangerous to himself and to the welfare of the country. It is sometimes said that the less a worker does, the more jobs he creates for other men. This fallacy assumes that idleness is creative. Idleness never created a job. It creates only burdens. The industrious man never runs his fellow worker out of a job; indeed, it is the industrious man who is the partner of the industrious manager—who creates more and more business and therefore more and more jobs. It is a great pity that the idea should ever have gone abroad among sensible men that by "soldiering" on the job they help someone else. A moment's thought will show the weakness of such an idea. The healthy business, the business that is always making more and more opportunities for men to earn an honourable and ample living, is the business in which every man does a day's work of which he is proud. And the country that stands most securely is the country in which men work honestly and do not play tricks with the means of production. We cannot play fast and loose with economic laws, because if we do they handle us in very hard ways.

The fact that a piece of work is now being done by nine men which used to be done by ten men does not mean that the tenth man is unemployed. He is merely not employed on that work, and the public is not carrying the burden of his support by paying more than it ought on that work—for after all, it is the public that pays!

An industrial concern which is wide enough awake to reorganize for efficiency, and honest enough with the public to charge it necessary costs and no more, is usually such an enterprising concern that it has plenty of jobs at which to employ the tenth man. It is bound to grow, and growth means jobs. A well-managed concern is always seeking to lower the labour cost to the public; and it is certain to employ more men than the concern which loafs along and makes the public pay the cost of its mismanagement.

The tenth man was an unnecessary cost. The ultimate consumer was paying him. But the fact that he was unnecessary on that particular job does not mean that he is unnecessary in the work of the world, or even in the work of his particular shop.

The public pays for all mismanagement. More than half the trouble with the world to-day is the "soldiering" and dilution and cheapness and inefficiency for which the people are paying their good money. Wherever two men are being paid for what one can do, the people are paying double what they ought. And it is a fact that only a little while ago in the United States, man for man, we were not producing what we did for several years previous to the war.

A day's work means more than merely being "on duty" at the shop for the required number of hours. It means giving an equivalent in service for the wage drawn. And when that equivalent is tampered with either way—when the man gives more than he receives, or receives more than he gives—it is not long before serious dislocation will be manifest. Extend that condition throughout the country, and you have a complete upset of business. All that industrial difficulty means is the destruction of basic equivalents in the shop. Management must share the blame with labour. Management has been lazy, too. Management has found it easier to hire an additional five hundred men than to so improve its methods that one hundred men of the old force could be released to other work. The public was paying, and business was booming, and management didn't care a pin. It was no different in the office from what it was in the shop. The law of equivalents was broken just as much by managers as by workmen.

Strikes Always Fail

A strike is a lose–lose event even if it delivers higher wages in the short run, because it reduces the business's ability to serve. However, Ford is quick to assign blame to employers who make strikes necessary through, for example, paying workers as little as possible.

* * *

Practically nothing of importance is secured by mere demand. That is why strikes always fail—even though they may seem to succeed. A strike which brings higher wages or shorter hours and passes on the burden to the community is really unsuccessful. It only makes the industry less able to serve— and decreases the number of jobs that it can support. This is not to say that no strike is justified—it may draw attention to an evil. Men can strike with justice—that they will thereby get justice is another question. The strike for proper conditions and just rewards is justifiable. The pity is that men should be compelled to use the strike to get what is theirs by right. No American ought to be compelled to strike for his rights. He ought to receive them naturally, easily, as a matter of course. These justifiable strikes are usually the employer's fault. Some employers are not fit for their jobs. The employment of men—the direction of their energies, the arranging of their rewards in honest ratio to their production and to the prosperity of the business—is no small job. An employer may be unfit for his job, just as a man at the lathe may be unfit. Justifiable strikes are a sign that the boss needs another job—one that he can handle. The unfit employer causes more trouble than the unfit employee. You can change the latter to another more suitable job. But the former must usually be left to the law of compensation. The justified strike, then, is one that need never have been called if the employer had done his work.

There is a second kind of strike—the strike with a concealed design. In this kind of strike the workingmen are made the tools of some manipulator who seeks his own ends through them. To illustrate: Here is a great industry whose success is due to having met a public need with efficient and skillful production. It has a record for justice. Such an industry presents a great temptation to speculators. If they can only gain control of it they can reap rich benefit from all the honest effort that has been put into it. They can destroy its beneficiary wage and profit-sharing, squeeze every last dollar out of the public, the product, and the workingman, and reduce it to the plight of other business concerns which are run on low principles. The motive may be the personal greed of the speculators or they may want to change the policy of a business because its example is embarrassing to other employers who do not want to do what is right. The industry cannot be touched from within, because its men have no reason to strike. So another method is adopted. The business may keep many outside shops busy supplying it with material. If these outside shops can be tied up, then that great industry may be crippled.

So strikes are fomented in the outside industries. Every attempt is made to curtail the factory's source of supplies. If the workingmen in the outside shops knew what the game was, they would refuse to play it, but they don't know; they serve as the tools of designing capitalists without knowing it. There is one point, however, that ought to rouse the suspicions of workingmen engaged in this kind of strike. If the strike cannot get itself settled, no matter what either side offers to do, it is almost positive proof that there is a third party interested in having the strike continue. That hidden influence does not want a settlement on any terms. If such a strike is won by the strikers, is the lot of the workingman improved? After throwing the industry into the hands of outside speculators, are the workmen given any better treatment or wages?

There is a third kind of strike—the strike that is provoked by the money interests for the purpose of giving labour a bad name. The American workman has always had a reputation for sound judgment. He has not allowed himself to be led away by every shouter who promised to create the millennium out of thin air. He has had a mind of his own and has used it. He has always recognized the fundamental truth that the absence of reason was never made good by the presence of violence. In his way the American workingman has won a certain prestige with his own people and throughout the world. Public opinion has been inclined to regard with respect his opinions and desires. But there seems to be a determined effort to fasten the Bolshevik stain on American Labour by inciting it to such impossible attitudes and such wholly unheard-of actions as shall change public sentiment from respect to criticism.

The Employer's Duty to Address Root Causes of Labor Dissatisfaction

Ford's statement: "The wages paid are always higher than any reasonable union could think of demanding and the hours of work are always shorter," shows why there was no identifiable effort to unionize his factories while he was actually running them. This also explains why British carpenters turned against their own trade union after the Ford Motor Company took over the automobile body plant in which they worked.

Unionization was, however, the natural consequence, exactly as Ford said it would be, when those in whose charge he left his company's management went against his principles during the late 1930s. Chapter 8 reported Upton Sinclair's (1937, p. 81) description of a no-layoff rule that had been established when Ford was actually running his company, but which his successors circumvented when productivity improvements made workers temporarily unnecessary.

* * *

Merely avoiding strikes, however, does not promote industry. We may say to the workingman: "You have a grievance, but the strike is no remedy—it only makes the situation worse whether you win or lose."

Then the workingman may admit this to be true and refrain from striking. Does that settle anything?

No! If the worker abandons strikes as an unworthy means of bringing about desirable conditions, it simply means that employers must get busy on their own initiative and correct defective conditions.

The experience of the Ford industries with the workingman has been entirely satisfactory, both in the United States and abroad. We have no antagonism to unions, but we participate in no arrangements with either employee or employer organizations. The wages paid are always higher than any reasonable union could think of demanding and the hours of work are always shorter. There is nothing that a union membership could do for our people. Some of them may belong to unions, probably the majority do not. We do not know and make no attempt to find out, for it is a matter of not the slightest concern to us. We respect the unions, sympathize with their good aims and denounce their bad ones. In turn I think that they give us respect, for there has never been any authoritative attempt to come between the men and the management in our plants. Of course radical agitators have tried to stir up trouble now and again, but the men have mostly regarded them simply as human oddities and their interest in them has been the same sort of interest that they would have in a four-legged man.

In England we did meet the trades union question squarely in our Manchester plant. The workmen of Manchester are mostly unionized, and the usual English union restrictions upon output prevail. We took over a body plant in which were a number of union carpenters. At once the union officers asked to see our executives and arrange terms. We deal only with our own employees and never with outside representatives, so our people refused to see the union officials. Thereupon they called the carpenters out on strike. The carpenters would not strike and were expelled from the union. Then the expelled men brought suit against the union for their share of the benefit fund. I do not know how the litigation turned out, but that was the end of interference by trades union officers with our operations in England.

We make no attempt to coddle the people who work with us. It is absolutely a give-and-take relation. During the period in which we largely increased wages we did have a considerable supervisory force. The home life of the men was investigated and an effort was made to find out what they did with their wages. Perhaps at the time it was necessary; it gave us valuable information. But it would not do at all as a permanent affair and it has been abandoned.

Sloganeering Is Not Leadership

W. Edwards Deming warned explicitly against reliance on slogans which, in the absence of genuine leadership by example, are meaningless words or phrases. To this, Ford (1922, pp. 204–205) added:

The best propaganda an employer can use is to do right now for his own men what he knows he can and ought to do.

… The best propaganda you can ever have is the reputation of being square, humane and thoughtful of others all the time. There are some things you can never *tell* men, nor *persuade* them of by speech or literature. But if the things are there, the men will *know* it—you may be sure of that.

The concept of stewardship also appears in this section: "… when one looks at a great productive organization that is enabling all these things to be done, then the continuance of that business becomes a holy trust." This is simply an extension of the principle that the job is paramount, as was shown in Chapter 6, to the idea that the organization's ability to serve is paramount. Stewardship meanwhile ties in with the concept of the Mandate of Heaven, which appears in the next section.

* * *

We do not believe in the "glad hand," or the professionalized "personal touch," or "human element." It is too late in the day for that sort of thing. Men want something more than a worthy sentiment. Social conditions are not made out of words. They are the net result of the daily relations between man and man. The best social spirit is evidenced by some act which costs the management something and which benefits all. That is the only way to prove good intentions and win respect. Propaganda, bulletins, lectures—they are nothing. It is the right act sincerely done that counts.

A great business is really too big to be human. It grows so large as to supplant the personality of the man. In a big business the employer, like the employee, is lost in the mass. Together they have created a great productive organization which sends out articles that the world buys and pays for in return money that provides a livelihood for everyone in the business. The business itself becomes the big thing.

There is something sacred about a big business which provides a living for hundreds and thousands of families. When one looks about at the babies coming into the world, at the boys and girls going to school, at the young workingmen who, on the strength of their jobs, are marrying and setting up for themselves, at the thousands of homes that are being paid for on installments out of the earnings of men—when one looks at a great productive organization that is enabling all these things to be done, then the continuance of that business becomes a holy trust. It becomes greater and more important than the individuals.

THE EMPLOYER AND THE MANDATE OF HEAVEN

This book has already introduced the Chinese leadership concept of the Mandate of Heaven, which says simply that a person derives his or her right to lead from service to the organization's stakeholders. Ford and Crowther (1930, p. 64) discuss the underlying concept very explicitly: "The leaders of a business are as responsible for the welfare of the people as the generals of an army are responsible for the welfare of the soldiers." The following discussion exemplifies this concept in business and industry; the rightful leader is the one who keeps the pay envelopes coming.

* * *

The employer is but a man like his employees and is subject to all the limitations of humanity. He is justified in holding his job only as he can fill it. If he can steer the business straight, if his men can trust him to run his end of the work properly and without endangering their security, then he is filling his place. Otherwise he is no more fit for his position than would be an infant. The employer, like everyone else, is to be judged solely by his ability. He may be but a name to the men—a name on a signboard. But there is the business—it is more than a name. It produces the living—and a living is a pretty tangible thing. The business is a reality. It does things. It is a going concern. The evidence of its fitness is that the pay envelopes keep coming.

Groupthink

Groupthink is a well-known organizational dysfunction in which a highly cohesive group of people will support a bad decision to avoid any disruption of the group's harmony. The destruction of the Space Shuttle *Challenger*, and the loss of its entire crew, is but one example. Nobody wanted to hear why the mission should be scrubbed because of bad weather, and the warnings of engineer Roger Boisjoly were accordingly ignored.

The application of Ford's principle (Chapter 6): "The work and the work alone controls us," helps overcome groupthink by putting the organization's goal ahead of temporary harmony. If everybody in the group puts the job first, criticisms of a proposed course of action apply to the action (inanimate object) as opposed to any person. Ford now adds explicitly: "What have your likes or dislikes to do with the facts?" If everybody adopts this attitude, then groupthink will not be a problem.

* * *

You can hardly have too much harmony in business. But you can go too far in picking men because they harmonize. You can have so much harmony that there will not be enough of the thrust and counterthrust which is life—enough of the competition which means effort and progress. It is one thing for an organization to be working harmoniously toward one object, but it is another thing for an organization to work harmoniously with each individual unit of itself. Some organizations use up so much energy and time maintaining a feeling of harmony that they have no force left to work for the object for which the organization was created. The organization is secondary to the object. The only harmonious organization that is worth anything is an organization in which all the members are bent on the one main purpose—to get along toward the objective. A common purpose, honestly believed in, sincerely desired—that is the great harmonizing principle.

I pity the poor fellow who is so soft and flabby that he must always have "an atmosphere of good feeling" around him before he can do his work. There are such men. And in the end, unless they obtain enough mental and moral hardiness to lift them out of their soft reliance on "feeling," they are failures. Not only are they business failures; they are character failures also; it is as if their bones never attained a sufficient degree of hardness to enable them to stand on their own feet. There is altogether too much reliance on good feeling in our business organizations. People have too great a fondness for working with the people they like. In the end it spoils a good many valuable qualities.

Do not misunderstand me; when I use the term "good feeling" I mean that habit of making one's personal likes and dislikes the sole standard of judgment. Suppose you do not like a man. Is that anything against him? It may be something against you. What have your likes or dislikes to do with the facts? Every man of common sense knows that there are men whom he dislikes, who are really more capable than he is himself.

The Right Leader Is the One Who Can Do the Job

Recall from Chapter 6, the statement (MacPherson, 2012) that every member of the U.S. Special Forces is expected to exercise leadership in accordance with the situation at hand. If an enlisted man is a subject matter expert in a specific situation, officers and noncommissioned officers will follow that man's directions. The directions are not the orders of a superior to a subordinate, but rather the requirements of the job for which the entire team is ultimately responsible.

* * *

And taking all this out of the shop and into the broader fields, it is not necessary for the rich to love the poor or the poor to love the rich. It is not necessary for the employer to love the employee or for the employee to love the employer. What is necessary is that each should try to do justice to the other according to his deserts. That is real democracy and not the question of who ought to own the bricks and the mortar and the furnaces and the mills. And democracy has nothing to do with the question, "Who ought to be boss?"

That is very much like asking: "Who ought to be the tenor in the quartet?" Obviously, the man who can sing tenor. You could not have deposed Caruso. Suppose some theory of musical democracy had consigned Caruso to the musical proletariat. Would that have reared another tenor to take his place? Or would Caruso's gifts have still remained his own?

19

What We May Expect

This chapter begins with a clear and easily understandable explanation of the barriers to universal prosperity, and then reiterates Ford's common sense principles for its achievement. It also introduces the concept of sustainable manufacturing, which Ford practiced long before anybody heard of it.

* * *

We are—unless I do not read the signs aright—in the midst of a change. It is going on all about us, slowly and scarcely observed, but with a firm surety. We are gradually learning to relate cause and effect. A great deal of that which we call disturbance—a great deal of the upset in what have seemed to be established institutions—is really but the surface indication of something approaching a regeneration. The public point of view is changing, and we really need only a somewhat different point of view to make the very bad system of the past into a very good system of the future. We are displacing that peculiar virtue which used to be admired as hard-headedness, and which was really only wooden-headedness, with intelligence, and also we are getting rid of mushy sentimentalism. The first confused hardness with progress; the second confused softness with progress. We are getting a better view of the realities and are beginning to know that we have already in the world all things needful for the fullest kind of a life and that we shall use them better once we learn what they are and what they mean.

Whatever is wrong—and we all know that much is wrong—can be righted by a clear definition of the wrongness. We have been looking so much at one another, at what one has and another lacks, that we have made a personal affair out of something that is too big for personalities. To be sure, human nature enters largely into our economic problems. Selfishness exists, and doubtless it colours all the competitive activities of life. If selfishness were the characteristic of any one class it might be easily dealt with, but it is in human fibre everywhere. And greed exists. And envy exists. And jealousy exists.

But as the struggle for mere existence grows less—and it is less than it used to be, although the sense of uncertainty may have increased—we have an opportunity to release some of the finer motives. We think less of the frills of civilization as we grow used to them. Progress, as the world has thus far known it, is accompanied by a great increase in the things of life. There is more gear, more wrought material, in the average American backyard than in the whole domain of an African king. The average American boy has more paraphernalia around him than a whole Eskimo community. The utensils of kitchen, dining room, bedroom, and coal cellar make a list that would have staggered the most luxurious potentate of five hundred years ago. The increase in the impedimenta of life only marks a stage. We are like the Indian [Native American] who comes into town with all his money and buys everything he sees. There is no adequate realization of the large proportion of the labour and material of industry that is used in furnishing the world with its trumpery and trinkets, which are made only to be sold, and are bought merely to be owned—that perform no service in the world and are at last mere rubbish as at first they were mere waste. Humanity is advancing out of its trinket-making stage, and industry is coming down to meet the world's needs, and thus we may expect further advancement toward that life which many now see, but which the present "good enough" stage hinders our attaining.

And we are growing out of this worship of material possessions. It is no longer a distinction to be rich. As a matter of fact, to be rich is no longer a common ambition. People do not care for money as money, as they once did. Certainly they do not stand in awe of it, nor of him who possesses it. What we accumulate by way of useless surplus does us no honour.

It takes only a moment's thought to see that as far as individual personal advantage is concerned, vast accumulations of money mean nothing. A human being is a human being and is nourished by the same amount and quality of food, is warmed by the same weight of clothing, whether he be rich or poor. And no one can inhabit more than one room at a time.

But if one has visions of service, if one has vast plans which no ordinary resources could possibly realize, if one has a life ambition to make the industrial desert bloom like the rose, and the work-a-day life suddenly blossom into fresh and enthusiastic human motives of higher character and efficiency, then one sees in large sums of money what the farmer sees in his seed corn— the beginning of new and richer harvests whose benefits can no more be selfishly confined than can the sun's rays.

There are two fools in this world. One is the millionaire who thinks that by hoarding money he can somehow accumulate real power, and the other is the penniless reformer who thinks that if only he can take the money from one class and give it to another, all the world's ills will be cured. They are both on the wrong track. They might as well try to corner all the checkers or all the

dominoes of the world under the delusion that they are thereby cornering
great quantities of skill. Some of the most successful money-makers of our
times have never added one pennyworth to the wealth of men. Does a card
player add to the wealth of the world?

PROSPERITY SHOULD BE WITHIN EVERYBODY'S REACH

The following material again contradicts the paradigm of business as a
zero-sum game, in which one supply chain participant's gain can come
only at the expense of another's loss. Ford contended, and proved unequivocally, that a business whose focus is on service to its stakeholders can create abundant wealth for all participants.

* * *

If we all created wealth up to the limits, the easy limits, of our creative capac-
ity, then it would simply be a case of there being enough for everybody, and
everybody getting enough. Any real scarcity of the necessaries of life in the
world—not a fictitious scarcity caused by the lack of clinking metallic disks
in one's purse—is due only to lack of production. And lack of production is
due only too often to lack of knowledge of how and what to produce.

This much we must believe as a starting point: That the earth produces, or
is capable of producing, enough to give decent sustenance to everyone—not
of food alone, but of everything else we need. For everything is produced from
the earth.

That it is possible for labour, production, distribution, and reward to be so
organized as to make certain that those who contribute shall receive shares
determined by an exact justice.

That regardless of the frailties of human nature, our economic system
can be so adjusted that selfishness, although perhaps not abolished, can be
robbed of power to work serious economic injustice.

Focus on Service, and Profits Will Take Care of Themselves

Recall that Ford's results in the language of money prove the truth in the
statement that, if the organization puts the job first, the money will take
care of itself. The following material reminds the reader that Ford began
with almost nothing, and that his company earned everything it had
"by unremitting labour and faith in a principle." This success included
not only automobiles and tractors but, as this book has already shown,

railroads and a world-class hospital. Ford's methods were equally successful in mining and every other enterprise to which he applied them, which
suggests strongly that all the United States needs to do to correct its current economic problems is to diligently apply Ford's universal code.

* * *

*The business of life is easy or hard according to the skill or the lack of skill
displayed in production and distribution. It has been thought that business
existed for profit. That is wrong. Business exists for service. It is a profession,
and must have recognized professional ethics, to violate which declasses a
man. Business needs more of the professional spirit. The professional spirit
seeks professional integrity, from pride, not from compulsion. The professional spirit detects its own violations and penalizes them. Business will some
day become clean. A machine that stops every little while is an imperfect
machine, and its imperfection is within itself. A body that falls sick every
little while is a diseased body, and its disease is within itself. So with business.
Its faults, many of them purely the faults of the moral constitution of business, clog its progress and make it sick every little while. Some day the ethics
of business will be universally recognized, and in that day business will be
seen to be the oldest and most useful of all the professions.*

*All that the Ford industries have done—all that I have done—is to endeav-
our to evidence by works that service comes before profit and that the sort of
business which makes the world better for its presence is a noble profession.
Often it has come to me that what is regarded as the somewhat remarkable progression of our enterprises—I will not say "success," for that word
is an epitaph, and we are just starting—is due to some accident; and that
the methods which we have used, while well enough in their way, fit only the
making of our particular products and would not do at all in any other line
of business or indeed for any products or personalities other than our own.*

*It used to be taken for granted that our theories and our methods were fun-
damentally unsound. That is because they were not understood. Events have
killed that kind of comment, but there remains a wholly sincere belief that
what we have done could not be done by any other company—that we have
been touched by a wand, that neither we nor any one else could make shoes,
or hats, or sewing machines, or watches, or typewriters, or any other necessity after the manner in which we make automobiles and tractors. And that if
only we ventured into other fields we should right quickly discover our errors.
I do not agree with any of this. Nothing has come out of the air. The forego-
ing pages should prove that. We have nothing that others might not have.
We have had no good fortune except that which always attends any one who
puts his best into his work. There was nothing that could be called "favorable" about our beginning. We began with almost nothing. What we have, we*

earned, and we earned it by unremitting labour and faith in a principle. We took what was a luxury and turned it into a necessity and without trick or subterfuge. When we began to make our present motor car the country had few good roads, gasoline was scarce, and the idea was firmly implanted in the public mind that an automobile was at the best a rich man's toy. Our only advantage was lack of precedent.

We began to manufacture according to a creed—a creed which was at that time unknown in business. The new is always thought odd, and some of us are so constituted that we can never get over thinking that anything which is new must be odd and probably queer. The mechanical working out of our creed is constantly changing. We are continually finding new and better ways of putting it into practice, but we have not found it necessary to alter the principles, and I cannot imagine how it might ever be necessary to alter them, because I hold that they are absolutely universal and must lead to a better and wider life for all.

If I did not think so I would not keep working—for the money that I make is inconsequent. Money is useful only as it serves to forward by practical example the principle that business is justified only as it serves, that it must always give more to the community than it takes away, and that unless everybody benefits by the existence of a business then that business should not exist. I have proved this with automobiles and tractors. I intend to prove it with railways and public-service corporations—not for my personal satisfaction and not for the money that may be earned. (It is perfectly impossible, applying these principles, to avoid making a much larger profit than if profit were the main object.) I want to prove it so that all of us may have more, and that all of us may live better by increasing the service rendered by all businesses. Poverty cannot be abolished by formula; it can be abolished only by hard and intelligent work. We are, in effect, an experimental station to prove a principle. That we do make money is only further proof that we are right. For that is a species of argument that establishes itself without words.

A Restatement of Ford's Basic Principles

In the first chapter was set forth the creed. Let me repeat it in the light of the work that has been done under it—for it is at the basis of all our work:

(1) *An absence of fear of the future or of veneration for the past. One who fears the future, who fears failure, limits his activities. Failure is only the opportunity more intelligently to begin again. There is no disgrace in honest failure; there is disgrace in fearing to fail. What is past is useful only as it suggests ways and means for progress.*

(2) *A disregard of competition. Whoever does a thing best ought to be the one to do it. It is criminal to try to get business away from another*

man—criminal because one is then trying to lower for personal gain the condition of one's fellow-men, to rule by force instead of by intelligence.

(3) The putting of service before profit. Without a profit, business cannot extend. There is nothing inherently wrong about making a profit. Well-conducted business enterprises cannot fail to return a profit but profit must and inevitably will come as a reward for good service. It cannot be the basis—it must be the result of service.

(4) Manufacturing is not buying low and selling high. It is the process of buying materials fairly and, with the smallest possible addition of cost, transforming those materials into a consumable product and distributing it to the consumer. Gambling, speculating, and sharp dealing tend only to clog this progression.

We must have production, but it is the spirit behind it that counts most. That kind of production which is a service inevitably follows a real desire to be of service. The various wholly artificial rules set up for finance and industry and which pass as "laws" break down with such frequency as to prove that they are not even good guesses. The basis of all economic reasoning is the earth and its products. To make the yield of the earth, in all its forms, large enough and dependable enough to serve as the basis for real life—the life which is more than eating and sleeping—is the highest service. That is the real foundation for an economic system. We can make things—the problem of production has been solved brilliantly. We can make any number of different sort of things by the millions. The material mode of our life is splendidly provided for. There are enough processes and improvements now pigeon-holed and awaiting application to bring the physical side of life to almost millennial completeness. But we are too wrapped up in the things we are doing—we are not enough concerned with the reasons why we do them. Our whole competitive system, our whole creative expression, all the play of our faculties seem to be centred around material production and its by-products of success and wealth.

There is, for instance, a feeling that personal or group benefit can be had at the expense of other persons or groups. There is nothing to be gained by crushing any one. If the farmer's bloc should crush the manufacturers would the farmers be better off? If the manufacturer's bloc should crush the farmers, would the manufacturers be better off? Could Capital gain by crushing Labour? Or Labour by crushing Capital? Or does a man in business gain by crushing a competitor? No, destructive competition benefits no one. The kind of competition which results in the defeat of the many and the overlordship of the ruthless few must go. Destructive competition lacks the qualities out of which progress comes. Progress comes from a generous form of rivalry. Bad competition is personal. It works for the aggrandizement of some individual or group. It is a sort of warfare. It is inspired by a desire to "get" someone. It *is wholly selfish. That is to say, its motive is not pride in the product, nor a desire to excel in service, nor yet a wholesome ambition to approach to scientific methods of production. It is moved simply by the desire to crowd out others and monopolize the market for the sake of the money returns. That being accomplished, it always substitutes a product of inferior quality.*

LOOK FOR MULTIPLE PRODUCT USES

Ford predicted a biofuel industry that would, for example, convert corn that was otherwise useless into tractor fuel. The idea is to find multiple uses for every product so, if one market goes soft, the product can be sold in another.

The following section also includes an assessment of the dysfunctional role of money. Ford (1922, p. 68) elaborates on this as follows:

> To make business wait on gold is like making the passenger traffic of a main line dependent on the facilities of a local branch with one train a day. If gold did the work it might be as acceptable as anything else; but it doesn't.

Crossen (2000) expands on this by discussing how a scarcity of gold in eighteenth-century France impeded commerce; the entire country was "waiting on gold." France had goods to trade, but shortages of a medium of exchange prevented the goods from selling. John Law, the architect of paper money, then "... proved that the value of money is an agreement among people, not an objective standard measurable in nuggets or ingots, a distinction that fostered future stages of wealth creation."

* * *

Freeing ourselves from the petty sort of destructive competition frees us from many set notions. We are too closely tied to old methods and single, one-way uses. We need more mobility. We have been using certain things just one way, we have been sending certain goods through only one channel—and when that use is slack, or that channel is stopped, business stops, too, and all the sorry consequences of "depression" set in. Take corn, for example. There are millions upon millions of bushels of corn stored in the United States with no visible outlet. A certain amount of corn is used as food for man and beast, but not all of it. In pre-Prohibition days a certain amount of corn went into the making of liquor, which was not a very good use for good corn. But through a long course of years corn followed those two channels, and when one of them stopped the stocks of corn began to pile up. It is the money fiction that usually retards the movement of stocks, but even if money were plentiful we could not possibly consume the stores of food which we sometimes possess.

If foodstuffs become too plentiful to be consumed as food, why not find other uses for them? Why use corn only for hogs and distilleries? Why sit down and bemoan the terrible disaster that has befallen the corn market? Is there no use for corn besides the making of pork or the making of whisky? Surely there must be. There should be so many uses for corn that only the important uses could ever be fully served; there ought always be enough channels open to permit corn to be used without waste.

Once upon a time the farmers burned corn as fuel—corn was plentiful and coal was scarce. That was a crude way to dispose of corn, but it contained the germ of an idea. There is fuel in corn; oil and fuel alcohol are obtainable from corn, and it is high time that someone was opening up this new use so that the stored-up corn crops may be moved.

Why have only one string to our bow? Why not two? If one breaks, there is the other. If the hog business slackens, why should not the farmer turn his corn into tractor fuel?

We need more diversity all round. The four-track system everywhere would not be a bad idea. We have a single-track money system. It is a mighty fine system for those who own it. It is a perfect system for the interest-collecting, credit-controlling financiers who literally own the commodity called Money and who literally own the machinery by which money is made and used. Let them keep their system if they like it. But the people are finding out that it is a poor system for what we call "hard times" because it ties up the line and stops traffic.

If there are special protections for the interests, there ought also to be special protections for the plain people. Diversity of outlet, of use, and of financial enablement, are the strongest defenses we can have against economic emergencies.

It is likewise with Labour. There surely ought to be flying squadrons of young men who would be available for emergency conditions in harvest field, mine, shop, or railroad. If the fires of a hundred industries threaten to go out for lack of coal, and one million men are menaced by unemployment, it would seem both good business and good humanity for a sufficient number of men to volunteer for the mines and the railroads. There is always something to be done in this world, and only ourselves to do it. The whole world may be idle, and in the factory sense there may be "nothing to do." There may be nothing to do in this place or that, but there is always something to do. It is this fact which should urge us to such an organization of ourselves that

this "something to be done" may get done, and unemployment reduced to a
minimum.

THE ROLE OF THE INDIVIDUAL IN THE ADVANCEMENT OF INDUSTRY

Ford's statement that "a man's real work is what he is chosen to do" is consistent with the Asian concept of karma or destiny, and also with the Roman concept of *fatum*. Fatum does not mean fate or fortune, but rather a divine calling. Paterno and Asbell (1989, pp. 43–45) explains it as follows with regard to Aeneas, the hero whose destiny was to found Rome:

> Destiny, the fatum, the divine word, the inner voice, whatever you want to call it, tells you where you have to wind up and what you're destined to do, but it doesn't tell you how to get there or how to do it. ... Through years of hardship and peril, Aeneas reluctantly but relentlessly heeds his fata until he founds Rome.

Paterno and Asbell emphasize that fatum does not include specific directions on how to achieve the desired goal, but only the absolute inner need to reach it. Ford (1922, p. 307) elaborates that a person who follows this path is an instrument of destiny, and an agent of the universe.

* * *

Faith is the sixth sense that completes all the others and it shows itself chiefly in loyalty to Duty, for Duty sums up all the creative work we do. Our career is our duty, and our duty is our contribution to life. Creative work is not a fine and pleasant frenzy; it is often doing what we would not choose to do, for we are chosen oftener than we choose. A man plodding along at what he knows to be his duty is an agent of the universe, in his right place.

* * *

If it was Henry Ford's fatum to transform the United States into the wealthiest and most powerful nation on Earth, and to create a prosperous middle class, he achieved it through diligent work and persistence. The latter personal characteristic includes a refusal to be beaten by temporary setbacks, and to keep trying until one succeeds. Persistence and perseverance are, in fact, aspects of the quality that Niccolò Machiavelli called *virtù*. Ford (1922, p. 148) described its aspects as follows: "And the texture of a man is his vitality, his energy, his character, his courage and his rock-bottom brain power." The lesson, therefore, is that a clear sense of fatum or destiny in combination with virtù leads to world-class success in any enterprise.

* * *

Every advance begins in a small way and with the individual. The mass can be no better than the sum of the individuals. Advancement begins within the man himself; when he advances from half-interest to strength of purpose; when he advances from hesitancy to decisive directness; when he advances from immaturity to maturity of judgment; when he advances from apprenticeship to mastery; when he advances from a mere dilettante at labour to a worker who finds a genuine joy in work; when he advances from an eyeserver to one who can be entrusted to do his work without oversight and without prodding—why, then the world advances! The advance is not easy. We live in flabby times when men are being taught that everything ought to be easy. Work that amounts to anything will never be easy. And the higher you go in the scale of responsibility, the harder becomes the job. Ease has its place, of course. Every man who works ought to have sufficient leisure. The man who works hard should have his easy chair, his comfortable fireside, his pleasant surroundings. These are his by right. But no one deserves ease until after his work is done. It will never be possible to put upholstered ease into work. Some work is needlessly hard. It can be lightened by proper management. Every device ought to be employed to leave a man free to do a man's work. Flesh and blood should not be made to bear burdens that steel can bear. But even when the best is done, work still remains work, and any man who puts himself into his job will feel that it is work.

And there cannot be much picking and choosing. The appointed task may be less than was expected. A man's real work is not always what he would have chosen to do. A man's real work is what he is chosen to do. Just now there are more menial jobs than there will be in the future; and as long as there are menial jobs, someone will have to do them; but there is no reason why a man should be penalized because his job is menial. There is one thing that can be said about menial jobs that cannot be said about a great many so-called more responsible jobs, and that is, they are useful and they are respectable and they are honest.

The time has come when drudgery must be taken out of labour. It is not work that men object to, but the element of drudgery. We must drive out drudgery wherever we find it. We shall never be wholly civilized until we remove the treadmill from the daily job. Invention is doing this in some degree now. We have succeeded to a very great extent in relieving men of the heavier and more onerous jobs that used to sap their strength, but even when lightening the heavier labour we have not yet succeeded in removing monotony. That is another field that beckons us—the abolition of monotony, and in trying to accomplish that we shall doubtless discover other changes that will have to be made in our system.

STANDARDIZATION AS THE SERVANT AND NOT THE MASTER

The concept of a quality system standard like ISO 9001 as the organization's servant rather than its master helps gain buy-in from the organization's workforce and management team. If the standard is merely something with which the organization has to conform to get a certificate with which to impress customers, it is indeed the master rather than the servant. It is also a costly and time-consuming annoyance because it demands the organization's resources and returns little of real value. If, on the other hand, the organization uses ISO 9001 as a framework with which to remove system-related deficiencies that undermine people's daily work, it becomes the servant rather than the master. Ford summarizes this principle as follows: "Factory organization is not a device to prevent the expansion of ability, but a device to reduce the waste and losses due to mediocrity."

Ford also makes it clear that the purpose of standardization is emphatically not to stifle worker initiative and creativity. Every production operator must, for example, follow the existing work instruction because it contains the best known way to do the job. This does not mean, however, that the worker cannot or should not look for a better way to do a job. Taylor (1911a, p. 67) elaborates on this as follows: "And whenever the new method is found to be markedly superior to the old, it should be adopted as the standard for the whole establishment." This is where the discipline of standardization propagates worker initiative and creativity rather than suppressing them.

A good quality management system will include a procedure (second-tier document) for best practice deployment. Ford and Crowther (1926, 85) describe this practice very explicitly: "... the benefit of our experience cannot be thrown away." The Automotive Industry Action Group (2006, pp. 137, 172) describes the Lessons Learned Database and Read

Across/Replicate Process for the purpose of not only holding the gains from a specific improvement activity, but also deploying its benefits to all relevant activities in the organization.

* * *

The opportunity to work is now greater than ever it was. The opportunity to advance is greater. It is true that the young man who enters industry to-day enters a very different system from that in which the young man of twenty-five years ago began his career. The system has been tightened up; there is less play or friction in it; fewer matters are left to the haphazard will of the individual; the modern worker finds himself part of an organization which apparently leaves him little initiative. Yet, with all this, it is not true that "men are mere machines." It is not true that opportunity has been lost in organization. If the young man will liberate himself from these ideas and regard the system as it is, he will find that what he thought was a barrier is really an aid.

Factory organization is not a device to prevent the expansion of ability, but a device to reduce the waste and losses due to mediocrity. It is not a device to hinder the ambitious, clear-headed man from doing his best, but a device to prevent the don't-care sort of individual from doing his worst. That is to say, when laziness, carelessness, slothfulness, and lack-interest are allowed to have their own way, everybody suffers. The factory cannot prosper and therefore cannot pay living wages. When an organization makes it necessary for the don't-care class to do better than they naturally would, it is for their benefit—they are better physically, mentally, and financially. What wages should we be able to pay if we trusted a large don't-care class to their own methods and gait of production?

If the factory system which brought mediocrity up to a higher standard operated also to keep ability down to a lower standard—it would be a very bad system, a very bad system indeed. But a system, even a perfect one, must have able individuals to operate it. No system operates itself. And the modern system needs more brains for its operation than did the old. More brains are needed to-day than ever before, although perhaps they are not needed in the same place as they once were. It is just like power: formerly every machine was run by foot power; the power was right at the machine. But nowadays we have moved the power back—concentrated it in the power-house. Thus also we have made it unnecessary for the highest types of mental ability to be engaged in every operation in the factory. The better brains are in the mental power-plant.

Every business that is growing is at the same time creating new places for capable men. It cannot help but do so. This does not mean that new openings come every day and in groups. Not at all. They come only after hard work;

it is the fellow who can stand the gaff of routine and still keep himself alive and alert who finally gets into direction. It is not sensational brilliance that one seeks in business, but sound, substantial dependability. Big enterprises of necessity move slowly and cautiously. The young man with ambition ought to take a long look ahead and leave an ample margin of time for things to happen.

THE NEED FOR SUSTAINABLE MANUFACTURING

The last paragraph of *My Life and Work* describes sustainable manufacturing very explicitly, and Ford practiced it at every opportunity. Woodyard (2010) reports that the 2011 Ford Explorer's body will be made from a soybean-based plastic, but Ford himself introduced a soybean-based car body 60 years earlier. Among the reasons was the need to conserve steel during the World War II, but the idea of using a renewable resource was evident even at that time.

Ford News (1923, September 15, p. 3) meanwhile describes the production of artificial leather from various forms of cloth, along with then-advanced safety precautions, such as using air switches and air-powered motors in the presence of flammable solvent vapors.

* * *

A great many things are going to change. We shall learn to be masters rather than servants of Nature. With all our fancied skill we still depend largely on natural resources and think that they cannot be displaced. We dig coal and ore and cut down trees. We use the coal and the ore and they are gone; the trees cannot be replaced within a lifetime. We shall some day harness the heat that is all about us and no longer depend on coal—we may now create heat through electricity generated by water power. We shall improve on that method. As chemistry advances I feel quite certain that a method will be found to transform growing things into substances that will endure better than the metals—we have scarcely touched the uses of cotton. Better wood can be made than is grown. The spirit of true service will create for us. We have only each of us to do our parts sincerely.

Everything is possible ... "faith is the substance of things hoped for, the evidence of things not seen."

Conclusion

This book has shown that Henry Ford's universal code can deliver world-class results in any human enterprise. Application of this universal code is, at its most basic level, simply action in accordance with impartial and inarguable laws of economic, physical, and behavioral science.

Ford called these laws the Constitution of the Universe, and they are no more debatable than the laws of thermodynamics. Kipling personified them as the equally implacable Gods of the Copybook Headings. A supply chain's stakeholders, and a nation's citizens, must realize that it is worse than hopeless to try to defeat or evade these laws through ideology, legislation, collective bargaining, or any other transient Gods of the Market Place. Enormous rewards, in contrast, await those who act in complete harmony with these laws and thereby gain their support.

The application of Ford's universal code to government should meanwhile be common sense. The government cannot disburse more wealth than the nation creates, and any delusion to the contrary can lead only to economic catastrophe and bankrupt social welfare programs. We cannot have more wealth than we produce, and the offshoring of manufacturing jobs is a clear and present danger to our national affluence and security.

The solution to problems, such as the United States' runaway healthcare cost, lies similarly in management and engineering science as opposed to ideology or legislation. *My Life and Work* has laid out the nature of this science very clearly. Ford proved that high quality, rapid delivery, and low cost are synergistic performance measurements in any enterprise, and this includes healthcare.

The greatest barrier to resolution of our nation's problems is, therefore, not the lack of a solution, but a general inability or unwillingness to grasp a proven solution that has existed for almost a century. If *My Life and Work* has removed that obstacle to progress and universal affluence, it has fulfilled its mission.

References

Anand, G. 2009. The Henry Ford of heart surgery: In India, a factory model for hospitals is cutting costs and yielding profits. *Wall Street Journal*, November 25. Online at: http://online.wsj.com/article/SB125875892887958111.html (accessed June 30, 2012).

Anderson, J. 2007. Ohio State opens new automotive production line research center. *Ergonomics Today*™. Online at: http://www.ergoweb.com/news/detail.cfm?print=on&id=2096 (accessed May 28, 2012).

Arnold, H. L., and Faurote, F. L. 1915. Ford methods and the Ford shops. New York: *The Engineering Magazine*. Reprinted 1998, North Stratford, NH: Ayer Company Publishers, Inc.

Automotive Industry Action Group (AIAG). 2006. *CQI-10: Effective problem solving, A guideline*. Southfield, MI: AIAG, http://www.aiag.org.

Bennett, H. 1951. *Ford: We never called him Henry*. (As told to Paul Marcus) New York: Tom Doherty Associates, Inc.

Burns, T. and Stalker, G. M. 1961. *The management of innovation*, London: Tavistock.

Cable, J. 2012. Made in the USA, the Honda way. *Industry Week*, May.

Chemical Week. 2011. Earthquake may cause shortage of electronic materials. March 28, Online at: http://goliath.ecnext.com/coms2/gi_0199-14788510/Earthquake-may-cause-shortage-of.html (accessed 11/4/12).

Clausewitz, C. von. 1976. *On war*. NJ: Princeton University Press, (translated by M. Howard and P. Paret. Princeton).

Coburn, T. A. 2012. *The debt bomb: A bold plan to stop Washington from bankrupting America*. Nashville: Thomas Nelson.

Covey, S. R. 1991. *Principle-centered leadership*. New York: Summit Books.

Crossen, C. 2000. *The rich and how they got that way*. New York: Dow Jones & Co. (Excerpts in the *Wall Street Journal*, Sept 19, B1, B4.)

Emerson, H. 1909. Efficiency as a basis for operation and wages. *The Engineering Magazine*.

Ford, H. 1922. *Ford ideals: from "Mr. Ford's page."* Dearborn, MI: The Dearborn Publishing Company.

Ford, H., and Crowther, S. 1922. *My life and work*. New York: Doubleday, Page & Company.

Ford, H., and Crowther, S. 1926. *Today and tomorrow*. New York: Doubleday, Page & Company (reprint available from Productivity Press, 1988).

Ford, H., and Crowther, S. 1930. *Moving forward*. New York: Doubleday, Doran, & Company.

Ford News. 1922–1923. Digitized by Google books.

Franklin, B. 1986. *The way to wealth*. Bedford, MA: Applewood Books.

Fraser, G. M.. 1969. *Flashman*. London: Barrie & Jenkin.

Gillibrand, K. 2009. Cap and trade could be a boon to New York. *Wall Street Journal*, October 21. Online at: http://online.wsj.com/article/SB10001424052748704500604574481812686144826.html (accessed June 30).

Godfrey, B. 2000. Managing key suppliers. *Quality Digest*, September.

Goldratt, E., and Cox, J. 1992. *The goal*. Croton-on-Hudson, NY: North River Press.

Gourley, C. 1997. *Wheels of time: A biography of Henry Ford*. Brookfield, CT: The Millbrook Press.

Greenhill, S. 2008. Secret of the Lusitania: Arms find challenges Allied claims it was solely a passenger ship. U.K. *Daily Mail*, December 20. Online at: http://www.dailymail. co.uk/news/article-1098904/Secret-Lusitania-Arms-challenges-Allied-claims-solely-passenger-ship.html (accessed July 2, 2012).

Halpin, J. F. 1966. *Zero defects*. New York: McGraw-Hill.

Hayes, R. H., Wheelwright, S. C., and Clark, K. B. 1988. *Dynamic manufacturing*. New York, The Free Press.

Heinlein, R. A. (ed.) 1980. On the slopes of Vesuvius. In *Expanded universe*. New York: Ace Books.

Hopp, W. J., and Spearman, M. L. 2000. *Factory physics*, 2nd ed. New York: McGraw-Hill.

Hoyer, R. W. 2001. Why quality gets an 'F': What happens when the bottom line overrides a focus on customer needs. *Quality Progress*, October: 32–36.

Hughes, D. J. 1993. *Moltke on the art of war: Selected writings*. Novato, CA: Presidio Press.

Huxley, A. 1932. *Brave new world*. London: Chatto & Windus.

Industry Week (staff article). 2011. Employees in U.S. aren't very happy. June 20. Online at: http://www.industryweek.com/articles/employees_in_u-s-_arent_very_happy_24897. aspx (accessed May 25, 2012).

Juran, J., and Gryna, F. 1988. *Juran's quality control handbook*, 4th ed. New York: McGraw-Hill.

Kilcarr, S. 2009. Lifting the load: Truck weight limits. *FleetOwner*, April 1. Online at: http://fleetowner.com/management/feature/truck-weight-limit-debate-0409/index.html (accessed 11/4/12).

Kipling, R. *The gods of the copybook headings*. Online at: http://www.kipling.org.uk/poems_copybook.htm (accessed August 8, 2012).

Knowledge at Wharton. 2012. Declining employee loyalty: A casualty of the new workplace. *Quality Digest*, May 18. Online at: http://www.qualitydigest.com/inside/quality-insider-article/declining-employee-loyalty-casualty-new-workplace.html (accessed May 26, 2012).

Krebs, M. 2012. Will higher gas prices boost hybrid, EV sales? Edmunds.com. Online at: http://www.edmunds.com/industry-center/analysis/will-higher-gas-prices-boost-hybrid-ev-sales.html (accessed June 28, 2012).

Levinson, W. A. 2002. The long and shoreman of it. From *Ideas in action with Jim Glassman*. Online at: http://www.ideasinactiontv.com/tcs_daily/2002/10/the-long-and-shoremen-of-it.html (accessed July 3, 2012). (Originally in *Capitalism Magazine*, October 2002.)

Levinson, W. A. 2006. On the road again. *Industrial Engineer*, January: 28.

Linebarger, P. M. A. 1954. *Psychological warfare*. Washington: Combat Forces Press.

Lorenzen, J. 1992. Quality function deployment. American Society for Quality section meeting, May 26.

Machiavelli, N. 1965. *The art of war*, New York: Da Capo Press.

MacPherson, S. 2012. Green Beret way to build lean leaders. *Industry Week* webinar, May 23.

Mege, C. J. 2000. Is there a HAM in your future? *Manufacturing Engineering*, July: 114–124.

Meldrum, A. 2005. As country heads for disaster, Zimbabwe calls for return of white farmers. *The Guardian*, May 20. Online at: http://www.guardian.co.uk/world/2005/may/21/zimbabwe.andrewmeldrum (accessed 11/4/12).

Miller, L. M. 1989. *Barbarians to bureaucrats: Corporate life cycle strategies*. New York: Fawcett Columbine.

Miller, R. B. 1985. Lecture for "organizational behavior." Union College Graduate Management Institute, Poughkeepsie, NY, September 9.

National Park Service. (nd). Thomas Blanchard. Online at: http://www.nps.gov/spar/histo-ryculture/upload/Thomas-Blanchard.pdf (accessed May 26, 2012).

Norwood, E. P. 1931. *Ford: Men and methods.* Garden City, NY: Doubleday, Doran & Company, Inc.

Nye, R. H. 1993. *The Patton mind: The professional development of an extraordinary leader.* New York: Avery Publishing.

Ohno, T. 1988. *Toyota Production System: Beyond large-scale production.* Portland, OR: Productivity Press.

Panchak, P. 2003. Lean health care? It works! *Industry Week,* November.

Paterno, J. V., and Asbell, B. 1989. *Paterno: By the book.* New York: Berkely Books.

Peters, T. 1987. *Thriving on chaos.* New York: Harper & Row.

Peters, T., and Austin, N. 1985. *A passion for excellence.* New York, Warner Books.

Robinson, A. (ed.) 1990. *Modern approaches to manufacturing improvement: The Shingo system.* Portland, OR: Productivity Press.

Sinclair, U. 1937. *The flivver king.* (Second printing, 1987.) Chicago: Charles H. Kerr Publishing Company,

Sorensen, C. E. (with Williamson, S. T.) 1956. *My forty years with Ford.* New York: W. W. Norton & Company Inc.

Stuelpnagel, T. R. 1993. "Déjà vu: TQM returns to Detroit and elsewhere. *Quality Progress,* September: 91–95.

Taylor, F. W.. 1911a. *The principles of scientific management.* New York: Harper Brothers. (1998 republication by Dover Publications, Inc., Mineola, NY.)

Taylor, F. W. 1911b. *Shop management.* New York: Harper & Brothers Publishers.

Vance, J. 1959. Dodkin's job. In *Astounding science fiction,* ed. J. W. Campbell, Jr.. New York: Street & Smith Publications, Inc.

Womack, J. P., and Jones, D. T. 1996. *Lean thinking.* New York: Simon & Schuster.

Woodyard, C. 2010. Mystery car 40: Henry Ford's soybean car. *USA Today,* June 29. Online at: http://content.usatoday.com/communities/driveon/post/2010/06/mystery-car-40-henry-fords-soybean-car/1#.T8P1RsV1i3g (accessed May 28, 2012).

Index